TALES OF WHITETAILS

TALES OF WHITETAILS

Archibald Rutledge's Great Deer-Hunting Stories

Edited by JIM CASADA

For Larry Lahay, with all best wishes.
To walk along literary trails of
whitetails with Old Flintlock as a
guide is to tread trails of
wonder.

Jim Casada

4/27/95

UNIVERSITY OF SOUTH CAROLINA PRESS

For Mom and Dad, who gently nurtured my interest in the outdoors; quietly endured anxious moments as I enjoyed nature's wonders in the solitude of the Smokies; and still share my love of field, forest, and stream.

Published in Columbia, South Carolina, by the
University of South Carolina Press

Printed in Canada

Library of Congress Cataloging-in-Publication Data

Rutledge, Archibald Hamilton, 1883–1973.
    Tales of whitetails : Archibald Rutledge's great deer-hunting
stories / edited by Jim Casada.
        p.   cm.
    Includes bibliographical references.
    ISBN 0-87249–860–3 (alk. paper)
    1. White-tailed deer hunting.   2. Deer hunting.   3. Hunting
stories, American.   4. Rutledge, Archibald Hamilton, 1883–1973.
5. Hunters—South Carolina—Biography.   I. Casada, James A.
II. Title.
SK301.R88   1992   92-20100
799.2′77357—dc20

CONTENTS

ACKNOWLEDGMENTS

Mine is a special debt of gratitude to Judge Irvine Rutledge, Flintlock's sole surviving son. He has taken a keen interest in this project from the outset and has supported it enthusiastically. Rob Wegner, America's leading authority on the history and literature of whitetail hunting, has contributed to my efforts in a variety of ways. Nick Lyons, as is ever his wont, has offered quiet wisdom and words of encouragement. Lou Razek of Highwood Books has provided assistance and insight from his unrivaled collection of outdoor periodicals. The fine folks in the Reference Department at Winthrop College's Dacus Library have helped procure what must have seemed to them an endless stream of research materials on interlibrary loan. Warren Slesinger, Peggy Hill, and others at the University of South Carolina Press have prodded me when progress was slow; provided support when it was needed. Finally, as always, Ann and Natasha have cared—and shared.

A NOTE ON SELECTION

As the bibliography which concludes this work indicates, Archibald Rutledge wrote prolifically on deer and deer hunting. While he has been accused, with some degree of justice, of killing the same buck repeatedly in print, even so he produced scores of fine, original deer stories. These were by no means equal in literary merit, yet the vast majority of his deer stories are both readable and entertaining—eloquent testimony to his deep devotion to the animal. There is also an enduring quality to his work, one which guarantees that so long as man takes to the hunting field, the best of Rutledge's writings will remain timely.

The selections which follow were chosen primarily with an eye on two criteria—as the most readable and most representative of his many tales of whitetails. Some are obscure; others well known. For anyone who wants to travel further with Rutledge, the bibliography will serve as a guide. Meanwhile, what follows is my personal choice of thirty-five of his finest writings on deer.

Tales of Whitetails

FLINTLOCK AFIELD:
A Life Devoted to Deer

Fascination with deer runs a bright thread through the fabric of Archibald Rutledge's life. Fortunately for posterity, one outlet of his passion for whitetails was in print, and arguably no American sporting writer has been more successful in capturing the myriad, and often elusive, meanings of the hunt. Deer figured in Rutledge's dreams, as they also, in one fashion or another, occupied many of his waking hours. Some of the happiest times of his life were spent hunting whitetails, and he also devoted countless hours as a nocturnal naturalist observing them from a specially built platform in a live-oak tree. Mementoes of hunts past surrounded him at Hampton Plantation, the family home in the Santee delta. Even during the better than three decades Rutledge spent at Pennsylvania's Mercersburg Academy as a teacher, he lived from Christmas to Christmas in anticipation of holiday deer hunts back home in the South Carolina Low Country.

Rutledge hunted deer for almost eighty years, and he wrote about them for more than sixty years. Throughout his adult life he meticuously maintained a hunter's diary, in which he dutifully recorded the details not only of every hunt but also of each encounter he had with deer. Some indication of the extent of his contact with whitetails is given by the fact that in 1952, better than two decades before his death, his records showed that he had "observed, in their native haunts, under almost all conceivable circumstances, more than 8,000 wild deer." Sadly, his diary, along with the manuscript of an unfinished autobiography, was lost late in his life when fire swept the family's "Summer House" near McClellanville. Rutledge managed to reconstruct and rewrite much of the autobiography, only to have it mysteriously disappear from his bedside at the time of his death. These losses notwithstanding, Rutledge wrote so prolifically on deer and had such a gift for recapturing the ethos of individual hunts that the corpus of his writings on whitetails is unmatched in the annals of American sporting literature.

His style was far removed from the transitory and frequently stale "how to" and "where to" approaches commonly encountered today. Rutledge's writings went far deeper than mere discussion of the essentials for being a successful hunter. He had an unrivaled knack for rendering the thrill of the chase, and his ability to set a scene was such that it placed the reader squarely amid the deep swamps, ridges of mixed pines and hardwoods, and dense thickets of palmetto and greenbrier that were the hallmarks of his hunting world. At times it seemed almost as if he enjoyed a symbiotic relationship with deer; certainly they sustained him from a literary standpoint and helped give meaning to his entire existence. He once wrote that "startlingly close, indeed, is the bond between human life and animal life of high intelligence," and he considered deer—"that noble, elusive, crafty, wonderful denizen of the wilds"—to be the wisest of game animals.

Rutledge followed, in the pursuit of sport, a life-style which to him represented important values such as honesty, manliness, and fellowship. His firm belief was that there was "much more to hunting than hunting," and he considered "renewed health, a more wholesome outlook on life, [and] a reverence for the miracle of creation" among the benefits of the quest. He praised whitetails in poetry, found in them inspiration for a sophisticated philosophy, and perhaps most important of all, immortalized the world of the hunter and the hunted in prose.

Stories on deer are liberally sprinkled throughout his books, and his whitetail writings appeared in the major outdoor magazines of his day on a regular basis. For some reason, however, he never wrote a book devoted exclusively to the animal. Indeed, with the single exception of *Bolio and Other Dogs* (1930), none of his books focuses on a single aspect of sport. Perhaps one explanation for the eclectic approach he took lies in the manner in which he created his books. Virtually all of his prose works, which comprise close to fifty volumes, consist of stories which had previously appeared in periodicals. Rutledge brought these pieces together in formats that suited his own tastes and those of his many readers. The best of the books, such as *Plantation Game Trails* (1921), *Days Off in Dixie* (1925), *An American Hunter* (1937), and *Hunter's Choice* (1946), are characterized by material which ranges widely across the gamut of shooting sports and natural history.

Comprising thirty-five stories, the present volume offers readers, for the first time, a clear focus on and easy access to Rutledge's best writing about deer, much of which has remained buried in books that are long out of print and expensive to acquire. But before we join Rutledge in hunts and haunts of long ago, some comment on the man who wrote the stories is in order to enhance the meaning of these tales for the reader.

By his own account, based on what his mother told him, Rutledge was only a few months old when he had his first noteworthy encounter with a deer. The family had a pet buck, known as Old Ben, which had been raised from a fawn to a lordly stag, sporting ten points on his antlers. Old Ben walked into a room where the tiny boy lay in his crib and curiously sniffed the infant. The baby, equally curious, grasped the buck's substantial rack. When Rutledge's startled mother walked into the room, it was to find her son swinging from the deer's antlers. The episode became a family legend, and later Rutledge wrote of it as an augury of what the future held in store for him. He firmly believed "that the old stag passed me the mystic word concerning the rarest sport on earth."

The Rutledge men had been sportsmen for many generations, and Colonel Henry Middleton Rutledge, Archibald's father, was a renowned deer hunter. He was reputed to have killed more than six hundred deer during his lifetime, and his record of thirty double shots (taking a whitetail with each barrel of his shotgun) had earned him widespread acclaim. In his son's estimation he was, "judged by his skill and by his sportsmanship, the best hunter I ever knew." Colonel Rutledge introduced his son to the joys of deer hunting when the boy was only six. The two soon became inseparable companions, and in time Rutledge would repeat this sporting link of hands from one generation to the next with his own sons.

Young Archibald Rutledge's first lesson from his father was that "a good hunter has to outquiet his game." It was a tenet he took to heart. Some of the most joyous moments of his life would be spent in quiet, contemplative solitude as he watched deer, unaware of his presence, wander through the forest and browse at the edge of fields.

His tutors also included a number of the plantation's black residents, whom he fondly referred to as "huntermen." These accomplished woodsmen helped him read nature's book in their knowing fashion, and he credited the best of them with knowing "what a buck will do before the deer himself does." Old Galboa, faithful Gabe Myers, and Phineas McConnor were among the most notable of these mentors, but for all of their undoubted influence they take a back seat to Prince Alston in the shaping of this master among deerslayers. Alston and Rutledge were the same age, and for a generation they were linked as tightly as brothers. This "companion to my heart," as Rutledge poignantly describes his friend, was a woodsman without peer. He was "as close to nature as any man in the world," and Prince's wife maintained, only half jokingly, that Prince could not be a true Christian. She said that for him "deer hunting was religion," echoing closely words the deeply religious Rutledge used to describe himself in another story. Small wonder that the pair were so close for all of the forty-four earthly years Prince knew.

Young Rutledge, his brother Tom, and Prince Alston enjoyed an idyllic life on the extensive, game-rich lands of Hampton Plantation. As a lad Rutledge became enamored of the hunt with that single-minded intensity peculiar to adolescents, and his passion grew stronger with the passage of time. Young Rutledge read and was influenced by the stories of Ernest Thompson Seton. He constantly questioned experienced hunters and listened to the stories of hunts past told during the gatherings of sportsmen that were an important feature of plantation Christmases. By the time he left home in late adolescence to enroll at Union College in New York, Rutledge was a highly accomplished deer hunter.

Almost four decades—from his matriculation at Union through the thirty-three years he spent as a teacher in Pennsylvania—would pass before Rutledge returned for good to the hallowed hunting grounds of his youth. Yet there is little question that memories of grand hunts he had known there, along with the anticipation of returning each year during the Christmas season, sustained him.

Although he wrote surprisingly little to this effect, it is clear

that from the death of his parents onward his goal in life was to
return to Hampton and restore it to the grandeur he associated
with the old plantation home during his childhood days. Meanwhile, in absentia, he yearned to return to his roots running deep
in the Southern soil. Lines from Rutledge's poem "Exile" reveal
something of the toll exacted by those long years away.

> So, from the old plantation, cityward
> We came, leaving the hollies and the oaks behind.
> We left the river flowing by our doors;
> The hounds to hunt without my hearing them;
> The wild azalea flaming in the woods—
> We unbeholding. And I left my gun,
> Forever standing lonely in the hall.
> About me now the city towers; the cries
> Of many voices sound, but make no song
> For me, a woodsman lost in Babylon.
> And yet above me still the pine trees soar.
> I cannot see for all that I have seen:
> The shadowy deer, furtively stealing forth;
> The old wild gobbler, that all night has slept
> In starlight, in the shrouded cypress crest.
> And sometimes, when the wind is in the south,
> I'm sure I smell the jasmine in the swamp,
> And hear the mallards clamoring in the marsh.

Rutledge's exile was eased by his annual Christmas visits to
Hampton, where Prince Alston and others patiently awaited his
permanent return. Those sojourns were fraught with meaning
for Flintlock, the moniker by which he was known, and his three
sons, Archibald, Jr., Middleton, and Irvine. He nurtured their
growth as sportsmen in much the same fashion that the Colonel
had once encouraged and rejoiced in Rutledge's own develop-
ment. He felt that the lessons that his boys learned from the
annual "Hampton Hunt" at Christmas played a vital role in shaping their characters. Also he relished the bonds formed during
their time together afield.

Among the tasks set for himself was the important one of
teaching his sons to be ethical sportsmen, for in his eyes "to be
a sportsman is a mighty long step in the direction of being a
man." His parental philosophy in that regard was straightfor-
wards. "If a man brings up his sons to be hunters, they will never

grow away from him. Rather the passing years will only bring them closer, with a thousand happy memories of the woods and fields."

Those memories, primarily of deer hunts, sustained Flintlock and his sons from one December to the next throughout the 1920s and 1930s. They hunted grouse, quail, and other upland game in Pennsylvania, but Rutledge knew that deer hunting as it was practiced in that state was not for him. The vast "pumpkin army" taking to the woods with high-powered rifles at the opening of each season frightened him. With customary frankness, he explained why, as much as he loved deer hunting, he chose to forgo it in the Mercersburg area which was his home away from home. "Most of these hunters had never seen a deer, and after a good many narrow escapes, I developed the suspicion that to my friends and neighbors I must have looked exactly like an old buck. Whenever a man begins to feel that he is a target, the chances are that his enthusiasm for hunting is going to wane." He might also have added that the tactics and techniques involved in Pennsylvania deer hunts were far removed from the dog (or occasionally, man) drives and use of shotguns Rutledge knew in South Carolina.

Finally, in the fall of 1937, with his sons grown and his years of teaching behind him, Rutledge returned to Hampton for good. Now a popular, well-established writer of national repute, as well as the Palmetto State's poet laureate, he was a man with a mission: to restore the home and grounds at Hampton to their former glory. Typically however, deer hunting was the first order of business. Even as family belongings were being unpacked after the move to Hampton, he called young Prince Alston (the son of his boyhood companion, who had died several years earlier) aside. Prince assured him that "some able bucks" were easing into the pea fields to feed at twilight. Such information was all that was required to get the hunter's juices flowing, and in short order the pair set out. Soon Rutledge spotted a fine buck at about fifty yards distance and fired with the double-barrel Parker 12 gauge which had been presented to him by students at Mercersburg Academy. When he and Prince rushed forward, they found that not one but two deer had been killed by Rutledge's single shot. The pair of hunters immediately agreed that "this was about as fine a homecoming as a man could have."

From 1937 on, Rutledge was once more in his element. The

Hampton Hunt knew its finest years, as each Christmas his sons came to join friends and relatives for several days of sport. At other times during the lengthy Low Country hunting season, which stretched from late August to the New Year, the squire of Hampton joined neighbors for the full-scale, carefully organized kind of hunt which he delighted in orchestrating. Some of his most pleasant moments, however, came when he ventured out alone, or with one of his huntermen, in the endless quest for whitetails.

During this same period he solidified his place as America's most masterful chronicler of deer stories. His eloquence matched his love for the hunt, and articles continued to pour from his pen in a steady stream. For all the pleasure that these activities provided, there was pain as well. Prince Alston's premature death had moved him deeply, and for the remainder of his life he regularly experienced sudden, bittersweet recollections of some exploit he had shared with his youthful companion. In 1943, Rutledge's son Middleton was killed in an automobile accident, and Arch, Jr., whom he fondly called Buckshot, also predeceased him.

Always, no matter what his travail, deer hunting gave him succor. "With me deer hunting is kind of a religion," he wrote, "and I have worshipped at this shrine ever since a grown oak was an acorn." Even in his final years the wonders of whitetails sustained him. They gave him a zest for life, as exemplified in a photograph taken after a shattered hip had ended the octagenarian's days afield. He holds in his old man's hands the rack of his finest deer, a massive thirteen-point buck he had killed in 1942. Rutledge's body is frail but those piercing, hawklike eyes, always one of his most prominent features, still burn brightly in fond recollection of what had been.

His had been a rich life, filled with a mystical attachment to deer that he expressed in hunting and writing. That whitetails held him mesmerized, constantly in awe, is beyond dispute, and his close link to the animal gave magic to his words. His writings on deer comprise a rich literary legacy—what Rob Wegner describes as the best expression of "the real meaning and the ultimate value of this animal for American cultural history." Certainly Flintlock had a rare gift both for sharing with others the incomparable pleasure whitetails gave him and for communicating his harmonious relationship with nature and with those who were his frequent companions on the hunt. In some stories the modern reader may be shocked by what would today might seem overt or racist remarks, but it must be remembered that the author's world on the lower Santee was one far removed from the world of today. Rutledge's devotion to his black friends, far from being paternalistic or condescending, always sprang from genuine love for them.

As we turn to his stories it is appropriate to remember that Rutledge now rests beneath the grounds of the Hampton he so loved. Moss-laden live oaks stand as silent sentinels guarding his grave. Mast from these mighty oaks, along with the grasses growing about the family cemetery plot, beckon the many deer which roam the plantation's expanses. These whitetails, lineal descendants of the bucks which brought so much wonder to Rutledge's life, still walk with sinewy grace in the moonlit shadows. Occasionally, in their nightly feeding forays, deer leave footprints on the hunter's grave. Those of bucks are deep and heavy, while does daintly "mince along in high-heeled slippers." One senses that Rutledge would have found the marks of their passage fitting, and those who read his tales of whitetails can take heart in the knowledge that the animal which filled his life with meaning still thrives amid the splendor of Rutledge's Santee paradise.

DEER IN THEIR WORLD

—————— Part I ——————

A rchibald Rutledge was an avid hunter, but there was much more to his interest in deer than the thrill of the quest or the joy of the sounds of bugling hounds hot on a whitetail's trail. A keen student of natural history, he delighted in study and observation of deer. Throughout the year, once he had returned to South Carolina for good, Rutledge would take long walks or horseback rides about Hampton Plantation. One of the primary purposes of these jaunts was to check on "his" deer. "One of my greatest delights," he once wrote, is "to watch wild things, and in that way try to learn more about the way they live, so that I might know better how to live myself."

From boyhood until he was bedridden in his final years, Rutledge learned by watching. Throughout his literary career, during moments of fond reflection, he would recall how he was prone to moments of school-boy daydreaming. Deer were inevitably the focus of these musings. Sometimes his thoughts turned to grand hunts, either real or imagined, but equally prominent were dreams of watching a mighty stag from a secret perch among the limbs of a venerable live oak. After he retired from teaching and came home to Hampton, Rutledge enjoyed reliving his boyhood. He erected a lofty platform in an ancient oak to use specifically as a deer observation post. There, perhaps accompanied by one of his faithful "huntermen," he would sit for hours or even the entire night, watching in silence as whitetails went about their nocturnal business.

Rutledge likewise made a careful study of deer habits and habitat, and he knew, from his own observations, together with tales handed down by his father and previous generations, that the deer of Hampton had followed certain trails and adhered to particular behavioral patterns for a span of two centuries. When-

11

ever he was afield Rutledge kept a keen eye out for tracks, signs of where deer had browsed, and in the mating season he was alert for telltale rubs and scrapes. Even when he was at home, working at his desk or enjoying the company of family and friends, the man's mind was never far from the animal he dearly loved. Throughout the house souvenirs of hunts past gave quiet comfort and functioned as decoration.

When he wrote, Rutledge liked to have antlers from memorable bucks close at hand in his study or on his desk. Antlers always fascinated him, and he wrote that in the Low Country of his youth, "A plantation home without its collection of stag horns is hardly to be found. . . . In some families, there is a custom, rigorously adhered to, that no deer antlers must ever leave the place, so that the antlers of every buck killed find their way into the home's collection. Such a frieze in a dining room seems to fill the place with woodland memories and serves in its own way to recall the hunts, the hunters and the hunted of long ago."

Ever a lover of history and family traditions, Rutledge saved the antlers from his own hunts. More important for us though, he viewed his countless experiences with whitetails as part of a lifelong exercise in acquiring deer lore. Through these experiences he came to know and appreciate the animal as few—whether hunters, biologists, or natural historians—have done. As the selections that follow suggest, Rutledge was as masterful in capturing the ways of wildlife as he was in portraying the hunting ethos. His ability to carry us to the wild world he knew so intimately is one of his finest accomplishments as a writer.

MY FRIEND THE DEER

It was the middle of May in the woods of South Carolina, and the time of day was noon. I was riding along leisurely, trying to drink in a portion of the marvelous beauty of the scene which stretched away from me on all sides; a scene in which bright birds flashed, wild flowers gleamed and glowed, and great trees seemed to shiver and expand in the ecstasy of their springtime joy. Suddenly my attention was arrested by a strange and beautiful sight. Far through a forest vista a doe came bounding along gracefully. She showed neither the speed nor the tense, wild energy of a deer in flight; therefore, I judged that she was not being followed. And as it is very unusual to see a deer traveling about at midday, there must be, I reasoned, some unusual cause for the doe's movements. Slipping from my horse I watched her approach. She was bearing to my left; and while still a hundred yards away she turned abruptly to the right, leaped, with a great show of her snowy tail, a hedgelike growth of gallberries, and then came to a stop in a stretch of breast-high broomgrass. As her running had not been that of a fugitive, so her pause was not that of a listener and a watcher. Instead of standing with head high and ears forward the doe bent her beautiful head, and from the slight movements of her arched neck I knew that she was nuzzling and licking something that could be nothing but a fawn. I tied my horse and quietly drew near, but, alas, generations of hunting have made deer incapable of distinguishing between a friend and an enemy. To a mature deer the scent of a man is the most dreadful of all warnings that death is near.

From *Plantation Game Trails* (1921).

13

As I came up the doe winded me, tossed up her beautiful head, leaped over the high grass, paused to look back, then bounded off again. If there is such a thing as reluctant speed that doe showed it. She went and went fast, but clearly she didn't want to go. Indeed, when three hundred yards off she came to a stop, and after that she did not increase the distance between us. As I approached the fawn the little creature stood up, swayed on its delicate legs, and took one or two uncertain steps away from me. But though startled, it was not frightened. It let me come up to it, stroke it, and prove my friendliness. Indeed, after I had turned away from it the delicate woodland sprite bleated faintly and followed me for a step or two. Far behind, among the glimmering aisles between the pines, the doe began to approach her baby as I receded from it. When I had mounted my horse and ridden some distance away, I caught a glimpse of the mother and baby together again.

This scene of the woodland illustrates a typical incident in what I shall call the "inside life" of our Virginia deer. American hunters are quite familiar with these beautiful creatures, as objects of sport; but few indeed, even of those who know the deer well in a general sense, have an understanding of the real nature and everyday habits of these most interesting creatures. Whatever I know of deer has been gained from many years of experience in the woods; and perhaps a statement of this experience will be of interest to those who care for details of an intimate nature of the lives of the woodland wildernesses.

The little scene described shows us much about the deer. After the birth of the fawn the mother will leave it in a sheltered, sunny spot and will go away to feed. This is a daily habit. Sometimes the doe will go several miles and will return twice or three times a day to nurse her fawn, the frequency of her return depending on the age of the fawn. When a fawn has thus been placed by its mother it will not leave the spot. I once knew this habit to be pathetically illustrated. A Negro worker in the great turpentine woods had brought me a fawn, and I was raising it on a bottle. It slept in the house at night; but early in the morning it would go in its wary, delicate fashion to a patch of oats near the house and lie down. There I always found it for its midday bottle; and there it would remain until I brought it in at dusk. Except when disturbed—by hunters, dogs, or swarms of flies— in all regions where deer are hunted they very seldom move

about in the daylight; but a nursing doe's mother instinct over-
comes her timidity, and she travels from place to place for her
food. When the fawn is very young she never leaves it at night.
This mother-and-child relationship lasts until the fawn is at least
six months old. I have seen a fawn—possibly a "late" one—
following its mother in December. The doe was started first; she
ran off a short distance and waited for the fawn to overtake her,
when both of them bounded off.

As deer secrete themselves by day it will be interesting
to follow them into some of these secluded sanctuaries in
order to discover what kind of cover they like best, and what
precautions they use to secure themselves from danger. Deer
retire to their fastnesses in the early morning; a man never
sees a deer in ideal surroundings unless he sees it coming
forth to feed at twilight, or returning in the misty dusk of
morning. Always an unsubstantial creature the deer is peculiarly so when seen in shadowy forests. In approaching the
place where he is going to lie down for the day a deer—
especially a wise old stag—will try to cross, and even to follow,
water. This always is an effective barrier to trackers. I was
once walking in a swamp, following a trailing hound, when
ahead of me I detected a slight movement. Against the gnarled
roots of a tree standing in shallow water a deer was lying,
literally curled up. It did not leave its refuge until I was
almost on it.

Favorite bedding-places for deer are hummocks or tiny islands in sluggish watercourses. Often, too, where the growth is
dense on the edges of woodland pools, a deer will walk across
the water and lie down on the other side. Then he will need to
be alert for danger from one side only; and that the side which
his tracks have not traversed. In sections where there are growths
of laurel, tamarack, scrub cedars, and other evergreens, these
dense coverts will be haunts of deer. Much, however, depends
on the season of the year and on the state of the weather. In the
winter, on clear days, deer seek for southern exposures, sunny
and wind-sheltered. I once started a drove of seven deer lying
in a tiny amphitheater made by fallen logs. The dense top of a
fallen tree is a favorite place with deer.

In violent storms, by night or day, deer will speedily make
for open stretches of woods, where they will not be in danger of
falling limbs and trees. After such a tornado it is no uncommon

thing to find many cattle killed; but I have known of but one deer to be killed in this way. If the weather is rainy deer will move about in the day in search of shelter. An old hunter told me that if a snowstorm sets in during the day, he always looks for deer under the densest hemlock trees on the mountain. One day I was going home through a heavy rain, when I was astonished to see a great buck cross the road ahead of me and go into a very heavy myrtle copse beside the road. Being unpursued and showing no signs of fear he was evidently merely getting in out of the wet. There was something positively bored about his expression; it resembled that of a chicken, which, being caught in a far corner of the yard in a shower, runs disgustedly for shelter.

During those periods in summer when gauze-winged flies are a torment, deer resort to the densest thickets, and at such times they do little lying down. I remember coming, on an August day, upon three deer—they were a family—on the edge of a heavy copse. Being unobserved and unsuspected, I saw the creatures behave in what must have been a most natural manner. There was continuous petulant stamping, much flicking up and down of the ends of tails—precisely after the manner of goats— and an impatient tossing up and down of graceful heads. The buck, which carried fine antlers, once lowered his stately head and made a sudden tumultuous rush through the dense bushes. Probably he did this to clear himself from the flies and in order to ease the itching which was making his velvety horns tingle. As soon as I showed myself two tall while tails and one tail-let rocked off in standard fashion into the thicket.

As deer are seldom seen by day except when they are disturbed, the time to observe them is at night; but, naturally, they are even less frequently seen then. In regions where deer are plentiful their shadowy forms are seen crossing old roads or clearings at dawn and at dusk. No one can have an accurate idea of the true life of the wild deer who has not observed the creature browsing by moonlight. Now that most of the animal enemies of deer have been practically exterminated in the whitetail's habitat—such enemies as wolves and catamounts—deer fear the dark less than the light. Their movements are bolder and freer; by daylight a deer is seldom aught but a skulker, a fugitive. In the Southern pine-woods I have watched deer at night, and they seem to me stranger, wilder, more dreamlike creatures than any I had observed by daylight.

Near our plantation house there was the ruin of an old Negro church. This stood in a circular clearing of about an acre in extent, surrounded on three sides by scrub pines, and on the fourth by low myrtle and gallberry bushes. For some reason the clearing had remained inviolate of growths of any kind. In the center was the ruined church, which was ringed by an arena of pure white sand. I discovered that deer loved to come to this place at night, partly because it lay between their daytime haunts and their favorite night feeding-grounds, and partly because deer seem to love open sandy places—"yards" they are sometimes called. I buried some rock salt in the sand by the old church, knowing that the deer would find it and come to it regularly. Then in the forks of a pine I built a suitable platform, about sixteen feet up. I should have hidden among the timbers of the old church but for the fact that a deer "travels by his nose." Both by day and by night a deer's eyesight is comparatively poor; it is not to be compared to the clairvoyant seeing power of a wild turkey. But a deer can generally wind and locate a man, if he is not well off the ground. During the still nights of good moonlight in November and December I spent many a solitary hour on this platform, waiting and watching for deer, and being richly rewarded.

In order that some time might elapse between my coming on the ground and the arrival of the deer, I always ascended the platform at sunset. I shall try to describe exactly what I saw and heard from this platform on a typical night.

Though near a plantation road it was at least three miles from any habitation. There were therefore absent many of those sights and sounds which characterize the Southern plantation twilight. Sometimes I could hear the melodious whooping of a Negro, but usually the only sounds were from the wild denizens of the woods. In the dim distance an owl would hoot; perhaps a fox would bark; and once I heard the cry of a wildcat, utterly savage. Then the risen moon would begin to steep the woods in light, and with the coming of the moonlight there seemed to be a cessation of the wild cries; there was movement in the forest, the mysterious movement of wild life that hunts by night or is hunted. Long before I could see anything, I could hear furtive steps, glimpse a swaying bush, and hear twigs crack. Animals of many kinds were prowling; the half-wild hogs and cattle that infest the Southern pine woods; the crafty raccoons, pacing along well-worn paths; the silent foxes, the very spirit of craftiness;

the hushed-winged birds that love darkness better than light. Last, after I had been on the platform nearly three hours, came the deer.

No other creature of the forest seems more a shape of the moonlight than does the deer. It is apparently possible for the largest buck to move through the dense bushes and over beds of dry twigs with no perceptible sound. A movement rather than a sound off to my left had attracted my attention; another glance showed me the glint of horns. A full-grown stag was in the act of jumping a pile of fallen logs. He literally floated over the obstruction, ghostlike, uncanny. I noticed that he jumped with his tail down—a thing he would not do if he were startled. Behind him were two does. They negotiated the barrier still more lithely than the buck had done. Even in the deceptive moonlight and at the distance they were from me—fifty yards—I could easily discern a difference in the aspect distinguishing the buck from the does; the stag was bold, proud, impatiently alert; the hinds were hardly less alert, but were meek followers of their master. All three of them were feeding; but at no one time did all of them have their heads down at the same moment. One always seemed to be on watch, and this one usually the buck. For a few seconds at a time his proud head would be bowed among the bushes; then it would be lifted with a jerk, and for minutes he would stand champing restlessly his mouthful of leaves, grass, and tender twigs. Often he would hold his head at peculiar angles—oftenest thrust forward—as if drinking in all the scents of the dewy night woods. After a while, moving in silence and in concert, the shadowy creatures came up on the space of white sand which stretched away in front of me. Now they paused, spectral in the moonlight, now moved about with indescribably lithe grace, never losing, even amid the "secure delight" of such a time and place, their air of superb readiness, of elfin caution, suppressed but instantly available. The steps they took seemed to me extraordinarily long; and it was difficult to keep one of the creatures in sight all the while. They would appear and reappear; and their color and the distinctness of their outlines depended on the angle at which they were seen. Broadside, they looked almost black; head-on, they were hardly visible. At no time could I distinguish their legs. When they moved off into the pine thicket, whither I knew they had gone to eat mushrooms, they vanished without a sound, apparently without exerted motion, and I was left alone in the moonlight.

In addition to his fondness for mushrooms the deer is also a great devourer of hazelnuts, chestnuts, acorns of many kinds,— especially those of the white oak and of the live oak—beechnuts, pine mast, and the like. Occasionally he will eat apples; and I have known peach-trees to be wholly stripped of their half-ripe fruit by deer. Of domestic crops the deer will eat anything green and succulent; he delights in wheat, rye, buckwheat, oats, al- falfa, rice, sweet potato vines, young corn, timothy, turnips, beans, and peanut vines. Deer have been known to pull up peanut vines in order to get at the nuts, which they greedily relish.

In order to obtain these green crops of the field and garden deer resort to some very crafty devices. A great hunting club in the South had planted several acres of peas to attract quail; the deer found the peas in the early summer, and every night a herd of six or seven jumped the six-foot fence. The fence was raised to eight feet, and this height the marauders did not negotiate. But possibly it was because they did not have to. Whenever I think of the jumping power of deer I am reminded of a shrewd remark once made to me by an old woodsman: "A deer can jump as far or as high as he has to." In this case the deer, to enter the field, got down in an old ditch, crawled under the wire fence, and found themselves in clover. And so baffling was the manner of the deer's entrance that the manager of the preserve could not account for it until he had sat up in an oak on a moonlight night and had seen the affair come off.

This striking instance of crafty intelligence may well serve to introduce the question of the deer's mental capacity. At the outset it can assuredly be said that the deer is so intelligent that it is impossible to classify his probable actions. As animals in- crease in intelligence the chances of their behaving in a regular, unvarying manner are decidedly decreased. It therefore becomes impossible for us to say that a deer will do this or will not do that under certain circumstances, for he has both a certain sense of judgment and at least a rudimentary power of decision. This intelligence is best illustrated by examples of the deer's clev- erness.

A buck in cover, if he hears what he takes to be danger

approaching, will carefully weigh his chances; though it is his instinct to run up the wind, he will dash down it if in such a course appears to be his way to safety. If from afar he hears the noise and decides that it means danger, he will probably slip craftily out; if the danger is near before he is aware of its approach, he may steal out silently, he may bound out with astonishing vigor and speed, or he may lie where he is, even though the peril be upon him.

After it has passed it is like him to leap up and sail off down the back track of his enemy. It all depends on what seems to him the wisest thing to do under the particular circumstances. A buck will send does or a young buck out of a thicket ahead of him or he may take the lead himself.

One day in the woods I walked within twenty paces of a buck which was lying down on the sand under some leafless scrub oaks. I probably should never have seen him but for the fact that, as he moved his head craftily, I saw the rocking antlers. He had his lower jaw flat on the ground, much like a crouching rabbit. He was planning to have me pass him by, but I disappointed him. Almost the instant that he discerned that I had seen him he bounded up and was gone. A friend of mine had a somewhat similar experience with a buck; only the buck did not wake up until my friend seized him by the horn, when there was a regular tableau. Whether this buck was deaf, I do not know; but the manner of his flight betrayed not the slightest impairment of any of his other physical powers.

When deer are hunted on sea islands, where their range is naturally limited, they will frequently leave their wooded haunts and take to the surf. I have seen a buck go two hundred yards out in shoal water and stand there for hours, with little more than his back and his antlered head showing above the water. Frequently, from a refuge of this kind, a deer will not come ashore until after nightfall. On reaching the beach after such an experience a deer is always plainly exhausted.

From these examples it is easy to infer the degree of a deer's intelligence—the brain power of this mischievous, playful, timid, curious, truculent creature.

I say he is truculent; and on occasion he undoubtedly is. A doe is never dangerous; but a buck in the mating season is a treacherous animal. It is his nature at such a time to attack. It is the time of love, of rivalry, and of combat; and a buck, with his clean, sharp antlers, his new dun coat, is a creature of ugly and uncertain temper. Keepers of preserves are frequently attacked; but I doubt if a buck in a wild state would ever attack a man unless cornered or wounded. If the records of men being injured by wounded deer be examined, it will be found that in the majority of cases the victims have been injured by the wild struggles of the deer rather than by any direct attack of the creature.

At close quarters the sharp hoofs of a deer's front feet are more to be feared than the antlers.

But while bucks very seldom bring man to an encounter, they are forever fighting their fellows, at least until some sort of caste system of superiority is established. In the course of these combats many fatalities occur, the most gruesome of which are the cases of locked antlers. The fighting of deer is playing with fire.

Often two bucks, in a spirit of frolic or of indolent urgings of strength, will put their heads together just to feel the tingle that must come when hard horn raps against hard horn. They may break off the bout in a friendly spirit, or, stirred by a painful wrench of the neck or a jab from an antler point, they may enter a battle which gradually increases in fury. This fierceness of the fray may continue even after the battle is ended; for sometimes the victorious stag will mutilate the body of his fallen rival. This he can do by retreating, turning, bounding back and jumping on his fallen adversary. Carcasses of such bucks have been found which have literally been cut to pieces. Wherever two bucks have been fighting, there will be an arena worn almost bare of verdure by their trampling hoofs. Occasionally on the scene of the encounter a broken part of an antler will be found. Few are the mature bucks that do not show evidences of their having been in battle.

His antlers are, of course, the pride and the glory of the buck. I read recently, in a book of natural history that has had a wide circulation, the following statement: "The older and larger the buck, the finer the crown of antlers he wears." This is not entirely wrong, but it is quite misleading. Deer antlers are directly related in growth to the reproductive processes; and a buck will wear his most massive crown when his physical powers are at their zenith. This usually comes, with the whitetail deer, between the fifth and the twelfth years. The size of the buck does not determine the size of his antlers, though the ruggedness of the life he leads may determine to some degree the architecture of his horns. Thus, the wilder the surroundings, the heavier and the more craggy are the antlers. Naturally, this is because in savage environment the deer has great need for his horns as defensive weapons.

In the old days deer had many enemies; and even now in the wilder portions of their habitat some of these enemies are present. Man is the chief; after him are cougars, wolves, wild-cats—which kill fawns—and possibly the more savage of the bears, though the smaller bears and deer are known to live amicably in the same woods.

But take it all in all, deer probably have fewer natural foes to contend with than almost any other of the wild creatures. Their closed season is long and is pretty general throughout the sections where the whitetail is found.

Occasionally a deer will be killed by a rattlesnake, but far more frequently will the rattler be killed. In sections where alligators infest lagoons, streams, and wood ponds, many deer are taken by these grim saurians. The fawns sometimes suffer from the raids of eagles, particularly golden eagles.

The only disease which makes any considerable inroad into the ranks of the whitetail is black tongue, or hoof-and-mouth disease—anthrax. This is a highly contagious disease, and it is singularly fatal to deer. In riding the woods where such a plague is abroad I have counted as many as eleven deer in various stages of the malady. Such deer act very strangely. Some attempt to run, but fall over. Some lie quite still. Others stand, shaking and shivering as with the ague. The superb normal health of a deer, which enables it almost incredibly to recover from terrible wounds, seems unable to combat this fell disease. Wherever it appears in deer forests its effects are disastrous.

Unless attacked by black tongue, or unless meeting an untimely fate, deer may live for thirty years; Millais, the British authority, says that deer live as long as horses. But the deer's existence is precarious, and few ever attain an age exceeding fifteen years. I have seen several ancient bucks taken, and they gave clear evidences of age: their hoofs were broad, stubby, and cracked; their muzzles were grizzled; their horns were small and scraggly; and even their motions in the woods were as near being decrepit as I suppose the motions of so alert and graceful a creature can ever become.

Such are some of the facts concerning the secret life of the whitetail deer. It is an animal vividly interesting; shy and crafty, swift and elusive, gentle and beautiful. There is no creature which seems more adequately to express the spirit of the lonely wood, the solitary lake, the silent mountain, the gloomy swamp.

He who sees a deer in its native surroundings sees all that is wildest in the wilderness, all that is most haunting in deep sanctuaries, all that is most delicately alluring in remote woodlands, in wild valleys, and on far mountains.

A Baby Fawn

Perhaps the most appealing of all babes of the woods is the fawn of the Virginia or whitetail deer. There is an old English superstition that if a fawn ever hears the human voice and feels the touch of the human hand, it will desert its own kind to follow man. This has some truth in it. At least, I have never had any trouble in "gentling" a fawn. It makes the most interesting, affectionate, playful, and troublesome of pets. I say "troublesome" because the fawn can jump almost anything. You cannot keep both a fawn and flowers, especially geraniums. He will not only eat the stalks and flowers, but he will take the most childish delight—especially if he be a little buck—in pushing off with his head every flower-pot on a stand. I think he enjoys hearing the pots fall and break.

One day I was driving down a pineland road with a companion, who happened to have a gun. As we neared a woodsman's cabin a fawn dashed out of a thicket, jumped the road, and ran into the yard in front of the cabin. My friend sprang from the buggy with his gun. I warned him not to shoot so close to the house, and of course I didn't want him to kill the fawn. As we came up, the owner of the cabin met us, and we asked him about the young deer.

"Oh, that," he said; "that's the baby's pet. I expect it's under the dining-room table now. It always hides there when it gets scared. He and the baby sleep together," he added, his voice softening in affection. "The fawn sleeps on the floor, and the baby lies down beside it and puts its head on the fawn's flank. If the fawn wakes when the baby is still asleep, the fawn will not stir; but if the baby wakes first, he will pull the fawn's ears. We call them the twins."

From *Wild Life of the South* (1935).

24

A WOODLAND COURTSHIP

One October day I was walking along the dewy sweet border of a deep bay thicket in the wasteland of the great Carolina coastal country. The sun was not yet up. Hale airs made the great pines murmur and wave, shedding with their melodious music aromatic odors—primeval forests fragrances that the heart is fain to dream may be the very breath of life, of death, or of love. Those three are, after all, the great trinity.

Down a dim forest pathway, overhung with misty grass tops, I saw a doe coming. She had not seen me. Indeed, she was in full flight; and naturally she was chiefly concerned with what was behind her rather than with what was before her. Lithe, exquisite, a veritable palpitation out of the great forest's heart, feminine in that mysterious sex's indefinable delicacy, on she came. She did not run as a deer runs from dogs or men—in mad, incontinent flight, with tail high and nervously jerked from side to side with the rocking of the haunches. The flight of this doe, beautiful to behold, was merely a part of the ancient hide-and-seek game of the female and the male. Having in it no fear, it yet possessed an alluring imitation of timidity—purposeful in its shyness, fatal in its modesty. Here was suddenly divulged the passionate, exquisite, infallible lure of Beauty's shadowy feigned avoidance.

Love's fugitive passed me; rocked lithely through a golden breast-high sedgefield; trotted through a red copse of huckleberry; paused; dodged through a small myrtle-bordered pond; passed up an old lumber road; paused once more to look back. Was this a flight? It was full of sweet delays of feigned escape.

From *Children of Swamp and Wood* (1927).

Hers was that flight which yearns for pursuit. She wanted to be followed, perhaps followed fast; but she didn't want to be overtaken—not yet. While unqualified to venture an opinion on so wide a subject, I believe it universally true of the feminine that capture is sweeter after long, arduous, dangerous, oft-frustrated pursuit. The game, at any rate, is one of stunning contradictions; and perhaps is not yet fully mastered by far wiser than I. It has to do with frantic, wild denials, with impetuous, intimate surrender. It has to do with much that is mystic. Some things are not meant to be explained.

The doe that I had been watching faded into the distant forest—vanishing in that silent and eerie fashion which is characteristic of deer. Of the tremulous spirit of the virgin wilderness are they; and I never see one without feeling that the ancient inscrutable forest has for a moment uttered a beautiful secret— a secret usually held inviolately within the deep wood's wise mothering heart. And now a second secret that heart was to tell; fast on the track of the doe came the stag.

In this rapturous season of love and of mating, the presence of a doe renders inevitable the presence of a buck. He may be miles behind, but he will follow. Sometimes, several does will herd, possibly feeling a sense of security in so doing. And for days and nights, for weeks—indeed, in some cases, for months— the long pursuit will continue. The virgin does hold out longest.

The buck that was following my doe was a handsome fellow, sheeny in his fresh dun coat, regal in his tall antlers. He was swiftly and shrewdly drinking up the alluring scent that lingered on the trail—"fair, speechless messages," relayed by the dew-hung bushes. It was odd to see him running with his head low, and with an intentness of purpose almost human. He came very close to me. He saw me. Of all living things, I was his fellest and most ancient enemy. Did he swerve from his direction? Did he quit the game? One of the Elizabethan dramatists, I believe, poignantly describes death as the mere giving over of a game that must be lost. But love is a game that must be won; it is not in the heart to give it over. Only a glance of haughty indifference the pursuing stag gave me—such a look as he might have employed to pierce a rival. His broad black nose, with red nostril-pits wide, never left the trail. He recognized me as something living which did not represent the goal of his passionate search. Less than nothing was I in his proud consideration.

With reason it might be supposed that one feature of this forest bridal, this woodland romance, that would lend a peculiarly alluring charm to it would be the fact that the courtship takes place in those dim hours of twilight and dawn, and in the silver hours of moonlight and of starlight. True, the deer is of the night; and during the gaudy hours of day is usually serenely couched in some lonely thicket. Much mating is done during that time of the day and night when the deer are usually feeding and moving. But so urgent is the impulse of the mating season that the bucks pursue the does throughout the day. I have, in mid-October, in the very heyday of the deer's courtship, observed a twelve-point stag, in all the bald literalness of bright sunshine, in all the utterly trite obviousness of high noon, pursuing in stern passion an elusive acquaintance. The doe I did not see; but she had not been gone long. He would overtake her; perhaps for a week he might follow. But in this kind of game, Nature dooms one to lose. Or do both win? Or does the fugitive win? The course of the male is cave-mannish, obvious, gauche, over-weening; that of the female is subtle, smacking of sorcery, witching in perverseness. I think she wins.

And now the scene changes, and we are among the wild Tuscarora hills of southern Pennsylvania. This is a strange region—close to the hoof-hearted hurry of civilization, yet intimately retired mistily among old mountains haunted by silence and by peace. Across one line of hills can be heard the roar of a Pennsylvania creeper; across another a fellow freight train on the B. & O. shrieks for a crossing. The air tingles with these blatant voices of Progress. Yet the same air, here in this fastness, is aromatic with the dusky fragrance of dewy hemlocks, with the odor of ripened wild grapes, with those vague but penetrant woodland spiceries of which, assuredly, nectar must be made. The tattered gold of yet unfallen leaves forms fragmentary arras marginal to mystery. Though an amethyst light is fast suffusing the lonely forest, heralding dawn, one great white star trembles like a gleaming jewel in the dark crown of foliage worn by a mountain pine. Still is the forest with primeval stillness; there is no wind, but the woodsy fragrances themselves seem to be breathing, uttering the poignant aromas of the fulfilment of nameless longings. Definitely, I smell shellbarks, damp pine-needles, wet mosses beside a tiny rill, and a profusion of odors sweet as that of an "indolent misty peach," heavy with summer's sweetness stored.

But it is of the love-story of the wild deer that I am wishing to tell; and on this quiet wooded hillside, here is the tale written indelibly. No man who runs can read it; but one who walks slowly, and who pauses long to observe, will translate somewhat as follows the silent but eloquent language of tracks.

Down the side of this shadowy glen, probably late yesterday afternoon, there came a stag. He must have been a sprightly fellow. His stepping was all on edge. His hoofprints, see, are shallow, and they are inclined to tip forward. An old buck is more likely to walk flat-footed. This cavalier is, in effect, walking on his toes, adopting an anciently approved approach to the lady of his adoration. Here, either something startled him or else the urge of the mystic season impelled him; for, look, he has taken a vibrant leap—eighteen feet by measurement. "How far can a deer jump?" I once inquired of a grizzled swamp-hunter. "As far as he needs to," came the comprehensive reply. A horse in an English steeplechase has cleared thirty-six feet; a man has jumped more than twenty-five; a deer has been known, rather unconcernedly, and over no obstacle, to leap thirty-two. A jump of eighteen is therefore merely a little frisk. I have measured the casual jump of a doe from her bed; airily she sailed sixteen feet. Think of that, from a lying-down position—and without the training of daily-dozen exercise!

Here our buck, reaching the open flat area of an old charcoal hearth, has stood for some time. A stag loves an open place in the woods. I have known deer to stand for hours on sand dunes, gazing at the sea. They like clearings, especially at night—and old roads, and pathways that offer clearance for horns. On the north end of this ancient woodland hearth, telling of a departed race of mountaineers, a wild grape had let down a tapestry of vines, loaded now with frosted purple clusters, deep in bloom. Lusciously they drooped—an affluent offering by the primitive mother. On some of these bunches the stag had champed negligently. But he was not interested in eating. He was not hunting grapes.

Leaving the hearth, he has followed the fragrant glenside to the lowest bench of the mountain. Here are secret thickets, the mournful beauty of an old clearing, now fast being reclaimed "by the forest"; here, under the girlish grace of silver birches, shimmering in the dusk, under the stubborn hardihood of many a mountain ash and towering poplar, there is a delicious glade. It is a deer rendezvous. I think it beyond dispute possible for creatures of the high intelligence of the deer to prearrange meetings. For example, I once had two stags come straight for me as I stood on a road. They saw me and checked up to reconnoitre. Separating, they passed me like lightning, one running on my right and the other a hundred yards away on my left. A half mile beyond the road they swung together again. And this happened where there was no regular deer run. Of the comings together in the mating season, perhaps the custom of being together in a certain place at a certain time of day has its determining power. But these secret children of the forest have resources of which we do not dream. A deer's sense of locality and of direction is perfect. He is not at all likely to have a wide range. A deer undisturbed, with a sufficient food-supply offered on his range, will likely live and die near where he was born. In home woods, a deer knows every tree and every thicket, every bypath and every road. A doe, secreting her fawn, may go miles away to food, may return by another route. But her reapproach to her little one is as infallibly accurate as the flight of a bird to its nest, as the turning of the mother toward her child.

In our mountain glade our sprightly stag had expected a doe. Here, you see, on the glimmering edges of it, he has paused, listening, looking, scenting the hale sweetness of the air.

Circling the glade, let us discover the doe track. Yes, here it is. After a long and palpitating pause, she minced timidly out of the bosky thicket. This buck had pursued her long and arduously, and she had ever eluded him. But such play comes to an end. She has at last relented; perhaps she cannot help herself. Here she has been nervously stamping her dainty feet. Why did not her lover come straight across to her? See, in her restless hope-and-fear mood, she has reached up and caught and broken that hickory twig that you see dangling about five feet above the ground. Many a time have I found such telltale evidence of a doe's tremulous sweet suspense, full of anxiety and of the delight of delay. Let us step into the arena of the glade. Now you see what has happened. This has been indeed an arena.

For a space of twenty yards the ground is torn up by vicious tramplings. The piles of gaudy leaves have been tossed about.

Young shoots of maple and of hackberry have been crushed down. Deep into the black sandy loam of the glade there are the savage scars of deeply driven hoofs. As Elaine read the shield of Launcelot, visioning his battles, so you may here read this record of a wild and lonely strife between two furious bucks. They have fought for more than life; they have contested for love. With wide horns clashing, with burly necks lowered, with legs spread and braced, here they have fought the business out. Look here on this young poplar. Its gray side is smudged with red; and here cling little tufts of white and dun hair. One of the rivals ran the other against this tree. Here, too, is a heavy splotch of blood on this old log. That probably means a rip in the side or in the neck from a sharp horn. For a long time they fought—perhaps for an hour. Then one yielded. Which one was it? Let us see which buck led the doe away. It is not hard to discover; for the bucks have very different tracks. Oh, see! Our friend of the sprightly step has won. He must have been too active for the old stag. The lord and master of the mountain is being replaced. The younger buck fought as lovers fight who are young. And now, into the silent shadows these forest lovers have wandered away. After long waiting, and following, after battle, after victory, love waits. Love is a long inheritance; and from its mystic joys the children of the wild are not excluded.

I described going into the mountain early in the morning and making the observation in question—eavesdropping, as it were. It is after twilight when I come out.

Over the mountain is shed the serene wild glory of the light of an autumn full moon. Its beauty hymns lyrically to the primitive in man. I am out on the lonely road now, a road leading back to the valley and to civilization. But though my face is turned homeward, with a primeval yearning my heart turns backward—there toward the peace of the silent hills—the glamour of the moonlit forest—back toward that beauteous bridal of the forest wilds, deep-veiled upon the hushed and fragrant bosom of the huge sequestered night.

TAMPERING WITH KINGLY CROWNS

During the past eight or ten years this business of tampering with kingly crowns has been exceedingly popular, and interest in the sport has been worldwide. I should like briefly to describe a variety of this recreation with which I am somewhat familiar; and it is more innocent than that of assailing the headpiece of a mortal monarch. In brief, I think it can be established that the growth of deer-antlers can be made subject to man's control. My discovery of this has been somewhat curious; and while the truth of it may not yet be established, I hope it may seem interesting and plausible.

During nearly thirty-five years of deer hunting and of roaming deer-haunts, I have never been impressed with anything more than the fact that in certain localities the stags seem to wear bigger horns than they do in other places, even though the latter may be quite near—say, within twenty or thirty miles. I know two small private preserves—not parks, but estates of two or three thousand acres, and in desperately wild country—where the stags grow antlers that are unbelievably large. So well is this curious fact known by sportsmen of the vicinity—near Charleston, South Carolina—that whenever a phenomenal head is seen at a taxidermist's or elsewhere, someone always says: "Oh, that must be from the Millbrook Place or from the Oakland Club. The deer there always have better horns than they can grow elsewhere." And to show what is meant by "better," I may say that many of these heads have a spread of from twenty-two to twenty-four inches, a beam-circumference of from five to six

From *Days Off in Dixie* (1925).

31

inches, and carry from twelve to eighteen-points. But it is the general appearance rather than any special feature which really impresses: the burly, rugged, craggy, massive aspect of these splendid antlers.

Once or twice I hunted where these great deer are found; and one feature of the landscape impressed me constantly. It is the so-called dredge cuts. The country lies close to the sea; and it is here that valuable mineral deposits in the form of phosphate rock are found. These workings have been going on for nearly a century, and as a result much of the forest, destroyed by the first workings, has now returned; but the whole region is deeply and strangely serrated by these profound dredge cuts, deep and wide ditches, now half filled with water, canals now a permanent feature of the forest. The deer in this kind of country love nothing better than to feed on the lush grasses that fringe these cuts, and they drink from these old canals. I had often wondered if they did not assimilate an unusual amount of lime into their systems by feeding and drinking where this marl rock had been mined, and where much of it that was not removed by the dredges remained exposed to various forms of erosion. That deer do thus assimilate lime I now believe there can be no doubt; and that its absorption affects the growth of their horns is, of course, a natural and easy assumption.

But while I was thinking over this business, I had a talk with a friend who had lately come from England, where he had been privileged to inspect a certain duke's deer preserve.

"The duke," he said, "has been experimenting with the horns of his red deer; and he has already produced antlers larger than any ever seen in the Kingdom. His keepers feed the stags turnips sprinkled with slaked lime. As you know, a deer, being of the goat family, will eat almost anything; and these deer take famously to lime, which acts directly on their antlers."

As lime is one of the chief constituents of horn and of bone, this theory seems altogether likely to prove true; and I believe I have found why the deer of a certain place are likely to have so much finer antlers than the stags of some other neighborhood. Have they not access to some alkali springs or some other source of lime? This belief may prove also why a buck of inferior proportions may sometimes wear a statelier crown than one a monster in size.

Hereafter, upon encountering a stag, the proper question to

ask will be, not "Have you had your iron to-day?" or "Have you had your vitamins to-day?" but rather, "Old scout, what about that lime? Have you been taking it regularly?"

This business I do not assert as gospel truth. I honestly just wouldn't swear to it. But I'd risk about a thousand berries off next week's salary bush that there's something in it. Nor, even if it's true, do I think this tampering can very easily be practised on wild stags of an unlimited range. Yet perhaps it wouldn't be harder to put lime on one's tongue than salt on one's tail; easier, by a mile. A buck has to get a certain amount of lime to grow any horns at all; and if he has access to a good supply, he'll not be bashful. He seldom is except when he is dodging bullets.

BUCKS ARE LIKE THAT

One day in the sunny pinelands of the South I was on a deer stand about 200 yards in front of a dense sweet bay thicket. Beside me was a Negro guide to whom, as I was to learn, the mysteries of deer nature were no mysteries at all. As the drive came on through the heavy copse an old eight-point buck stole out of the fragrant greenery of the junglelike bayhead. On he came softly. He was neither running nor walking; he appeared to glide without sound or perceptible effort.

Then suddenly the buck came to a halt, and there stood at his full height. By that time he was within 160 yards of me, and facing my way. I was amazed at the height to which he lifted his head. As the only breeze stirring was from him to me, I knew that he would not wind me; yet, despite the clamor of the Negro drivers behind, who were ardently heaping imprecations on the whole race of bucks, there he stood, the master strategist of the wilderness.

My guide and I were concealed in the heavy cover of some young pines.

"Why does he keep standing there like that?" I whispered to my dusky companion.

"He is readin' his book," the Negro told me.

That was it: he was taking time to weigh all possible chances. Before coming to a decision that he knew might be critical, he had sense enough to estimate everything. Then followed a maneuver for which I was totally unprepared, though I have hunted deer systematically for nearly fifty years and though last Christmas I hung up my one hundred and third stag.

From *Those Were the Days* (1955).

The buck sank out of sight in the yellow broomsedge. He just subsided, tall horns and all. It seemed incredible that a creature so large, with such big antlers, could suddenly fade into grass hardly over two feet high. But he did. No witch ever vanished more completely.

"What is he doing now?" I whispered to my Negro.

"His book tells him to play a trick. His book is full of tricks," the Negro assured me.

Knowing less then about an old buck's ancient craft than I was to learn a few minutes after, I felt sure that the drivers would push him out to me. But five minutes later, when they broke through the thicket, my guide touched my arm.

"See him yonder?" he asked, pointing far over to my left.

Barely discernible above the golden sea of the broomsedge I saw the ivory tips of moving horns. He had literally crawled around me under cover of the grass. Neither his head nor any part of his body could be seen. At nearly three hundred yards, when he was completely out of the drive, he leaped up and was gone into the glimmering woods.

Bucks are like that; and your chances in hunting them are diminished in proportion to your failure to read their "books" with them.

It is generally and perhaps naturally supposed that deer, when hard hunted, will retire as deeply into the wilderness as they can go. They may, if in the depths of the wilds they find security; but as often they may attempt the ruse of coming even closer to civilization than they usually range. Once I had a very curious confirmation of this truth.

On my plantation in Carolina we had hunted for several weeks a famous stag, Roland by name, for such is an old buck's personality that he often acquires a proper name. At last he vanished completely, and I supposed that other hunters had killed him or that he had taken refuge on the vast and primeval Santee Delta, which is a natural sanctuary for all such fugitives.

But one day, just after my hunting party had broken up, an old Negro came to me to ask why I had stopped hunting the renowned old Roland. I said that we had been unable to find him. He then told me that for ten or twelve nights the buck had slept in some tall weeds close to his cabin. Leaving his bed at dusk, he would roam the woods feeding, and at the break of day he would come out of the wilderness to lie down beside the old man's humble home. I was somewhat incredulous of the story; but on visiting the place with my informant I found eleven fresh beds, and the tracks to and from them were unmistakably Roland's.

One December day, as I made my way almost silently through knee-high huckleberry bushes, a misty rain was falling. There was no wind. As I was in good deer country, I was on the alert; but as so often occurs when we hunters are most alert, nothing happened. This stretch of bronzed bushes in the lone pinelands of my plantation had always been a favorite bedding place for bucks; and it happened to be bucks in which I was at that moment especially interested.

At last, for some reason, I paused and looked back; it may have been instinct that made me do so. As I turned slightly, out of those low bushes a gray form launched itself as a torpedo leaves a submarine. It was a ten-pointer, fifty yards behind me, coming out of a bed that was not fifteen steps from the line of my walk. He had deliberately let me pass him; and he never moved until my pause and turn gave him a certain pitch of suspicion. He gave me a fair shot, and I killed him.

Then came my two Negro drivers, who had been on the far side of the low but dense copse. We held a jubilation. We hung up the buck; we built a fire and dried off. The boys whooped and sang as though they had discovered a still.

After nearly half an hour of this racket I said, "I'm going over here to see if I can't find this old boy's bed."

He had fallen only about twenty yards from where he had gotten up.

In going to investigate, I left my gun leaning against a tree. Well, as I drew near the place where my stag had been couched, to my amazement out ripped a second and a much larger one. They had been lying side by side; I know it because I found both beds. Both had let me pass them at first; then one had made a break for liberty. But the other had stayed right where he was, in spite of all the noise we made; and he never would have left that spot unless I had literally kicked him out of bed.

Such incidents serve to raise the question, pertinent to every deer hunter: What may I expect my buck to do? I do not know that I can answer that question adequately, for experience has taught me that nearly every buck is a distinct individual. I might say that all bucks, like all men, are created unequal. As intelligence increases in animals, the only thing that you really have a right to expect is an infinite variety of behavior. And I don't know but that's the real reason why deer hunting is so fascinating. To put an old lean-flanked, rough-shod veteran of this kind on the spot, you have to be smarter than he is; and outguessing a buck is a feat in mental gymnastics.

While deer, like human beings, sometimes make fatal mistakes, yet you might as well count on your buck's being smart; and unless you are on to some of his wildwood tricks, he is going to outwit you. In the hope that I may make a few profitable suggestions to those who have fallen under the spell of the whitetail, I recommend that you make careful calculations of some of the master stratagems of this king of the wilderness.

I have already told that your buck may let you pass by him. We hear a lot about the wildness of deer, and we suppose that means a deer will be up and away long before you come near him. Never believe it. Repeatedly I have walked and have ridden within a few paces of a couched buck, and I have done it when the wind was in his favor. He was not asleep and he was not dumb; he was just estimating chances. An experienced stag knows that to jump up in front of a man usually means to be shot at, and I believe that many a hunter would be perfectly incredulous if he could know the number of deer he has passed by. Is not the same thing true with quail and with grouse and even with rabbits?

I think a good deal depends on the line of the hunter's approach. If he is going straight for his game, it is far more likely to leave its bed than it is if his normal course will take him some yards to one side of the couched bird or animal. For my part, so true do I believe this to be, that, if I am attempting to get up on game, have little cover, and am pretty sure that it is aware of my coming (and the chances are always in favor of its having detected your presence), I always change my course so as not to appear to be directly approaching the hider. I also assume an elaborate air of nonchalance and innocence, as if I were looking for buttercups, or were an Englishman going nowhere.

Depend upon it, game detects danger in a hunter's too earnest attitude. The Negroes on my plantation never carry guns, and they can go in and out among the game just as if they were wild creatures themselves; but let me appear, and the game turns on all its strategy.

Now, that buck you are after is almost like a human being in his intelligence; and in some important respects he will make some human beings look like descendants of a long line of morons. For example, he knows the woods as we can never hope to know them. Where food is adequate and cover sufficient, the range of a whitetail is likely to be very limited; and it frequently happens that one or two old stags will rule a certain domain. And every foot of that wild country they know intimately. They seem to know every rock, tree and bush. They know exactly where to pause, skulk, turn; and they know where they can make time running. One of the reasons why natives usually have better luck in deer hunting than strangers in a certain territory is that they have come to a knowledge of the terrain that is somewhat comparable to that of the game they pursue.

I have said that your buck may let you pass him. One day I was hunting in open sand-hill country where the ground was practically bare and where the only trees were small scrub oaks, then leafless. Coming up over a sudden rise, my eyes instantly caught, forty yards away, an old buck lying on the white sand, utterly exposed.

At the time I had been whistling for my dog, so that the deer had had ample warning of my approach, even before he saw me. There was absolutely no chance for me to hide. There I was, in full sight. And did that buck leave for parts unknown, as you would expect him to do? He did not. What he did was to flatten his jaw to the ground.

When he had heard me coming, he had evidently changed his position. Like all deer when they lie down, he had been couched on his side; now he was flat on his belly, his knees buckled under him, and his hind legs set in a wide stance. I have often observed that deer, if they have any warning at all of the approach of an enemy, will take this position, from which they can make a projectile-like getaway.

It was comical to watch this wily old master. Here was a ten-point stag trying to make himself look like a rabbit. To make him get up (I somehow get no thrill out of shooting anything in its bed), I kept whistling for my dog. Every time I whistled he would flatten himself lower; when I stopped, he would ease up a little. What betrays the presence of a deer in a case like this is the rocking of his horns.

After a time my dog came up from the other side, and he

and the buck started a race after all records. I brought the deer down on about his fourth jump. I think it best, if possible, not to shoot at a stag until he has a few jumps out of his system. You may miss him. I have.

His first jump seemed to me so prodigious that, when I was fully satisfied that his jumping days were over, I went back to where he had been lying, and measured carefully that first leap. It was an inch or two short of twenty feet, and that from a lying-down position! I once heard an amateur excusing an atrocious miss by saying that it was not really his fault; that he had had his sight on the deer, but that it jumped over his shot. At this alibi a grizzled old woodsman remarked, "Buddy, after this don't shoot at the jumps; shoot at the deer."

It is not only by the stratagem of lying still and letting the hunter pass him that the sagacity of a buck is shown. He may stand still and do the same thing; or, standing still, he may not move until you have worked yourself into a disadvantageous position. It has been my experience that a deer is one of the hardest things in the world to see, even when he is standing right before you—that is, if he has assumed the spectral stillness which is one of his life-insurance policies.

On many an occasion I have tried to show people deer in the woods. They would usually see all the stumps and bushes before they would make out the deer. One day I was going to take up a deer stand. Finally I reached the spot, and sat down on an old pine log in the sun. Then I let my gaze wander over the open pinelands.

About a hundred yards away I saw what at first I took to be a part of an old pine-top. A little later, looking at it again, I said, "Now, if I were a greenhorn, I'd take that thing for a buck standing up over yonder. You can see how the dead branches make his horns, and that big bay bush makes his body, and the play of sunlight and shadow complete the illusion."

Perhaps ten minutes later I happened to look at the object again. It had not moved. And it was a buck! He had been standing there all the time, his consummate craft consisting merely in becoming statuesque.

It is hard for a man, under any circumstances, to remain absolutely motionless; but for a wild deer it is second nature, and the deer hunter must not always be listening for the noise made by his game. He must listen to the silences as well. And he must not always be looking for movement; he must accustom his eyes to spotting a deer that by absolute stillness is merging himself in with the general aspect of the forest.

Of course, you naturally listen for the coming of your buck. But no one except a tyro will expect him to make much noise unless he happens to be in full flight, when your chance at him isn't going to be good anyway. For a creature so large, the deer makes less noise moving about than any animal I know. On a still day I have had deer come downwind to me without my being aware of their approach, although they came within twenty yards. Really, a gray squirrel makes more fuss in the autumn leaves. A buck, especially if he is uneasy, is a shadow-footed creature; and when he puts on his creepers of silence, don't count on always hearing his coming.

It would be supposed that in season bucks will haunt only the densest thickets. I have found it otherwise. I have nearly always found them on the edges of heavy swamps and copses. They don't like to break out of darkness into light, and be suddenly and fully exposed to peril. Bucks love to lie in those little bushy leads that make out from thickets, and even in very exposed places, the advantage to them being that they are not likely to be caught unawares. I once roused an old stag from a cairn of rocks on the tiptop of Tuscarora Mountain, from which commanding eminence he had a view for miles. It would have been impossible for a hunter to approach within shooting distance of him.

A buck loves to haunt watery places; I have seen one curled up on a tiny hummock in the middle of a lagoon. I believe that he was aware that water had the power to deaden his scent. A wise old stag will often deliberately walk across a shallow pond or lagoon before lying down. Perhaps, too, if he has water on one side of him, he knows that he has protection from that direction, and has to watch only one way for an enemy's coming. I once saw two old bucks lying down in the sunlight in a thin patch of young pines. They lay back to back, so that each faced in a different direction. That was a perfect double-team arrangement for the sentinel business.

As most hunters know, the buck has an ungallant habit of sending out the doe ahead of him. As in most states the open season runs concurrently with the mating season, bucks and does are then naturally found together; and depend upon it, if you see a doe, or several of them, there should be a buck coming. But he will come last. I once saw three does entering a wheat field at dusk. They hesitated at the edge. The old ten-point stag, eager and hungry, yet always wary, came up from behind, lowered his antlers, and deliberately pushed the does on ahead of him. But he let them feed for ten minutes or so before he himself joined them.

A buck has a weakness that should be understood; at least, if the hunter knows his deer, it may prove a weakness for him. If he makes up his mind to reach a certain place, why, that is where he is going. After he has made his determination, and has put on some speed, nothing can turn him. I have seen a buck run over drivers, dogs and hunters in his stubborn resolve to get to the place he has selected as a sanctuary.

Because of this habit it is always hard to drive a buck. You can drive him in a certain direction if that happens to be the direction he wants to take; but if it is not, you might as well count on his doubling. I think it a wise plan to ascertain these favorite sanctuaries and to drive accordingly. If a deer is on the full run, and you have time to pull the feat, it is easy to get ahead of him. He has his mind so set on reaching a fixed goal that he is not likely to pay attention to you and your maneuvers. I have known many fine stags to be killed in this way that otherwise would never have afforded the hunters a shot.

Your buck is up to all sorts of tricks. He can be depended on to do the unexpected. Well, study what some of these unexpected stratagems are, and then they will no longer be surprises to you. It is now almost fifty years since I shot my first stag, and I am still trying to learn how to kill a buck. If you know something of what he may do, or may not do, you will at least be joining me in the primary grade.

WHAT EVERY DEER HUNTER SHOULD KNOW

Some things about the wilderness I have learned from long experience—but much has come to me by way of warning and advice from those who are older and wiser than I about the variable and often mysterious ways of nature and her wild children. So now I'd like to pass along a few of the cardinal principles of deer hunting, with special reference to the whitetail. His haunts may vary in character, his size may differ with the locality, and the method of hunting him must suit the nature of the country, but the animal himself is one and the same creature, wherever you find him. All things considered, the whitetail is perhaps North America's premier big game animal.

In some states deer are driven by hounds; in some, by men; and in others they are stirred from their daytime beds by hunters who keep moving through the animals' haunts. Not infrequently, as the shooting season is usually coincident with the mating season, bucks and does may be moving about a good deal—even in the daytime. In any case, the wisdom of these warnings that old woodsmen have given me should be heeded, whether a buck is hunted in Maine or in Texas. The amateur, covering a likely place, has a good gun or rifle and good ammunition, and his intent and purpose are correct. But he may miss a shot, and miss also a chance to shoot, if he is neglectful of certain cautions.

Beware of the deer that try to slip by. If whitetail bucks always acted in a standard fashion, none would survive. But they are different. Once I came upon two bucks lying fairly close together. I walked up to one and killed him; the other lay just

From *Those Were the Days* (1955).

where he was for fifteen minutes. Then, when I was bending over my kill with my back turned, the other buck got up and made his escape.

But now and then a wary old stag will attempt to clear out of the country at the first sight, sound, or scent of danger. Many a time I have hardly taken my stand, the drive not even having begun, when a sly buck would come sneaking out. From the moment he is posted the stander should be alert and ready; and he should give all his attention to the business at hand.

Some time ago I read an article about what a certain writer saw on a deer stand. He did not see any deer at all—he was telling about the wood rats, the toads, the various birds he had noticed while sitting still in the forest. He was a good naturalist, but not a deer hunter. Only recently I took my stand, when I heard two fox squirrels chasing each other on a cypress behind me. I turned my head to look. When I faced ahead again, within forty yards of me stood a grand buck—a ten-pointer, I am sure.

He had arrived early, silently, unannounced—and he had me at a disadvantage. He saw me turn my head. I knew from the way he looked that he had made me out. The whitetail was in a little opening between two dense clusters of trees and bushes. Caught napping, I made a mistake. I knew that if I could get my gun on him, I could kill him where he stood. But I did not want to jerk the weapon up for fear of throwing my sight off. So I eased it up.

I had not edged the gun an inch before my quarry whirled and was gone behind the hopeless obstruction. I know now that I should have waited him out. The deer might have afforded me a shot; if not, the blame would not have been mine. But I scared him, and that's bad! Had I not been fooling with squirrels in the first place I would have seen him, and would have had my gun on him when he stopped so obligingly.

Once a stander complained to me that a fine buck had come to him before he had loaded his gun. "It *wasn't time* for the deer to come out," he alibied. He was trying to pass the buck to the buck. All I know is that the whitetail by-passed him, and left him to do the explaining!

Don't be conspicuous, and don't move. Lately I have heard that deer are color blind. I have no information about this. However, I have always heard, and believed to some degree, that a deer's eyesight is comparatively poor. Certainly it is not so keen as that of the wild turkey, but it is much better than a man's. If both man and deer are moving, the animal will always see the man first.

Old woodsmen tell me that on a crossing a stander should try to blend himself with some natural feature of the landscape. Stand with your back to a tree or a rock; never behind solid concealment. You will have to show yourself sooner or later—and at your first motion the deer will make you out. I love to sit on a stump or a log, but not right in the open. I try to get a little camouflage in front of me—like a bush or a bunch of grass—provided it's not too thick to interfere with my own outlook. One of the largest bucks I ever shot I killed while sitting on a low pine stump with a bunch of fennel before me. This buck finally did see me, of course, but only when it was too late to do him any good!

A fidgety and restless stander rarely gets a shot. He must be motionless. If he doesn't move and the buck doesn't wind him, he may have to shift to keep the old boy from running him down and trampling him! On several occasions I have had deer come so close that I could have touched them with my gun. And that, by the way, is one frequent cause of missing: the hunter is too close to his game. Standers who smoke, who walk up and down, who just can't keep still—these are the men who are going to have to tell their precious little women at home that they just did not have the heart to shoot at their bucks. As a matter of fact, the hunters were no doubt crazy to shoot, but their inability to do anything but move killed their chances.

An old hunter once said to me, "To kill a deer easylike, you got to ketch him unbeknownst." You'll never do that if you use your crossing as a regular parade ground.

Study the approach. On one occasion one of my plantation Negroes—Old Gabe—posted a friend of mine on a good stand. He was no hunter, yet he took the business seriously.

"Gabe," he said, "before you leave, tell me—from just what direction will the buck come?"

Gabe gave him the general idea. This old dusky hunter never dreamed that any man would count on expecting a deer to come out here, and not there. Often, you know, they come out 'way yonder. After a while I heard a great bombardment. However, on coming up to the stander, I saw no buck. My friend was in what I strongly suspected to be a pretended rage. He was cursing good Old Gabe.

"A glorious buck," he lamented, "but it did not come out to me as Gabe said it would. It's all his fault."

Gabe said nothing; but he eyed the blasphemer, and there was a world of pity in his look.

Being posted, a stander should look over the landscape and get ready for a shot. Often, a crossing is a gap between hills, or it may be marked by paths which the deer themselves have made. Many hunters stand on the very crossing. I think it wiser to stand to one side, within easy range. The wind, of course, often determines where a man should stand in relation to a crossing. Human scent should be kept away from the path of the buck's probable approach.

I have known some hunters to take up their stands in trees. This practice is not uncommon in regions where deer lurk in dense rhododendron jungles, and are rarely visible to a man on the ground. An elevated position takes care of the scent problem also. But it creates two others: the cramped position, and the special angle at which a downhill shot has to be made. If a man is afoot, and wounds a buck, he probably will have a better chance to kill it than if he were in a tree.

When is the right time to shoot? My youngest son asked me that question when I was about to leave him alone on his first deer stand. It is a good question. Isn't it likely that there is always one psychological moment for a shot? I don't know much about love affairs; but some lovers part too soon, and some meet too late. It takes judgment of a fine sort not to shoot too soon or too late.

I believe the stander first has to determine how close the buck is coming. Time and again I have known an amateur to empty his gun or his rifle at a buck that was either not within range, or else had not yet reached the right spot. A head-on shot is perhaps the most difficult; and when your buck first appears he may be head-on. Don't chance him then unless there definitely isn't going to be any other opportunity. Wait a minute or two, and he is almost sure to present a decent target. Don't put up your gun while he is looking in your direction; wait until he puts his head down, turns it, or moves so that his head is behind a tree.

If he is coming, you had better let him get pretty close, for your chances increase as the distance diminishes. Then should you miss him the first time, or hit him ineffectively, he cannot get out of range before you have fed him something more. I might add that if a whitetail goes down—yet still seems to be much alive—it is both wise and merciful to shoot him again. A wounded buck can be dangerous; besides, he has the most disconcerting way of getting up after an apparently mortal wound and making a clean get-away.

Listen for them. A great many woodsmen have told me that in deer hunting they depend much on their hearing. Unless in wild and unrestrained flight, the deer is a singularly noiseless animal. But he does crack the brush, and his hoofs do rustle the leaves. Often such a noise is the first warning that makes the hunter aware of the game's approach, and it gives him a chance to get ready. In my part of the country—South Carolina—deer usually lie in dense evergreen thickets of pine, myrtle, and sweet bay. Sometimes a buck will steal through these without any perceptible sound.

Old hunters, I think, agree that yearlings and does make more noise than bucks. The former plunge about as if noise meant nothing to them. Of course, if the wind is blowing, your ears will not be able to serve you well. On windy days I never like to hunt deer. It might be supposed that the noise made by the wind is to your advantage—but as a matter of fact, all game is skittish then. This is especially true of big-game animals, which count largely on their hearing for insurance. They seem to know that the wind robs them of one of their senses.

Hold that crossing. Watching a crossing for hours—when nothing at all seems to be doing—may seem a dreary business, but in the long run it is the wise thing to do. Deer stands are not chosen at random. Whitetails really pass these places. But you have to be a good waiter. If you do not have the patience, it might be better to go home. Few things irk me more than to have a stander quit his crossing, only to have a fine buck come to it after its guardian has left. I once saw two regal bucks go over a crossing when the stander, wearying of that place, had moved about 200 yards away, taking up his watch at a place where, I think, no deer has ever run for the last 1,000 years.

In hill country the stander must make allowance for the way a deer climbs a slope. Once I was on a high ridge when I saw a whole herd of whitetails coming. They seemed to be heading for a point 100 yards to the right of the crossing. I thought myself smart to sneak behind the brow of the ridge so as to get directly in front of their line of march.

On my new stand the footfalls seemed to be growing fainter, and when I peered over the crest of the ridge, there were the seven deer calmly going over my crossing! I did not know, or had forgotten, that when they are traveling naturally, deer climb in a zigzag fashion. Hold your stand—for when you see them coming and think that they are too far one way or the other, the first thing you know they'll turn and come right to you.

Not enough has been said, I think, of the engineering genius of big game. One of the high officials of the Pennsylvania Railroad told me that when their tracks were laid over the high Alleghenies, the railroad right of way hardly varied at all from the ancient game trails made by deer and buffaloes. These wise animals knew the grades, both up and down!

When you miss out. If you fail to hit a buck, or if through your own fault you don't get a shot, try to figure out what was the matter.

At my age, however, I grieve less about missing than I used to. There are reasons for that too. A noble buck invests the forest with a certain mystery and primeval charm. If you kill him, something is gone from those particular woods. If you miss him, he's still there, and you may have a chance at the old rascal again!

FLINTLOCK AFIELD WITH FAMILY AND FRIENDS

—————————— Part II ——————————

F or Rutledge, one of the key ingredients of the deer-hunting experience was camaraderie. The fun and fellowship of the sport took many forms for Flintlock, but always there was togetherness. As his son Irvine Rutledge movingly chronicles in his memoir, *We Called Him Flintlock* (1974), the annual holiday hunts at Hampton held a treasured place in Archibald Rutledge's existence. Rutledge's brother, Frederick, in his little-known book, *Fair Fields of Memory* (1958), also looks back fondly at the glories of hunting deer at Hampton. For the full span of a generation the holiday whitetail hunts were an annual tradition, and even as he reveled in the pleasures of being afield Rutledge harked back to similar outings in the family's history.

The Hampton Hunt, as Flintlock and his sons called the annual holiday outing for whitetails, began shortly after World War I. In the words of Irvine Rutledge, who saw in the hunt a magic akin to King Arthur's Camelot: "Although hunting had been the order of the day at Hampton since its building in 1730, it was about two hundred years later that there came into being what we knew as *The Hampton Hunt*. As soon as all three sons were old enough, Flintlock and the three of us hunted together along with our deer drivers Gabriel and Prince, and Prince's three sons, Prince, Will and Samuel, and also Richard and old Steve."

The Hampton Hunt's days of crowning glory ended abruptly in 1943, when Middleton Rutledge was killed. With his death a spark in his father's soul was extinguished for good. The same period also saw the dark days of World War II call the writer's other sons to patriotic duty. Hunting, particularly during the Thanksgiving and Christmas seasons, resumed after the war's conclusion, but as Irvine Rutledge says, "it was never quite the same." Nonetheless, Flintlock continued the ritual hunts with Irvine and Archibald, Jr., until the latter's death in 1959, and the venerable writer persisted in the chase until 1967, when he was forced to end his own hunting career.

Hunting with his sons gave Flintlock some of the most joyous moments of his life and provided material for some of his finest stories. And there were memorable hunts with friends as well, for an integral part of rural Low Country hospitality was hosting, and being hosted by one's neighbors, on carefully orchestrated hunts. Rutledge delighted in pre-hunt strategy sessions, deciding where each hunter would take his stand and what section of Hampton Plantation's vast acreage would be driven on a particular day. Long before he returned to Hampton for good, Rutledge had reached that stage of maturity in a hunter's life where he derived as much pleasure from the success of others as he did from his own.

Rutledge cherished every moment of each hunt even as he stored the experience in his mind for future resurrection in print. The hearty pre-dawn breakfast; the hushed wishes for good fortune as hunters took their stand and drivers moved into place; the mad excitement of anticipation after a noble stag had been rousted from his bed; and the satisfying tiredness of a post-hunt meal in which venison was the main dish—all offered grist for his literary mill.

These sensations, and much more, he captures in his enduring stories of the quest. For Rutledge, joining those he loved in hunting whitetails was a constantly renewing exercise in friendship and an outlet for the warmth of shared endeavor which has linked hunting man in communal existence throughout time. In the stories that follow we share Rutledge's pleasure as vicarious participants in the timeless pursuit of whitetails.

THE BOY AND THE BUCK

Though it is pleasant to recollect and to recount one's own success in the woods, I have found a deeper satisfaction in affording sport to others,—if the others really appreciate it. I recall one winter's day watching an effete gentleman's behavior on a deer-crossing. On his lap was a box of bonbons. He was reading a newspaper. A fine stag came to him. He shot it, and calmly continued reading the stock market. The spectacle filled me with a sense of desecration. He had killed a buck, but that fact meant nothing to him. If hunting means nothing to a man, he simply should not hunt.

Among my happiest memories is the one of the stalk of the great marsh-stag,—the day I acted as guide for the lad who had never before had a shot at a deer.

Mysterious and weird lay the sea-marsh before us, an immense solitary tract, lonely and beautiful. In the mild sunshine of the Southern winter it glinted softly. Over the massive wall of yellow pines to the eastward the sun had risen, and now was dispersing the mists that all night long had hung over the huge wasteland. Here and there in the marsh were scrub cedars, patches of myrtle, copses of bulrushes, sunny beds of golden broomgrass. Through the marsh ran many a telltale path, deep-trodden by generations of wild dwellers. Where the marsh gave way to certain sandy spaces, there were innumerable tracks. There the wildcat had set his crafty print; there the wild gobbler had indicated with exactness the size of his shoe; there the wary raccoon had paced thoughtfully, leaving tracks like the impresses of tiny human hands; and there the deer had roamed: fawn tracks

From *An American Hunter* (1937).

there were, tracks of timid mincing does, tracks of sprightly young stags, and those blunted, deep-sinking, often slovenly tracks of the master-bucks.

My little boy and I were examining these tracks, and were trying to decide how old each one was; and, in the case of the bucks, how good was the crown that each one carried. He was out for his first deerhunt; and here we were at the beginning of a perfect day, in the very heart of the deer country on Bull's Island, which is probably as romantic a spot as is left anywhere in America. And in some ways it is a good deal wilder and more primitive than many of the exotic isles of the South Seas.

While this barrier island is rich in wild life, to secure it is no easy matter. The cover is semi-tropical in its denseness; moreover, most of it is evergreen, so that the coming of winter is small help to the hunter. The jungles of such a sea-island resemble the jungles of Guatemala or of the Congo. Nor, for all its abundance and for all its cover is the wild life tame. It has always seemed to me that a wild thing is often just a little more timid in heavy cover than he is in thin cover; for in the former he cannot tell how close his enemy is upon him, whereas in the latter he can definitely mark out with his eye a zone of safety. The deer and the turkeys on Bull's Island have the same wildness common to all members of their races.

And here we were to stalk a stag,—we two. A manful business it is, especially when, as in this case, the country is so wild and so lonely and so apparently inviolate. We, and the caretaker, Richard, were the only human beings on the island. I was very fond of Richard, and I rather hoped he would finish his work in time to join us on the sea-marsh.

To kill a deer in a place like this requires careful figuring. In cover so abundant and so thick, the mere chance to shoot is always slight, and the chance of connecting with the game, even slighter. Conditions for good stalking always include fairly open country. Here it might be the case of snap-shooting; and I have never known a good hunter who did not hate to have to do snap-shooting. In such work, the worst shot may succeed, and the best shot fail. However, a hunter, being a mortal man, has to take the chances and the odds of this life as they come. And if he, under adverse circumstances, can lay a scheme to outwit his game, he has done well.

Our scheme was partly determined by the height of my boy.

Twelve years old, he was rather under the normal height for that age. Most of the cover was from five to eight feet high. But there were certain ridges running down through the marsh that were fairly open; and their elevation gave a hunter on them a far better chance than if he were in the marsh itself. But the ridges were lined by sweet myrtles, which make about as dense a screen as can be imagined. If anything crossed the ridge, the chance at it would be the chance of a second,—from the time when the deer left one green wall of myrtle until it entered the other. Still, though slight, the chance would be there; but it was not such a chance as even a hardened hunter would call a bargain.

It seemed best to put the boy on this ridge,—straight, sandy, with a few live-oaks growing on it, and walled by the myrtles mentioned, while I ranged the marshy thickets to leeward, feeling ahead of my little watchman there. I explained the business to him, and he seemed to comprehend; but one is obliged to have misgivings when the cover is tall, the young huntsman very young, and the deer—as he always is—crafty, elusive, and, even when fairly discerned, so startling as to be disconcerting even to veteran nerves. But such was the plan.

"I'm going in here to the left," I explained, "to ramble out these beds of broomgrass and these hummocks of red cedar. You keep straight on down the ridge, walking slowly. Try to keep me located, and then keep just about opposite to where I am. If anything gets up, I'll try to let you know. Don't get excited. Remember, you are the one who has the gun. If anyone should get excited, it's the deer."

Almost as soon as I entered the sea-marsh, from a dense clump of bulrushes out rocked three does. They headed toward the distant sand-dunes. So little noise they made that I verily believe that I should never have detected them had I not seen them. There was a wind in the sedges making an incessant sibilant music; and these deer stole away so softly that what little sound they made seemed one with the song of the sea-wind in the reeds. Suddenly behind me I heard something. I turned swiftly, thinking that a buck that had been lying with the does was about to make his getaway by the back door. But it was only Richard. With a catlike tread he came forward,—a veritable part of the mysterious sea-marsh,—at home, confident. Tall and black and rangy he stood; by no means a poor physical figure. Richard is really a good hunter; the ways of wild things are to him as an open book. And even if he does make it easy for me to believe in Evolution, I am fond of him.

"Where is the big hunterman?" he asked with a smile.

I explained my plan of campaign while he listened with respectful deference. All the time I felt a sense of my inferiority to this humble black man; for he knew this country and these deer far better than I did. Yet he offered no criticism.

"I will walk this out," he finally said; "and if you will go into the marsh the other side of the ridge, you might get a shot too. If the old gunnerman on the ridge should happen to miss a buck, he will come to you."

The plan seemed good; therefore I left Richard to do the driving while I recrossed the ridge, pausing for a moment to explain the new scheme to the boy, whom I found manfully holding the sandy white passages between the myrtles. It was not as if he had not seen deer before, because, almost as soon as he could walk I had had him on deer-stands with me; and he had acquired, through the sharpness and strength of those early impressions, some pretty definite ideas concerning this wildest and most interesting of our big game animals. He was not like the bride whose husband wanted to have her learn about the woods and the dwellers therein. On their honeymoon, spent in the wilds, he was telling her about deer, and happened to remark that at that time, in August, the fawns had dropped their spots.

"Lovely!" she exclaimed. "Oh, Jim, wouldn't it be wonderful if we could go out into the woods together and find some of the spots that the cute little things had dropped!"

Across the ridge in the wild thicket Richard was making some noises, the like of which I never expected to hear in this world. A Negro can whoop, and a hound can bawl on the trail, venting soulfully his marvelous music. Here was a combination; and the result was as if an entire pack of an entirely new breed of hounds had suddenly "yelled on the view" in that wild and lonely place. No self-respecting stag could long keep his bed with such alarming music radioed from Richard's vast and tireless throat. Indeed, hardly had he begun when things commenced happening. One of Richard's long-drawn yowls turned to a yelp, then to a sharp whoop to us. I heard the myrtles behind us crash just as I left the ridge. Then, a moment later, a hundred yards down the ridge, behind us, two bucks flashed across the opening, and were gone. They were farther from the boy than from me;

and neither of us shot. But through an opening in the myrtles we could watch the two great creatures leaping through the sea-marsh,—now wholly in sight, now swallowed by the brown waste of sedge. One of them had a splendid crown of antlers,—and even at that distance I marked that they were both freakish and regular: freakish because they did not "basket" forward in standard fashion, but rather stood almost straight up; and regular because such horn-architecture is characteristic of nearly all the bucks from this interesting island. Those who do not believe in the power of heredity and in the transfer of salient characteristics would be disconcerted by the really extraordinary similitude of all these antlers. Indeed, so decided is it, that one day, far off on the mainland, in looking at a collection of antlers, I pointed to one pair and said, "They are from a Bull's Island deer." The owner assured me that they were.

We watched the two bucks until they had cleared the marsh and had vanished into the pine forest to the north. The hunter is privileged to see many a memorable sight: a regal grouse hurtling himself magically over the tops of golden autumn trees; a flock of mallards drawing from afar, the sunrise tinting their plumage, straight into the decoys; a wild gobbler, tall and stately, standing erect as he listens almost to the sound made by the beating of the sportsman's heart; and the lordly spectacle of stag in full flight. I never get quite used to this last sight. It thrilled me as a boy more than any other scene of the wildwoods; and surely, if Methuselah was a hunter (I think he must have been, his life was so prolonged), a buck crowding the canvas must have sent the thrills up his thousand year old spine.

I passed through the myrtles on the north side of the ridge and forthwith entered the bulrushes. It was hard going in there, with no Pharaoh's daughter to pull me out either. But I kept at it, though with a feeling that there are some places through which a hunter is not intended to go. Every now and then, ahead of me on the ridge, I could catch a glimpse of my little sportsman, trudging forward, his gun ready. I was in much more intimate touch with Richard, whose bawling would make the wildest bull of Bashan hang a much-diminished head. He whooped with a certain primitive savagery that must have gone straight to the place where a deer keeps his fears.

Far ahead now I could see the end of the ridge, beyond which lay a vast and melancholy stretch of sea-marsh, through which wound a sluggish salt creek, sparkling dully in the warm winter sunshine. I felt that if we did nothing before reaching that marsh, we were liable to do nothing at all.

Richard now began to rail at the deer, and to cast at them aspersions, animadversions, revilings, and the like. I recall that he suggested that they were split-hoofed, big-horned, big-eyed, whitetailed, lazy, triflin' sons of sea-turtles. Such epithets will make some men fight; but they will make deer run.

"Look out, Cap'n!" I heard Richard yell, his chimpanzee mouth spread to its fearsome capacity. "Look out, little Cap'n! For God's sake, look out! De ole man's comin'!"

Such a warning at such a time, vociferated as only a Negro can, gave me a sudden rise in temperature, accompanied by chills. I strained my eyes to see the deer. I looked for the boy, to see how he was taking Richard's warning. I called to him to get ready. I saw the boy halt on the ridge. Off to his left I saw the white flash of a tall erect tail. Then I saw a rack of chestnut-colored antlers. How he was going! Richard must have been full on him when he jumped. From his course I knew he would cross the ridge ahead of the boy. But it would be at an angle away from him. And the distance would be discouraging,—seventy-five or eighty yards,—a long shot for the gun he was using. I moved forward in those thrilling seconds. I was not now far behind the boy, but off to his right.

In all likelihood, the stag would not run down the ridge when he reached it but would cross it, plunge through the myrtles, and run through the marsh for the deep woods beyond, just as the other two bucks had done. In that case, I would have a shot, and a better one than the boy, who would be offered only a flashing chance as the stag ripped across the opening on the ridge.

Again I saw the buck. He was now almost to the ridge; and he seemed to have pulled down the gas-lever some more. In about five seconds he would be across the ridge and ahead of me in the marsh. I put my gun to my shoulder. The boy, of course, would miss the buck, and I would kill him. You know how we old hunters reason such things out, giving ourselves all the credit that's coming to us.

I put my gun up, I say; and when I heard the boy shoot, I tightened my grip, feeling that my chance had come. Through the wall of myrtles I looked for the inevitable rack of horns, the long body, the tall flag. Grimly I waited, determined that the *whole* family wasn't going to miss that stag, even if he was a long way off, even if he was trying his best to imitate a cyclone.

But, wait as I would, no buck came. Puzzled, I lowered my gun. The deer must have run down the ridge. The boy probably ran after him, trying to catch what he had missed. Children act like that. After waiting a few minutes longer in a rather dreary frame of mind, I sauntered up on the ridge. Far ahead I saw Richard. But the boy was not in sight. Uneasy, I ran forward. I saw Richard turn into the myrtles to the right. In a moment or two I had joined him. He was with the boy, who stood, hat off, happy as only a young hunter can be, proud as only a young sportsman can be who shows his father his first fallen stag.

There lay the big buck, dead from a clean shot at eighty yards. A fine creature he was,—burly and old, his last race run, his last jump ended.

"I'se glad the young Cap'n done got the shot," Richard said in his gentle humble way. "I knowed he was a true gunnerman."

The boy may live to kill many another buck; and he may hear higher words of praise. But no other buck will ever mean so much. And no praise will ever be sweeter than the dusky Richard's.

My own feeling is that it is a fine thing for a man to kill a stag; but he will get a bigger thrill if he can lead his boy to the same achievement. And I believe that that old teacher had more in his mind than formal education when he said "Teach the young idea how to shoot." I for one have taken his advice literally.

MISTS OVER MONTGOMERY

Montgomery Branch, a swamp two miles long but very narrow, and Montgomery Hill, the adjacent high pineland, constitute one of the most dependable deer-drives on my plantation—a 3,000-acre tract on the lower reaches of the Santee River, in South Carolina. The chief objection to it is that it is hard to stand.

About seven men, good men and true, should be at the head of the drive; but even if I have that many deerslayers to post, the flanks have to be left open. Then, too, the whole rear is unprotected. As the river is not far away in that direction, and as a wary old buck has a decided leaning toward water, despite drivers and hounds that may be in his way, the chance of shooting at Montgomery are by no means in proportion to the chance of jumping deer in that justly renowned drive.

Yet the same thing might be said of many another deer drive in the country, unless it is so small that it can be completely surrounded. Even in such a case, deer often escape a regular ring of guns, not only because they may be missed, but because they may succeed in sneaking or skulking past a stander. And we all know that sometimes the fatal malady of buck fever assails a stander, so that when his Big Moment comes, he forgets why he is there.

It was early in the real deer season in South Carolina; it was mid-November. Although our deer season opens on the fifteenth of August, and extends to the first of January, comfortable deer hunting does not begin until the first frosts have laid the mosquitoes and sent the snakes into winter quarters.

From *Those Were the Days* (1955).

On this memorable hunt, I had with me one of my sons, Irvine, and a friend of his named Mack. Although we made but three standers, we decided to try the famous Montgomery, taking our chances that the bucks would run to the stands that we chose. I had to leave four of these crossings open. I put Mack at the renowned Laurel Tree Stand, so called because a century or more ago some wild bird dropped a laurel seed there, and now there is a great tree, seventy feet tall. Deer love this run, and I have slain many there. To me it appears certain that they steer their course by the laurel tree.

All close observers of the ways of nature have noticed how both birds and animals seem to guide their flight or their running by some natural and rather conspicuous object of the landscape, such as a huge tree, the junction of a trail and a road, a tarkiln, a sawdust pile, an elevation, or a depression. They know the woods and the sky-routes better than we do; and there is no reason why they should not remember and heed ancient landmarks and signposts of the wilds.

My son I put at the Green Bay Stand. It is a choice place, being the focal point of many runs. I went on beyond him to the Boggy Bay Stand, which is on an open pine ridge, level and straight, between two sweetbay branches.

In front of these stands is Montgomery; and behind them is the fetid wilderness of the Bog Ocean, the greatest natural sanctuary for deer known to me. It is about four miles long by two miles wide; and it is not penetrable by man. I, indeed, have been through it; but I went almost on hands and knees under black canopy of bushes and vines, following deer paths, and likely at any moment to run foul of a diamondback. Hounds may run the edges of the ocean, but they don't like the forbidding aspect of the place, and they soon come out. To my certain knowledge, more of our deer have been saved by the existence of this abysmal wilderness than by all the game regulations. Especially in these days, some kind of sanctuary, natural or artificial, is absolutely essential to the survival of game.

I realized that I am slow in getting this hunt started; but I want you to have an accurate idea of the layout of things; then you will be able to follow my story with a clear idea of the situation.

I had told Prince, my head Negro driver, to give us, after we left him with the yowling pack, a half hour to get on our stands. No sooner was I settled on a dead pine log right in the middle of the ridge than I heard his opening whoop far back at the tail-end of the drive. And when Prince whoops, his voice is enough to make jaded opera-goers tingle. It was just after daybreak! it was still; it was warm; and the woods exhaled all kinds of dewy fragrances, in which scents of myrtle and pine and bay were mingled. Soon I heard the dogs begin to trail: the ding-dong chop-mouth of Annie Oakley, the strange high tenor of Ring, and the deep rolling bell of old Warcry. There would be something doing before long. And all conditions were good except for a lacy mist that mantled all the dreaming woods. I could not see distinctly for more than a hundred yards; and in deer hunting, I like to be able to see all the way. I especially object to this business of having big-horned bucks bust right into my face out of a fog. But a hunter has to take conditions as they are.

After a little while Prince's amiable yodeling gave place to a sudden yelling as if a bear or the Law had caught up with him. I knew he had roused a stag, and had seen him. Now, if that buck would only do the generous and manly thing and choose the right stand, we'd hear a gun shoot. The hounds bore away northward toward Mack, but I heard no cannonade from him. But while I was listening intently for the blare of his blunderbuss, I saw silent shapes in the mist straight ahead of me. They were coming my way, and they were coming fast. Their sanctuary of the Bog Ocean was only two hundred yards behind me. On they came, three of them, as if they were going to jump the log on which I was sitting. They acted as if they had a heavy date with me. Twenty feet dead ahead of me they suddenly checked their run. Only then could I see distinctly and disappointedly that they were does. They suspected something; but as the wind was coming from them to me, and as I hadn't moved, they had not made me out. Such were their positions in relation to one another that I believe I could have dropped the trio with one barrel. I looked hard for horns, even for little spikes, but it was of no use.

Next to the way a lovelorn man or woman looks on the object of his emotional upset, there is no harder looking in this world than the way a hunter searches a deer's head for the happy glint of horns. It could not be in this case. I can kill a deer; but I can't change one's sex. However, as every Old Timer knows, the coming of ladies to a man's deer stand in November is a good sign: the Old Man himself may be following.

After a pause of several moments, the does passed me in long leaps, describing those soundless graceful arcs so characteristic of the whitetail in flight. I waited. The dogs seemed temporarily out of hearing. The drivers must have bogged down somewhere, or else must have discovered a still, at which they had lingered for refreshment. You know how it is when a promising hunt suddenly appears to go stale. It was with the kind of hope that is fast ebbing that I watched the puzzling mist ahead.

Yes, after five minutes of acute discouragement, O my fellow hunters, what is that I see? It's surely something, but it looks disconcertingly like a ghost; as a ghost-slayer I have no ambitions. What is that long gray shape sliding through the fog yonder, speeding low to the ground in what appears to be effortless speed, and magnified by the mist into a huge spectral shape? So-o-o! Here he comes, the herd-bull himself. He's a great stag with a glimmering rack. Then far away, but behind this buck and evidently on his track, I could hear Ring's peculiar high-pitched voice—a kind of sketchy screech, but bearing glad tidings. This is Ring's first season, and he has not settled himself down to the business of bawling. He just yip-yips excitedly. But he's bringing Town News.

Here comes my buck. But the wily old rascal isn't running the path of the does. He is streamlining it far to my left, through the low huckleberry bushes that fringe the edge of the branch. If he doesn't change his course, I am going to have a shot, and a comparatively open one; but it will be long. Now, for a shotgun, what is a long shot at a deer? Well, after forty yards uncertainty begins; after sixty, the chances are somewhat against a clean kill; after eighty, if you kill your buck, you are mighty lucky; and after a hundred yards, if you nail him to the mast, you're a liar.

True, I have killed a deer at 108 measured yards with an old Westley-Richards muzzle-loader, with 32-inch barrels; but that sort of thing is not in the cards. One reason why so many men miss deer with a shotgun is the fact that they do not know distances in the woods, and they ask the impossible of their good guns. Seeing game, however far away, they blaze away at it with their blunderbusses. The chances are that it is far out of range. This buck looked as if he were going to run broadside at sixty yards. I should kill him; but you know what it takes to break down a wild buck's miraculous vitality.

In shooting a buck that is on the full run that is within fair range, and is presenting his broadside, I generally shoot for his nose, if he is stretched out, or a foot in front of his neck if he is jumping. You really have to lead a running deer. Really capable of a mile a minute for a certain distance, he is probably going from twenty to forty miles an hour; and during the second that it takes you to pull the trigger, he's speeding out of the line of your sight.

When this buck was almost broadside, I held dead on his black nose, giving him the choke barrel of my old thirty-inch gun. At the blare that shattered the misty stillness, he blundered terribly, went down so far that his antler-tips ripped up the pine straw. I thought he was really down. But not so. He was up and away, sailing with all canvas crowded for the gross sanctuary of the Bog Ocean. Because of the bushes and the intervening trees, perhaps because of my own surprise that he did not stay down, my second shot was ineffective. I could not see that he winced or changed his stride. As a matter of fact, my second barrel seemed to have the effect of cheering him on.

If a running deer ever changes his stride at your shot, depend upon it, he is hit. This is a much more certain sign of his being wounded than the clamping down of his tail. I have seen many mortally wounded deer go off with tails as high and flaunting as ever. Perhaps a deer pulls down his flag only when he is hit in a certain place; but where that place may be, I do not know. That this deer was badly hit, I was certain; for four times I saw him stumble badly on his great run for the darksome safety of the Ocean. Yet the old wildwood strategist gained his sanctuary; and there I was with my thoughts, with my guest and my son soon to arrive, expecting big news. And the wounded buck had gone into the one place into which I was afraid to turn the hounds. It might be hours before we could get them back from the mysterious fringes of that bushy labyrinth. My chance, I felt, had come and gone. My reputation as a shot was tarnished. And there were mists over Montgomery in more senses than one.

Walking over to where the buck had blundered, I saw that he had indeed torn up the ground; but not a drop of blood did I see. That fact was disturbing. I followed the track for a hundred yards; still there was no trace of blood. Maybe the old rascal fell down from fright, I thought. Maybe it was a clean miss. Yet I did not see why he should have fallen several additional times unless he happened to be of a highly nervous temperament; and nearly fifty years of deer hunting have not led me to expect a buck to collapse emotionally just because he is shot at. A man might do that, but not a veteran stag.

Disconsolately I turned back to my stand; the drive was still on, and I had to cover my crossing. Suddenly I heard a squeal right in front of me. It was Ring, hot on the buck's trail. More trouble was this; for I did not know whether to stop him. If I didn't, he might find my deer; if I did, there would be no such happy chance. If I did not stop him and he didn't locate my buck, Ring might be gone all day, and my pack impaired. But this sensible hound spared me the pain of a decision. Seeing me coming toward him, and being somewhat strange in those woods, and perhaps not liking my looks anyway, and looking for a buck and not for a glum-faced hunter, he halted, appraised me, and then went flying back to Prince, who, poor fellow, was now whooping confidently, since he had heard my gun. Slowly I walked back to my stand, wondering if I was not getting too old to hunt. I felt a hundred. I didn't even have a good story to tell my fellow hunters. In hunting deer in this way, when standers are far apart, when one lets go both barrels, it is natural for all the others to expect to see bucks piled up when they approach him. I had nothing but a futile kind of story; not even a drop of blood to back up my tale of the old master's falling and blundering.

The rest of that drive seemed to me interminable; yet I was not especially eager for it to come to an end. I had a sorry part to play. I felt that the worst was yet to come, so to speak. Finally Prince and the other drivers stopped whooping; and they, together with Mack, Irv, and the hounds came trooping expectantly, with disconcerting confidence, toward me. I was especially ashamed to face the hounds. They have a way of saying nothing, but they say it with profound disgust.

Clearing my throat, "Well," I began, "I hardly know what to tell you. He was a very fine buck, an eight-pointer. I believe I shot him down, but he's gone into the Big Ocean. And I'm afraid that if we put the dogs on him, they'll get away. I don't want to break up the hunt."

Like the good deer hunter that he is, my son asked me exactly how the buck acted when I shot him. I told him. Heroically, he believed me. But Mack and the dogs and the drivers were silent skeptics.

"Let's try Annie Oakley on his track," Irv suggested. "She's slow, and she'll not go far by herself."

We went over to where I had made my first shot, and there tried to get Annie interested in the track. But it had been more than an hour since he had passed, there was no blood, and Annie was cold to my entreaties. Then Prince took a hand. You ought to see him cajole a hound! He began to talk to Annie as if they were in a world entirely apart from ours; he whistled softly, he called her endearing names, he vamped her doubting soul into doing just exactly what he wanted.

While we held Ring and Warcry on the leash, Annie took the trail, silent, and hardly going out of a walk, with head high, winding on the bushes and on the dewy needles of the little pines. Straight down the ridge she went, we walking at a natural pace behind her. I could tell that she was following exactly the course of the escaped buck. Only fifty yards from the forbidding borders of the Big Ocean, where the mists of the morning had hidden him from my view, there is a heavy growth of bays and gallberries jutting out on the ridge from Boggy Bay. These bushes form a curious little thickety head of dense greenery. To our surprise, Annie suddenly turned sharply to the left into this copse. The moment she was out of sight, we heard a tremendous commotion. At the moment, I did not associate this racket with my buck, thinking that he was far, far away, and that Annie had run into some other deer, or into a drove of wild hogs. But Irvine thought more quickly than I did. With the first sound in the bushes, he dashed round the head, so as to get between it and the Ocean. The very next second I heard him shoot. And it was all over.

"I really didn't have to shoot him," he said as we came up to him, standing beside a fine eight-pointed. "I could have caught him, but wanted to play it safe. See, you had broken his left foreleg, and had put seven other buckshot in him."

We can learn something of woodlore from nearly every hunt. Here was the case of buck that had been fatally wounded; yet when I last had seen him, he left me with the impression that I should see him no more. But for Irv's suggestion that we try Annie on his bloodless trail, we never should have found him; yet at one time I had walked within thirty feet of him. I doubt if he ever would have left the place where he lay down. Regarding the broken foreleg, I might say that, in running, a deer's forelegs, when not thrust forward, are momentarily folded back against his sides, or at least parallel with his lower shoulders, so that a shot intended for his heart is often intercepted by a leg.

As we stood there about the fallen buck, satisfied with his size and with his heavy and craggy horns, and with the strange hunt that had produced him, I noticed that the mists had begun to vanish from Montgomery; and for me they vanished in more ways than one! But why didn't I kill that stag dead with the first shot? It was the old, old story: it might have been done, but, after forty yards, uncertainty begins. And, after all, a deer is a creature of amazing stamina and vitality, while a gun is only a gun, and a man is only a man. Indeed, when I saw that old wildwood master coursing Oceanward, I felt a good deal less than a man, and a good deal like no hunter at all.

JOEL AND THE MARSH-BUCK

Being at home for a few days, I naturally sought out some of my hunting cronies to get the latest sportlore from them. It was Joel Raybourne who seemed all solemnly jazzed up on the hunting business.

"Have you seen any twenty-point bucks this year, Joel?" I asked.

"Bucks!" he exclaimed, with just a tinge of anger in his voice. "Do you know them marsh-bucks have darned nigh ruined me this season? They've turned the tables on me; I haven't been after them, but they've been after me."

"Taken a fancy to you, have they?"

"To my sweet potato patch. I've got two acres next to the big myrtle thicket behind my house, and it pretty nearly looks like a new-ploughed field."

"Tell me about it," I urged.

Joel told me. And that reminds me of what a regular Methuselah of a deer-hunter drawled out one day when he listened to one of Joel's stories: "Lordee!" he exclaimed in his soft, expressive Southern drawl, "can't he tell 'um?" He can. And the beauty of the thing is that he can tell 'um straight. Now he told me of finding a huge buck dead, apparently of old age, among the lonely sand-dunes of Murphy's Island. He described the beauty and symmetry of the horns, and when I went to his house he actually showed me the antlers. Some substantiation, I call that. Therefore, when he began to tell me of this venison and sweet potato curry—this warfare that would back Jack D—— and Georges C—— off the horizon—I knew that the thing was so.

From *Days Off in Dixie* (1925).

A hunter who tells the matter to you straight is the man to grapple to your soul with hoops of steel. For a long time, meaning twenty years or more, I have thus figuratively grappled Joel to me.

"These bucks," Joel was explaining, "aren't the regular deer of the pinelands. I mean that they are larger and burlier. They come to the mainland in the mating season, which is also the sweet potato season; but they are marsh-deer. They spend the whole day in the marsh, and it would take a field-trial hound to bring one out. I have stood on the back beach of one of those sea islands over yonder and have seen as many as five of these big fellows come out of the reeds at one time. They generally come out just about sundown; but last week I saw one in my field, and the sunlight was glinting on his clean-rubbed and polished horns."

"But, see here, Joel," I mildly remonstrated, "what good does all this do us? It seems to me that you haven't said anything yet. You haven't spoken the word. You are like a fellow who takes his best girl driving and never even holds her hand. You are like a man who talks about juleps when he doesn't have even the smell of one on his premises. You're a sad disappointment, Joel. As a hunter, you're failing in your old age."

"Say when," he answered with an understanding grin.

With such game in prospect, the time to go is usually right away. I, at least, under such circumstances always acquire a heated feeling that some other hunter will slip in ahead of me and steal the whole bankroll, or that the game, by mental telepathy, will get the ouija board word that the devil and all is camping on their trail and will forthwith utterly vanish. Every sportsman knows the alarming feeling. But in this case it was not justified in me, for it really took two unusual fools like Joel and me to plan the thing we did plan; and while demented ones are a crop that never fails in any region, we are of a somewhat padded-cell variety when it comes to deer hunting, and therefore have not many rivals.

The huge and melancholy marshland which harbored the deer we wanted to get is a formidable kind of place. Indeed, along the whole South Atlantic seaboard it is almost unique, for it is a super sea-marsh. Joel said it would take a fine dog to bring a deer out of it, but the fact is a dog will not willingly follow a deer into this marsh. On almost countless occasions I have known deer from the pinelands to make for the great marsh, which they consider a sort of sanctuary, and in almost every instance, regardless of how hot the pursuit might be, the result is always the same: as soon as the hounds reached the borders of that mysterious and forbidding domain they would break off the race.

I think the real reason for this is not any weird misgivings that the dogs may have concerning the entering of so strange a place, but rather the mere simple fact that salt marsh is very cruel to a hound's feet. Even the most willing and sagacious dog will be shy of the inevitable punishment which awaits him if he runs a trail into the almost boundless reed-land here described, that stretches many a mile from the coast to the far sea islands. And so fully aware are deer of the discomfort that hounds suffer in pursuing them into this inviolate region that they usually slow down the moment they have passed within its bounds. I once knew an unwounded buck to turn and whip off two perfectly good hounds about a hundred yards inside the marsh.

In planning for our little feat, it was clear that we need lay no scheme for the invasion of the marsh. And in passing I may say that I am most heartily glad for such a place: a region surrounded by hunters, but made by nature safe for game. Whatever Joel and I did would have to be done outside the marsh; and the marauding bucks did not emerge until dusk or thereafter.

"What's your idea, Joel?" I asked. "Are we going to drive them into your barnyard, or are we going to lassoo them and gentle them as those fellows in the West do to their wild ponies?"

"You come out to-morrow afternoon at about five o'clock and I'll teach you a lesson in deer hunting," he answered. "Bring your gun; and, though I don't think you'll get home until morning, you needn't bring your nightie, et cetera."

There is always something peculiarly romantic and alluring about a visit to Joel's home. It is a lonely place, God knows, and being on the coast somehow links it up with the peculiarly vast and ancient wildness of the ocean. His house is surrounded by live-oaks; behind it are fields of cotton, corn, and potatoes; before it stretch the interminable reaches of the savage marsh. Mosquitoes? Great New Jersey! Joel's place is the fountain-head for the true armor-piercing variety. The Disston Saw Works and the Bethlehem Projectile Department and the Savage and the Winchester Arms people ought to go to Joel's and learn a thing or two of hacking and penetrating and destroying. And when I say that I love to go to this solitary plantation despite the pests there, it ought to be understood that there are many compensating charms.

Five o'clock found me and the mosquitoes at Joel's. The things do not bite him—because they are prohibitionists, he says. They ate me alive—ravenously, joyously. But when I am deer hunting, I don't mind losing a life or two.

"I've got it all built," said Joel.

"The pen?" I asked.

"The platform," he replied. "Now let me explain," he went on, as he saw by my face that I feared we might be taking liberties with the law, "that this thing is all right. Fire hunting is prohibited; we are taking no fire. And, if it seems unfair to take advantage of a buck after nightfall, why, just look what these marsh devils have been doing to me for a month past. I won't get enough sweet potatoes from those two acres to flavor a baby 'possum."

"All right," I agreed, "I'll join you; only I hope your platform is out of reach of these mosquitoes."

"They'll likely forage you some," was his comforting answer.

Leaving Joel's house on the borders of the lone marsh we repaired to the invaded potato field, a quarter of a mile away, and ere we reached it the sun of the late October day had sunk below the sea horizon. The atmosphere was cool and clear. The woods bordering the plantation fields were exhaling a damp fragrance, in which the spicy odor of the sweet myrtle prevailed. There was no use for Joel to show me what the deer had done. They were Germans, and they thought his field was Belgium. The lush growth of the vines had been mowed clean. The tall sandy ridges of the rows had been trampled and dishevelled. The crop was undoubtedly badly injured, but I saw that Joel would get something more than he had hinted to me. However, we agreed that the marauders ought to be chastised.

Joel's platform was in a stout scrub pine that was growing on the line of the old rail fence that sagged its way decrepitly along the darksome borders of the forest. The platform itself was of rough boards and was nailed insecurely to the tree some fifteen feet off the ground. I eyed it appraisingly.

"Our roost," said Joel.

"That's where we'll camp-meet with the mosquitoes, is it?"

"That's where. Let's go up. Not long ago I saw a buck in

the field there before this time in the evening. Now, you can't chew or smoke or talk. And you really oughtn't to fight those mosquitoes very rapid. We want to put the Maxim on the sound and motion business."

"All right," I agreed as we began to clamber up the tree. "I have never, of course, seen a deer, but I understand that it is an animal having both eyes and ears."

"You said a spoonful when you said ears," Joel commented.

Soon we were seated on the platform, and I had a curious feeling that there was nothing further for me to do than to sit there and let the mosquitoes bite me. But, in truth, there were not so many at this elevation; besides, there was beginning to creep over me that indefinable thrill that a man feels when he is on a good deer-stand. And if ever a place seemed a sure-shot one to me, it was this platform of Joel's overlooking the potato patch and, beyond that, the lonely marshlands where dwelt the gentlemen for whose reception we were prepared.

Sunrise and sundown are the two times of the day when a hunter is most likely to be afforded intimate glimpses of wild life; and I have therefore always loved to be out early and late. Those are the times to see things retiring into their daytime haunts or coming forth from them, and, usually, there is a naturalness about game at such times that one does not see in it at high noon when it is roused for flight. A man gets a chance to observe what I should call some of the refinement of motion, some of the delicacy of feeding, some of the grace and beauty of behavior that characterize many forms of wild life when undisturbed.

Twilight found us seated silently on the strange structure among the heavy branches of the burly young pine; twilight with its tints and glows and afterglows faded and left us there. Darkness fell over the wide sea-marshes, over the huge oaks surrounding Joel's house, and over the field that lay before us. With the darkness came the voices of the night: the plaintive piping of the plover from the beaches, the human whistling of the curlews and willets; the weird intoning of the great horned owls in the deep forest behind us. Once I heard a fox bark raspingly. A mocking-bird, which is a singer full of song in October, gave a delirious burst of melody. Then a silence settled over the lone country. It was eerie and full of wonder. Suddenly I felt something brush my ear; at the same time a warning hand was laid gently on my arm.

"I hear them coming," said Joel's voice in the faintest whisper. "Get your gun up pretty well now; shoot if you make one out; and don't undershoot."

"I can shoot," I whispered back, "but who in blazes can see? I can't even see the ground. You do it."

Then, even as I whispered, over the old fence, about thirty yards below us, I distinctly heard a deer come across. How in the world am I to describe a sound so faint, so floating, so characteristic of one of these elusive, shadowy creatures? A burly buck can give the leader of a ballet an object lesson in dainty dancing. I was sure I heard the buck jump over. I heard the soft swish as he landed gently in the tall broomsedges bordering the fence. I strained my eyes for sight of the deer. But blank darkness filled my gaze. The stars were out, and when I elevated my sight I could distinguish the ragged outline of the trees against the night sky. But the potato field was a reproduction of the Black Hole of Calcutta. I again intimated this fact to Joel. He leaned up against me.

"I see one," he said.

"Shoot!" I urged.

"It will have to be by dead reckoning."

"That won't matter to me."

I shall never forget my tingling feelings as the woodsman beside me raised his gun. I could barely distinguish the barrel by the faint glinting of the starlight upon it. I could hardly tell the direction in which it was pointing. A shape appeared to float into my vision; but as suddenly and as vaguely it vanished. Clearly, we were dealing with phantoms. But then I distinctly heard some animals feeding almost beneath our stand. I heard the soft champing of succulent leaves and stems; I heard the impatient stamping of browsing deer. My personal experience with phantoms is limited; but I am sure that they do not feed in so material a fashion. Eagerly, yearningly, I tried to make them out. And while I thus struggled mentally and physically to bring the objects into my vision, Joel's gun blared forth on the silence and darkness.

I almost jumped off the platform. But I recovered my balance. The air was filled with acrid fumes. There was a sound of running in the field. Twice I heard short, fierce snorts, and once a weird whistling sound. There was some lively crashing through the myrtles, and then once more silence fell, and a deeper darkness seemed to prevail.

"I got him," Joel announced.

"Are you sure?" I asked. "Did you see him when you shot? Do you think he fell in the field?"

"I had to shoot him by dead reckoning; that is, partly by sight, partly by sound, but mostly by dumb guesswork. Yes; he fell in the field. Let's go down. I guess that's all for to-night. I heard them run all the way to the marsh."

Leaving the tree, we returned to the house and procured two lanterns. Then we came back to the place. Joel led the way to where he thought the buck had fallen. It was as he had said. The deer lay between two potato rows. He was a magnificent animal and in his full prime. His great dark horns bore thirteen clear points. His size was splendid. Joel and I admired him by lantern-light.

"He's one of the old marsh-bucks I have been telling you about," he said; "he fell in his tracks."

"He never even asked who threw the brick," I agreed.

There remains a word concerning the propriety of such hunting. I should not recommend it as a steady practice. But I am glad that I had the experience; and Joel's provocation had been great. Besides, a marsh-buck is not an ordinary critter: he's so exclusive that he has to be treated rudely sometimes. In any event, all my misgivings were forgotten when, on the following morning, as I was saying good-bye to my host, he said:

"This is Tuesday. You come out Thursday to dinner. We'll have some sweet potatoes out of that field, and they ought to go all right with this venison. . . . Don't think hard of me for shooting him at night. He was burgling on my premises. . . . By the way, I put the horns and the hide and the saddle and a haunch in your buggy for you."

HUNTER COME HOME

You might be interested in knowing how a man who lives on a plantation in the wilderness of coastal Carolina gets ready for a deer hunt, especially one which he hopes to give his soldier boy, returning from his long exile from home, the time of his life. I knew that my youngest son would enjoy most a good deer hunt in our own home woods. Long before his arrival, early in December, I began to get ready to give him what I hoped would be a real homecoming.

For two weeks before he came I did no hunting. I kept the woods quiet. It has always been my experience that, while deer will desert their favorite haunts if much disturbed, yet they love their homes and will return to them quickly if they are given a chance.

Almost every day I would walk out the old mazy plantation roads, searching for signs. And I was not looking for ordinary deer tracks. You know how it is; I wanted to find out where some of the old masters had been using. This was not easy to do, for, the mating season being about over, the bucks were not roaming much. As the crops of both pine-mast and acorns had failed, and the deer knew it, their tracks were not plentiful under the great pines and the live-oaks. In fact, I have known certain bucks to resort regularly to such places over a long period of time. While I did not find as many signs as I hoped for, there were plenty, and some had been left by old stormers.

The second thing I did, as my boy's coming approached, was to watch the wind and the weather. In my part of the country deer usually lie down all day, and just where they lie depends

From *Those Were the Days* (1955).

on the weather. On cold, sunny days they like the broomsedge on high sun-bathed hills. On rainy days I find them in dense cover, and at such times they often change position from time to time.

On days of high wind they lie on the lee slopes, especially where fallen logs afford them additional shelter. On balmy still days they may just drop down anywhere for a siesta. However, like all other wild creatures, deer carry personal and private barometers; and often where they lie may be determined not by what the weather is, but by what the weather is soon to be. Their positively occult information on what's coming makes an ordinary weather man look like the dumbest guesser in all the world.

To further insure sport, I checked over the hounds: Red Liquor, Sambo, Blue Boy, and Big Mike. As far as I could tell, all they needed was to be let out of the yard. Here, however, I want to say that whenever I mention the use of hounds in deer hunting the boys are inclined to ride me.

Well, if I were hunting in strange territory, the very first thing I should do would be to find out how the local nimrods went to work. Some use the rifle and no hounds; some use the rifle and hounds; we use the shotgun and hounds. What causes the difference is the character of the country. In my dense swamp country, jungle-like even in winter, there is no such thing as stalking. We have to use hounds. To use high-powered rifles would be a very dangerous thing in level country; these express bullets, you know, make no local stops.

Besides, I have found that where hounds are not used for deer it is only because their use is forbidden, for good and proper reasons. Yet all normal hunters love to hear a pack run. Imagine the difference between hearing and seeing a fine pack yowling after a fox or a rabbit, and the same pack after an old bruiser of a buck. The excitement is bound to be greater because the game is so much nobler.

Finally, when hounds are used, you rarely have the potshots that are so common in still hunting. An old stag, riding the bushes at thirty miles an hour, with a clamoring pack setting your nerves a-tingle, makes no easy target. As far as downright sport is concerned, hunting with hounds has the edge over stalking. Of course, this is only an opinion. Yet this kind of hunting has behind it age-old traditions, and certainly is not the low-down performance that some men who have never tried it think it is.

As a final preparation, I checked my African pack, my drivers. My son's arrival would permit us to hunt early Saturday morning. Plantation Negroes never work on Saturday, and rarely on any other days. I knew I would have my foreman, Prince; I could count on that great ape, Steve, shambling along in primeval style; on Evergreen, Wineglass and Sam'l.

My son arrived safely and on time from his separation center in the North. He had left me a private; he returned a captain. For two years he had been in England, France and Germany. Like millions of other boys from our country, he had seen a good deal that was pretty ghastly. But of all this he said nothing. He did not seem to have changed, only to have matured. I guess no one will ever be able to tell just how glad these boys were to get home. Our feelings are nearly always deeper than our power to express them.

After considering the weather and the sign that I had been studying, I decided, first to drive what we call Montgomery Branch. This is a mile-long swamp and watercourse, with dense pine and bay thickets. On either hand are open pinelands. As we had but two standers, I thought it wise to stand the two sides of the head of the branch. My son and I would be within long gunshot of each other, directly opposite each other, yet neither could see the other. A perfect jungle intervened between us.

In this kind of hunting the drivers and dogs, of course, put in at one end and the standers shut off the other. I debated with myself a long time before posting my captain. I felt reasonably certain that we could rouse a buck. I had told Prince and Wineglass to hold the center of the drive, while Evergreen, Sam'l and Steve flanked so as to keep the deer from flaring out at the sides. But if the old master were at home, and if he made a straight run, on which side of head would he break out? Angels and ministers of grace could not have answered that question.

At last I posted Irvine on the south side, while I took up the stand on the north. And no sooner were we in place than things began to happen far down the drive. The morning was cool and quiet, so that one could hear everything that was happening. And when you get a gang of Negro drivers together on a still day, you are going to hear something. As the African Nandi and Masai curse the lion they surround and are going to kill with their assagais, so my Negroes begin driving by amiably blaspheming all bucks. And each one feels it his duty to try to outdo all the others in the energy and the picturesqueness of his language.

They had been driving but a few minutes when I heard Big Mike (who by the way, though a Labrador retriever, is a wonderful deer dog) carry a deer far away to the eastward, hopelessly out of the drive. He must have gotten past Steve, for I heard that huge gorilla trying to turn him and the cruel jeers of his fellow drivers advising him that if he could do no better he might as well go home. Now Sambo and Red took a trail on my side of the branch. It was cold and mazy, and they did not seem able to straighten it out properly. I knew that if they stayed with it long enough they would jump the deer, but I was afraid he was not in our drive.

Suddenly I heard little Blue Boy, a beagle, coming straight down the drive toward us. I could hear him all the more clearly because the drivers had eased up on their racket in order to investigate the possibilities of what Red Liquor and Sambo were claiming they had discovered. My Blue Boy and I had hunted for three seasons, and had found him to be a quite matchless deer hound. I got him originally in this way. A beagle fancier had him, along with about twenty others. Blue was the very best of the lot. But his owner wanted him for exhibition purposes only; and he told me that, for the class in which he belonged, Blue's tail was a half inch too long! As for me, when it comes to a dog I really want to hunt, give me the nose. I don't worry about tails.

Blue held a straight course, and he was taking something to my son. I could not hear him so well, as he was running in the thickets, but soon he cleared the cover. Immediately I heard Irvine shoot once. It was a tantalizing thing for me to be so near yet not to know what had happened. I figured he must have killed something, or else he would have fired again.

I heard him talking to Blue; then I heard him taking Blue back into the head of the drive. What had happened? Had an old buck started out, been missed or wounded, and turned back? Whatever it was, I knew I had to hold my stand. For a few minutes I heard nothing whatsoever from Blue Boy. However, Wineglass, on my side of the drive and not far ahead of me, began to whoop as if he had been converted. Evidently he had walked up a deer. He had, and here they came to me—two old does and two yearlings, with no dog following. They passed me at a leisurely pace, within twenty yards, and without ever seeing me.

I was very curious over the meaning of Blue's race, the single shot, his being put back into the drive, and his present silence. The drivers were now in full cry again, and coming pretty close. Suddenly I heard Blue, and he was coming my way. Almost before I had time to get my gun up, a beautiful buck sailed out of the thicket ahead of me. He was running on my right, and he was in high gear; moreover, he was kiting through pines that were thicker than a man likes to have them when he is trying not to miss.

Blue was right after this buck, almost under his tail, and the buck was not trying to hide his purpose of getting out of that hot corner with all expedition. At my first barrel he fell flat. Blue was running so fast that he actually ran up on the prone deer's body, whereupon the old stag righted himself, got off the ground and started away. I had to shoot him again; at least I did so, for when a hunter sees a buck trying to get away, the sensible and the merciful thing to do is to end the business then and there.

I never understand just how it is done; but however far off hounds may have strayed, and however far away Negro drivers may be, at the blast of a gun they all suddenly appear on the scene of action. So it was now, with the bushes breaking in every direction and hounds and drivers emerging.

When I crossed the thicket to Irvine's stand, I found him with a shaggy eight-point buck that Blue had brought straight to him. Beside him was the delightedly smiling Sam'l. We brought this buck over the branch and laid him beside mine. Mine was only six-point, and I had had to shoot him twice. Irvine's was the finer deer, and he had done the task assigned with one shot. But you understand that is as it should have been.

What happened was probably something like this: these two bucks had probably been lying together, and came to the head of the drive together. One came straight out and ran into my sharpshooter's ambush (my son taught sharpshooting in the Army). The other buck dodged back. His intent was probably to make a run straight back for the river, two miles away. But the drivers had pretty effectively closed off that avenue of escape.

Providentially, Irvine, instead of tying Blue beside his dead buck, had put him back in the drive, having a hunch, as he told me, that there might be something more in there. Blue did not then open until he got on the second buck, which proceeded to try my side of the drive, with the aforesaid result.

We had taken to the woods at eight o'clock in the morning. By nine we were at home with two fine bucks. Such a thing had never before happened to Irv and me, nor is it likely to happen again—at least not just that way. And that's why it's a hunt really to remember.

A CHRISTMAS HUNT

On the old plantations of the Deep South, many of which are still in operation, and still in the hands of their original owners, there is an old tradition of having a big deer hunt on Christmas Day. On these ancient estates Christmas is probably as picturesquely celebrated as it is anywhere in the world. The Christmas found there has an old English flavor; it is the jovial Christmas of Shakespeare, of the Cavaliers of Dickens. There are manifest the high spirit, the boisterous but wholesome cheer, the holly, the mistletoe, the smilax in wreaths; the roaring fires of oak and pine; the songs, the laughter, the happy games, and all the other festive enjoyments of the days of long ago. Whatever else may be said of those who settled the South from the court of King Charles I, who, according to Edmund Burke, "had as much pride as virtue in them," they certainly knew how to make themselves happy at Christmas; and this fortunate characteristic they have bequeathed to their far descendants. While their rollicking spirit may not be so nearly akin to that of the Original Christmas as the stern joy of the sober-hearted Puritans, their hearts were warmer, and their homes were full of laughter and of light. The Puritan had the lilies and the snow and the wintry starlight of mystic love and devotion; the Cavalier had the roses, the red wine, and the ruddy fireside of human affection.

Quaintly, and very humanly, the chief business on Christmas Day on an old Southern plantation is not going to church. While the women naturally think religion should come first, they do not greatly demur when their husbands, brothers, and lovers, like the attractively boyish barbarians men always really are, decide to take to the woods.

From *Those Were the Days* (1955).

While there is a proverb in the South that Christmas is hard
on a hunter's aim, yet that is no deterrent to the annual gathering. Friends and neighbors will meet on Christmas morning at
one of the great plantations—some coming in cars, and some on
horseback; and behind the latter will be trailing their deerhounds
in the order of their enthusiasm. On such an occasion all the
packs of the countryside hunt together. I have known as many
as eighty hounds to be used on one such hunt. The presence at
one of these gatherings of some plantation owners who hunt on
Christmas only, and who have never been known to hit anything,
offers the wags of the party a rarer sport than deer could afford.
About such a holiday company there is a spirit of wholesome
irresponsibility, of genial laxity, that Southern hunters, who usually take their sport with gravity, almost as if it were a religious
rite, do not usually manifest.

As the wildwoods into which they are going is too rough for
cars, all the hunters and the Negro deer drivers are mounted,
though it must be confessed that many of them ride mules and
horses that are hardly fit for the plow. But what is lacking in
the elegance of equipage is compensated for by good cheer—by
Christmas cheer, which is unique, wherever it is found. As the
hunters ride away, to the winding of horns and the soulful yowling of the deer hounds, they appear like some cavalcade of old,
riding away into the shadows of the past.

Since I have mentioned the hounds, and since they form so
integral a part of the Christmas hunt, I think it well to make
some remarks about them. The deerhounds of the South, usually
Walkers or else Redbones, are really foxhounds trained to hunt
deer. Such is the density of the cover in the rural South, even
in midwinter, with gray moss shrouding the impenetrable jungles; and where, even on higher ground, evergreens such as the
scrub pines, sweet bay, cane, and gallberry prevail, that deer
stalking such as is practiced in the North and West is never
possible. The hunter is compelled to use hounds.

I love a hound. He is the philosopher among dogs. He has
a profound and genuine distrust of the general scheme of things
in this life. Melancholy of an ancient and appealing sort is his.
What makes his pessimism worthy of regard is the fact that it
has its source in remarkable sagacity. His honest and steadfast
refusal to be optimistic not only lends to his character a noble
severity but also gives to his philosophy the serene charm of

truth. He invariably seems to me to belong to an older and wiser generation which regards the behavior of all other living things as an exceedingly juvenile performance. A hound is the only dog that can make me conscious of my own shortcomings. Fixed by his grave appraising eyes, I shrink into my true stature. A sensitive and reflective soul, his spirit has a savor of astute meditation.

The hunters, drivers, and hounds having gathered, it must be decided what drive to take. Shall it be Boggy Bay, or the Long Corner, or the wilds of Peachtree along the South Santee River, or the Huckleberry Branch? Usually the master of the hunt makes the momentous decision. The Negro drivers, knowing these wildwoods better than white men, know exactly where to go and what to do. And with them go the hounds. They all circle until they get to the back of the drive; then they start toward the standers.

These, meanwhile, have been posted on crossings or stands. These are regular runs that deer have made since long before the Revolution. The master of the hunt will post each stander; and if he is at all strange to the country, will carefully describe a buck's usual direction of approach. If a stander is familiar with the drive, he will merely be told, "Take the Laurel Tree Stand," or "The Crippled Oak," or "The Three Sisters."

It is rather wonderful but it is true that both birds and animals steer their courses through the air and through the forest by natural objects of the landscape. I have often observed that wild ducks will pass directly over certain solitary pines and cypresses that stand in the marshlands; they fly right over my house, though they have to leave the line of the river to do so. Such objects must be landmarks to them. All over the pineland forests of the South are flat-topped mounds, standing about three feet above the floor of the forest. These are ancient tarkilns, dating back to colonial days. I never knew a tarkiln that was not a good deer stand.

There's tradition and some romance about the old names of deer-stands in the Deep South. Thus we have the Doeboy Stand, named long ago for a hunter who forgot or disregarded the buck law; the Shirttail Stand, named for a major miss executed there; the Savanna Stand, taking its name from the character of the swampy landscape there; the Ten-Master Stand, where a famous buck was killed far back about 1840; the Handkerchief Stand, where an unfortunate old gentleman, hearing the hounds starting his way, and finding his glasses a little misty, took them off to wipe them, and shook out his handkerchief almost in the faces of two eight-point bucks that had come up to him without his knowing that they were near! And there's the Green Lady Stand, honoring a Diana who, long ago but within my memory, all dressed in Lincoln green like Maid Marian, killed a noble buck with a rifle, the buck being on a dead run, after seven male standers had shot at him with their shotguns and had missed him.

I remember one Christmas Day when it was my turn to entertain all the nimrods of the neighborhood, I decided to drive the great Wambaw Corner, an 800-acre tract of pure wilderness, surrounded on three sides by creeks, and a place famous for its bucks. I did not have so great a crowd of hunters with me—just eighteen. I do not care for a huge pack of hounds; among so many dogs there will be some notable liars that will start the others off on false trails; there is difficulty and there is confusion in handling a yowling multitude; then, at the very beginning of the hunt, a doe or a yearling may be started, and the whole pack may get away on it. I therefore left at home about two-thirds of the hounds that had been brought to this meet, and selected twelve tried and true hounds to do the work. Among these were at least three that would run nothing but a buck; it is not generally known, I think, that there is a difference between the scent of sexes in whitetail deer, and perhaps in all animals of the wilds, and perhaps those that are domesticated as well.

I had four Negro drivers: Prince Alston, my plantation foreman and my best deer hunter; Will, his brother; Steve, who made up in enthusiasm for a piece of Christmas venison for what he lacked in wildwood sagacity; and Old Testament, an ancient crafty Negro, to whom the secrets of nature are like an open book.

Having sent these men with the hounds to the other end of the drive, far back to the lonely edges of the Santee River, I posted my standers on such famous places as the Forked Dogwood, the Gum Tree, the Savanna, the Mossy Oak, the Rattlesnake Stand. This last took its name from the fact that a hunter of the long ago, posted there, had come to him, not a buck but a huge diamondback rattlesnake. It goes without saying that the hounds were not running it!

In about twenty minutes the drive started. The drivers

spread out across the big peninsula began to whoop as if they had found religion or a cache of liquor. The dogs began to tune up. While they were still a mile away, I heard one of the standers shoot. I knew what this meant: a wary old buck had slipped out ahead of the hounds. While does and yearlings will rarely leave their beds until actually routed out, a wary old stag will attempt to steal away at the first whoop of a driver or voice of a dog; and he does so with a noiseless stealth peculiar to him. I have often known a stander to lose a shot because he had not loaded his gun the minute he was posted.

When one is familiar with his hounds, if weather conditions are favorable, he can recognize, even at a great distance, the voice of each one. I remember trying to describe the music of a pack of deerhounds in these lines:

> There's a short low tenor,
> And a yipping kiji;
> There's a bell-mouth ringing
> That a buck has got to die.
> There's a dingdong chop-mouth
> Always in the noise;
> There's a bass with no bottom,
> And a rolling gong voice;
> There's a bugle with a break,
> And a bugle with a scream;
> And a high wailing tenor
> Like a trumpet in a dream.

It is not only the dogs that tell us when a fine stag has started; for the drivers make the wildwoods ring with their natively melodious voices—sometimes chanting admonitions such as, "'Tis the Ole Man comin'! For God's sake don't miss him!"

Now we hear the pack divide: that means two or more deer are afoot. One buck heads for the creek, but from the swing that the hounds make, I can tell that Prince has turned the buck; and now he is heading straight for the standers. The other dogs begin to circle, but Old Testament gallantly takes care of that situation. Later he told me that he had turned two bucks by throwing pine knots at them, "and by jumping high in the air," he added. And he's close to eighty years old.

In such a situation, any other deer lying between the two oncoming packs and the standers would be roused, and would likely come our way, I knew. But quite often a wary old stag will object to being driven, and will race back through drivers and hounds. Once when I protested to a driver that he had failed to drive a buck out to me, but had let the deer almost run over and trample him, he said, "An old buck, he gwine where he gwine."

As the clamoring hounds got within three hundred yards of the road, the shooting began. I think in all there were some twenty-one shots fired. Some dogs got away after bucks that had been missed. But as yet no man knew what any other man had done; for there is a stern rule that a hunter must never leave his stand until the master of the hunt winds his horn, signaling that the hunt is over. And the signal may not be given for some time; for it is just like a buck that has passed the line of standers and is followed by hounds to circle right back into gunshot.

On this occasion, however, no deer turned back; and the dogs went out of hearing. When, therefore, the drivers had come out to us, I blew my horn. Then we gathered to report what had been done. I found the usual number of glad faces and red faces. The very first man who shot had killed a nine-point buck as he was stealing out far ahead of the drivers. There were five other bucks killed, one a huge twelve-pointer that had been known to harbor in that drive for years, a regular hart royal that we had always called the Bushmaster.

To get all these deer tied behind saddles, and to round up all the hounds by blowing for them takes time. And of course every successful hunter wanted to tell about his buck; those who had missed were not too keen about going into details.

Our return to the plantation was in the nature of a triumph; but I think the sternest joy was felt by our drivers, not only for the part they had so well played, but because of the solid satisfaction of the assurance of plenty of venison for them and for their families. Steve especially rejoiced; for he has an indefinite number of children—about fourteen, I think.

We gather in the backyard of the plantation, which overlooks the river, and rehunt the whole drive, and other drives as well, as the drivers dress the deer. Prince is delegated to feed the hounds. He had on the ground a long cypress board, and this was, at least in his own mind, divided into spaces, one of which was assigned to each ravenous hound. Bringing forth the pot of steaming food, I remember that he addressed his famished army about like this:

"How come you can't find your place, Music? Ain't you know you have a place at table between Buck and Ringwood? Don't you dare cross that line, Check. You stay away from Mate's dinner. Gambler, you ain't gwine to get a thing if you edge up on me. Red Liquor, if I ever bat you with this big spoon, your jaw will ache until New Year's Day."

During this admonitory address, Prince would be ladling the food on the big board, a portion for each hound; and he had them so trained that, until the banquet was properly spread, not a dog would dare to begin, though certain lean melancholy faces would loll forward languishingly.

With the sharing of the venison, the Christmas Hunt is over; and I say good-bye to my rural friends and neighbors. After this parting, I stroll toward the river, where I see a yellow jasmine blooming, and where a mockingbird is singing. In a patch of warm sunlight I come upon Bugle, an old hound too old now to hunt, fast asleep. Yet his feet are errantly moving, and joyous muffled barks proclaim that even in slumber he is running a buck. Dreams will never let him be, especially when plantation hunting comes to its climax on Christmas Day. I know his memory is full of noble images of stags that he has sped across the river's tide—stags that now for him are swimming forever and forever.

A BLACK BUCK

While our summers were nominally spent on the seacoast, hardly a week passed without our visiting the plantation; and our trips there became more frequent as the summer waned. During the time of our plantation boyhood, the deer season opened on the first of August; but this was no particular menace to the deer which abounded in the pineland. For the mosquitoes, flies, and snakes kept nearly every hunter out of the woods. Also, in August the hunter of the pinelands is liable to be exposed to intense heat and to sudden and dangerous thunderstorms. But if a man be a hunter born, he will tolerate an astonishing number of inconveniences in order to gratify his sense of sport.

One of the most picturesque and memorable hunts that my brother Tom and I ever enjoyed occurred in mid-August; and since its incidents are so typical of that old plantation life which we once knew, I shall describe it.

For August hunting, a three o'clock start in the morning was necessary; for before the actual hunting began, we had a drive of nearly ten miles, and we must do our most active work before the heat of the day set in.

While on the plantation the day before this hunt, we had interviewed our ever-faithful companion in all our adventures, the Negro boy Prince, and had told him to meet us at five o'clock next morning near the old Brick Church. We said we would bring the hounds with us from the village; so therefore it would not be necessary for us to go into the plantation until after the hunt.

It had been a still, cloudless August night, giving promise

From *Tom and I on the Old Plantation* (1918).

88

of a day like it. We drove out of the village at three o'clock, and I remember how fast asleep the houses seemed. The cotton-fields to our right were starred with their opening bolls; the cedars above the village lane were dreamy in their soft purple light. Before us, out of which now breathed the ancient sweet odors of the coming dawn, the dark pine forest lay; while above it glittered, large and lustrous, the morning star.

Into the dim woods we drove, and to us came the ineffable sweetness of the wild blossoming forest. Our buggy made no sound in the sand; our wise and tolerant hounds trailed beside us, in the paths made by walkers, like shadows in the dusk of the pineland. As we were leaving the skirts of the village, we had persuaded a friend's dog to join us; it being the immemorial privilege of hunters in the Santee county to blow their horns when starting out, with the understanding that all dogs not tied when that sonorous summons came were at liberty to join the joyous departing cavalcade. Not wishing to wake the people, we did not blow until near the woods; and pretty soon a fine hound joined our two.

It was a little after four o'clock when we met Prince by the Brick Church. The day was breaking, and through the fragrant pinelands the bobwhites were beginning to call. We greeted the Negro with that subdued hilarity that is the peculiar property of hunters who are on the hunting ground; while he, as eager as we, sat on his mule, chuckling and grinning.

"Prince, what's that thing you're riding?" Tom asked; not really for information, but because such a foolish question sometimes brought forth from Prince a witty answer.

"Dis is a mule, boss," was Prince's reply; "a good mule, too, sah, 'caze she only throwed me twice dis morning."

"Did she hurt you, Prince?" I questioned, knowing well enough that he was bantering us, but a little concerned over what might really happen if my brother or I should try his mount.

"No, sah, I was very lucky, 'caze both times I hit right on my head."

After a short consultation, we tied our horse by the Church, and turned the hounds over to Prince. It was then that we noticed for the first time that Prince had a dog following him; a mangy, skulking mongrel, lower even than "a cur of low degree."

"Look here, Prince," my brother said, just a little provoked, and yet a little amused at the incongruity of having a dog like that associating with our somewhat well-bred, and certainly haughty, hounds: "Why did you let that 'critter' follow you?"

Prince appeared somewhat abashed.

"Just seems he was obliged to follow me, Mas' Tom. And dat dog is a fine trailer; yes, sah, a fine trailer."

"What can he trail, Prince?" I asked, "wood-mice?"

"He can trail a ham-bone, boss. But dat ain't no huntin' dog, sah. Dat's a society dog. Can't you notice he walks just like he had on his Sunday clothes?"

Leaving us laughing at his foolery, Prince whirled his mule and rode away under the pines, the hounds trailing knowingly after him.

We set out down the road to take our stands for the first drive. The sun had not yet risen; and the woods were cool and beautiful. As we walked together down the broad grassy drive, we loaded our guns, and spoke of the chances of jumping deer in the Briar Bed, the famous thicket toward the head of which the Negro had taken the dogs.

On the stands of that drive we waited half an hour, without experiencing any more excitement than that occasioned by the persistent deer-flies with which the woods were at that season infested. Nor did our following drive of the Thickhead branch prove more successful. However, when Prince came out in the road, it was clear to us that he had seen something, for he was smiling the suppressed yet elaborately hidden smile of one who wishes to tell a secret.

"My dog done tree in yonder," he announced with pride, pointing back toward the dark outline of the Thickhead.

"What was it, Prince?" we asked in unison.

"He done tree a ground-mole," he said.

We then fell to discussing what drive we should try next.

"A big, able, black buck used to navigate in the Smallpox Corner. And he sure has got a brush-heap on his head." Prince was serious enough when he said this; so we decided to try that drive.

Since the stands were on the road ahead of us, and since this thicket with the sinister name had often proved a favorite place for deer, we sent Prince ahead with the dogs, as he had to make a far circuit before putting them in.

Smallpox Corner is on Montgomery plantation; it is a dense thicket of bull pines, scrub oaks, myrtles, and gallberry bushes, with spaces here and there of tall broomsedge. It lies between the old road leading into Montgomery and the famous Montgomery Branch, a broad watercourse of the pine woods, supporting so wild a jungle growth that, at least where we were, near the lower end of it, deer seldom entered it. If there was anything in the Corner, it would probably come straight out to us.

But we did not have much hope that the dogs would jump deer. It was ten o'clock on a sultry August morning, and the cicadas were shrilling insistently. The sandy ridges in the woods were as dry as pepper; the savannas and branches were steaming. The birds were silent; even the great pines, so sensitive to the least breath, were without movement and without music. It truly did not look promising, but we were going to try it.

Hitching the horse in a clump of scrub pines beside the road, we walked slowly down to the stands. There were but two of them; Tom decided to take the one on the brow of the sandy hill, while I went to the one near Montgomery Branch, sixty yards away. Unless the deer doubled in the drive, he would surely run to one of the stands thus covered.

For a half hour we stood patiently by our chosen pines, while the day grew hotter, and the sultry stillness more intense. There was a little wood-spring near my brother's stand, and as I now looked up, I saw him drinking from it with a bay-leaf. I saw the glint of the cool water on the silver sides of the leaf; and I could not resist the inordinate thirst that that glance awakened, though I knew well enough that one of the cardinal rules in deer hunting is that a hunter should, under no conditions, leave his stand until the dogs have come up. Leaving my gun leaning against a pine, I walked up the slope toward the spring. After satisfying our thirst, we, becoming overcome with drowsiness on account of our early start from home that morning, lay down under a little bushy-headed live-oak, with our hats over our eyes, and talked in a sleepy way, wishing that Prince would hurry up and come out, so that we could get to the sheltered coolness of the big plantation house.

We may have gone half asleep under that oak; at any rate, we were particularly shut out from the world, until a sudden wild whoop from Prince startled us, and woke all the echoes of the dreaming woods. The next moment we heard the three hounds strike the trail. But high above their chiming chorus we heard the melodious voice of the negro driver, pleading, insistent:

"'Tis the ole buck! 'Tis the ole black buck! Don't let him get by! O—O don't let him get by!"

At Prince's first shout we had bounded to our feet, and on that instant we saw the deer coming, he then being some three hundred yards away. At the speed he was going, he would cross the stands in five or six seconds. My brother, in his excitement and fearing that I would not get to the lower stand, for which the buck was heading, in time, dashed down the hill, leaving me at the upper crossing, with no gun.

Immediately beyond the road, there was a long burnt-over stretch of woods, and through this the buck was coming, his great speed unimpeded by brush or vines.

He was indeed a magnificent creature, with his tall symmetrical antlers in velvet; and he was the only buck I had ever seen which had black hair growing heavily on his chest. I understood why Prince had called him the old black buck. He came bounding along in his graceful, powerful way, every muscle of his shapely body subservient to his will. He was heading straight for my brother. I could see this so clearly that I was reconciled to not having my gun, and stood still by the spring, waiting for Tom to shoot.

Meanwhile the woods were ringing with the music of the following hounds, and Prince's voice sounded melodiously through the clamoring air:

"'Tis the ole buck! 'Tis the ole black buck! Don't miss him! O—O don't miss him!"

On came the splendid creature, flashing over the fallen timber and over the blackened spaces where the recent fire had eaten away bushes and young saplings. I saw my brother put up his gun. I held my breath in excitement. My intense pride in his excellent marksmanship was about to be fully justified.

Either winding him or seeing him, or doing both things at once, the great buck veered swiftly away from my brother and from within the deadly range of his gun. Then, literally crouching in his run, with the marvelous speed of which a cornered deer is capable, he skimmed off at a tangent, which brought him heading directly for me. Tom could have made the shot, I think, long as it was, for he had an old Westley-Richards muzzle-loader;

an English gun of wonderful carrying power; but he was unselfish, and he did not want to spoil my chance. It is only once in a long while that a man gets a fair shot at such a deer as that one was. I saw Tom lower his gun and look up the hill toward me.

"My gun's down there!" I cried. "Shoot, shoot before he jumps the road!"

I gestured wildly for him to shoot, shouting, I now suspect, somewhat incoherently; but the dogs were already in the burnt ground, and Prince and his sonorous pleading voice were out of the thicket and under the open pines. Before my brother understood my predicament, the buck leaped the road, not fifteen feet from where I stood, and swiftly vanished into a dense copse of young yellow pines. A minute later I stopped the dogs. Then holding them in leash, I walked down the slope toward Tom. Each of us had, I am sure, less to regret than we had at first suspected.

"Man alive," said Tom in good-natured admiration, "wasn't he a beauty? He was really too pretty to shoot."

And since I could concur heartily in his opinion, our hunt, though unsuccessful, ended most happily.

THE LADY IN GREEN

For a very long time we have had on the plantation a Negro named Steve. For a generation he worked for us; and he is with me to this day. While we usually had certain Negroes who could be counted on to accomplish even difficult material tasks, in what might be termed the realm of the psychic, Steve reigned supreme. For some reason, he was at his best when something esoteric and peculiar had to be accomplished. My Colonel early recognized Steve's strange talent, and occasionally called on him to exercise it.

Thus when the lady in green came to us for a visit, and came with the hope of killing a regal buck, I felt called upon to enlist the darksome strategy of Steve.

"Steve," I asked, "have you ever seen a woman wear pants?"

"I ain't done seen it, Cap'n," he responded, a fervent fire of recollection kindling in his eyes, "but I has done seen some wimmins what act like dey wears dem."

"Has your Amnesia ever worn them?"

"When I is around home," he assured me, "she don't ever wear anything else but."

"Have you two been falling out again, Steve?"

"Cap'n," he answered solemnly, "for yeahs and yeahs we ain't never done fell in."

"I guess she doesn't like your playing around with all these young girls, and leaving her at home."

"I tole her dat woman and cat is to stay home; man and dog is to go abroad. She didn't like dat atall, atall."

From *Hunter's Choice* (1946).

"Well," I said, "this is Friday. Monday will be Christmas Day. I know just one way I can get you out of the dog-house where Amnesia has put you. Wouldn't you like to get out for Christmas?"

Steve licked his lips, a sure sign that he is about to take the bait. Besides, as I had beforehand been of assistance to him in the vital manner of domestic reconciliations, he regards me as a kind of magician.

"Tomorrow," I told him, "will be Saturday, the day before Christmas Eve. I will help you, but I expect you to help me." I was testing his loyalty in a large way.

Haunted by a sense of his own helplessness and by the mastery of his huge Amnesia, he appeared pathetically eager to do anything. In fact, such was his yielding mood that I had to be careful what I asked him to do, for he would do it. Steve can resist anything but temptation.

"I'm giving a big deer drive tomorrow," I said. "There will be twenty men and one woman—but I hear she wears pants."

"Great Gawd," was Steve's comment.

"Green ones," I went on.

"Jeedus!"

"Now, Steve, you know that old flathorn buck in the Wambaw Corner—the one that has been dodging us for about five years?"

"You mean him what hab dem yaller horns, flat same like a paddle?"

"He's the one."

"Cap'n, dat's a buck what I knows like I knows the way to another man's watermelon patch," Steve assured me grinning. "What you want me to do? And how Amnesia suddenly gwine take me back because of what you is planning for me to do?"

"Well," I told him, "you've got a job, all right. I don't want to be unfair to these men, but ordinary bucks will do very well for them. Your business is to get the *buck with the palmated horns* to run to the lady in green. If you will do this, I will give you a whole haunch of venison, a ham out of my smokehouse, a dollar in cash and a dress for Amnesia. How about it?

Steve was stunned. When he came to, he said, "Boss, when I gits to heaben, I ain't gwine ask, 'How 'bout it?'"

"Of course," I told him, "I will put her on the Crippled Oak Stand. You know that is the favorite buck run. Just how you are going to get him to run there I don't know, but you probably can figure it out. Oh," I added, "I will not hold you responsible for her killing the buck. Being a woman, she'll probably miss it anyway. But I want you to give her a chance to shoot."

I could see that Steve was already deep in his problem. Knowing the woods like an Indian, so familiar with game that he can almost talk with it, familiar also with the likelihood of big game's acting in ways unpredictable, Steve was pretty well equipped for his task. I could almost see how he would enjoy this particular job.

"One more thing," I told him: "this lady doesn't shoot a shotgun. She always uses a rifle."

"Cap'n," he sensibly asked, "does you think she knows a deer? If she don't, I mustn't get too close to dat rifle."

"I have never seen her," I told him, "and I don't know whether she is a real huntress. All I know about her is what I have been told. But she's the daughter of one of my best friends, a gentleman from Philadelphia. I want her to have a good time. Think of what it would mean if she could kill the crowned king of Wambaw Corner!"

"I sure loves to please wimmins," Steve mused, "but so far I ain't done had too much of luck."

As we parted I kept pounding home his job to him: "Drive the buck with the flat horns to the Crippled Oak Stand. Drive him there if you have to head him off. And remember the haunch and the ham that will be yours if you manage it right."

Not long after daylight the following morning the crowd of Christmas hunters assembled in my plantation yard. As the season was nearing its close, every man I had invited came. And there was the lady in green. When I saw her, I was ashamed of the way in which I had bandied words with Steve about the nature of her attire. She was slender, graceful and very lovely. She looked like Maid Marian. Clad in Lincoln green, with a jaunty feather in her Robin Hood's cap, she was the attraction of all eyes. I could see that all the men were in love with her, and I didn't feel any too emotionally normal myself. There was nothing about her of the type of huntress I had described to Steve. She appeared a strange combination of an elf, a child and a woman; and though I do not profess to know much about such matters, that particular combination seems especially alluring, perhaps dangerously so.

While my Negro drivers were getting their horses ready, and while stately deer hounds, woolly dogs and curs of low degree gathered from far and near on account of the general air of festivity and the promise of some break in the general hunger situation, I got everybody together and told them that we planned to drive the great Wambaw Corner; that we had standers enough to take care of the whole place, we had drivers and dogs, we had deer. The great, and really the only, question was, Can anybody hit anything? That is often a pertinent question in hunting.

Wambaw Corner is peculiarly situated. A tract of nearly a thousand acres, it is bounded on two sides by the wide and deep Wambaw Creek. On one side is the famous Lucas Reserve, an immense backwater, formerly used for waterpower, but now chiefly for bass and bream. In shape this place is a long and comparatively narrow peninsula, with water on three sides. On the south runs a wide road, along which I usually post my standers; but when I have enough (or too many), I post them along the creek. The chance there is excellent, for if a buck is suspicious there's nothing he'll do quicker than dodge back and swim the creek.

With the woods still sparkling with dew, and fragrant with the aromas from myrtles and pines, I posted all my standers. I had sent my drivers far down on the tip of the peninsula, to drive it out to the road. I had also had a last word with Steve.

"Only one mistake you might be can is makin', Cap'n," he told me: "I dunno how 'bout wid a gun, but with a rollin'-pin or a skillet or a hatchet a woman don't eber seem to miss. Anyhow," he particularized, "dey don't neber miss me!"

"Have you got our plan made?" I asked him. "You've got five other boys to drive. That just about sets you free to do what you want to."

"I got my plan," he said. "And," he added darkly, "if so happen it be dat I don't come out with de other drivers, you will onnerstan'."

In a place like Wambaw Corner there are at times a great many deer. They love its remote quiet, its pine hills, its abundant food, its watery edges. I have seen as many as six fine bucks run out of there on a single drive, a flock of wild turkeys, and heaven knows how many does. I have likewise seen wild boars emerge from that wilderness—huge hulking brutes, built like oversize hyenas, and they are ugly customers to handle.

I know that there was sure to be a good deal of shooting on this drive, certain to be some missing, and possibly to be some killing. Everybody seemed keyed just right for the sport. I had men with me who had hunted all over the world, grizzled backwoodsmen who had never hunted more than twenty miles from their homes, pure amateurs, some insatiable hunters but rotten shots—and I had the lady in green.

After I had posted the men, there being no stand for me, or perhaps for a more romantic reason, I decided to stand with my Maid Marian. She seemed like such a child to shoot down a big buck; yet she was jaunty and serene. When I had explained to certain of the standers as I posted them just how an old stag would come up to them, I could see, from the way they began to sweat and blink, that they were in the incipient stages of nervous breakdowns. But not so my Sherwood Forest girl.

Her stand, by the famous Crippled Oak, was on a high bank in the pinelands. Before her and behind her was dense cypress swamp, in the dark fastness of which it was almost impossible to get a shot at a deer. If the buck came, she would have to shoot him when he broke across the bank, and likely on the full run—climbing it, soaring across it, or launching himself down the farther bank. All this I carefully explained to her. She listened intently and intelligently.

She appeared concerned over my concern. "You need not worry," she assured, for my comfort. "If he comes, I will kill him."

"Have you killed deer before?" I asked.

"No," she admitted lightly but undaunted. "I never even saw one."

My heart failed me. "This one," I told her, hoping that Steve's maneuvering would be effective, "is likely to have big yellow horns. He's an old wildwood hero. I hope you get him."

About that time I heard the drivers put in, and I mean they did. A Christmas hunt on a Carolina plantation brings out everything a Negro has in the way of vocal eminence. Far back near the river they whooped and shouted, yelled and sang. Then I heard the hounds begin to tune up.

Maid Marian was listening, with her little head pertly tipped to one side. "What is all that noice?" she asked with devastating imbecility.

Tediously I explained that the deer were lying down, that

the Negroes and the dogs roused them, and that by good fortune an old rough-shod stag might come our way.

"I understand," she nodded brightly. But I was sure she didn't.

Another thing disconcerted me: I could hear the voice of Prince, of Sam'l, of Will and of Precinct; Evergreen's voice was loud on the still air. But not once did I hear the hound-dog whoop of Steve. However, his silence did indicate that he was about some mysterious business.

In a few minutes a perfect bedlam in one of the deep corners showed that a stag had been roused. The wild clamor headed northward, toward the creek, and soon I heard a gun blare twice. But the pack did not stop. There was a swift veering southward. Before long I heard shots from that direction, but whoever tried must have failed.

The pack headed northeast, toward the road on which we were standing, but far from us. I somehow felt, from his wily maneuvers, that this was the buck with the palmated horns. Ordinary bucks would do no such dodging, and the fact that he had been twice missed would indicate that the standers had seen something very disconcerting.

Watching the lady in green for any tell-tale sign of a break in nerves, I could discover none. She just seemed to be taking a childish delight in all the excitement. She was enjoying it without getting excited herself.

About that time I heart the stander at the far eastern end of the road shoot; a minute later he shot again. He was a good man, a deliberate shot. Perhaps he had done what I wanted Maid Marian to do. But no. The pack now turned toward us.

Judging from the speed of the hounds, there was nothing the matter with the deer; judging by their direction, they were running parallel to the road, at a little over a hundred yards from it. It was a favorite buck run, and at any moment he might flare across the road to one of the standers at the critical crossings. Ours was the last stand on the extreme west. It seemed very unlikely that he would pass all those crossings and come to us. Now the hounds were running closer to the road. It sounded as if the buck was about to cross.

It is now just fifty years since I shot my first buck, and I have hunted deer every year since that initial adventure. But never in all my experience as a deer hunter have I heard what I then heard on the road, on which I had twelve standers. Judging from the shots, the buck must have come within easy sight, if not within range, of every stander. The bombardment was continuous. Together with the shots, as the circus came nearer, I could hear wild and angry shouts; I thought I heard some heavy profanity, and I hoped the lady in green missed this.

She was leaning against the Crippled Oak, cool as a frosted apple. I was behind the tree, pretty nervous for her sake.

"Look out, now," I whispered. "He may cross here at any minute."

My eyes kept searching for the buck to break cover. Suddenly, directly in front of the stander next to us, I saw what I took to be the flash of a white tail. The stander fired both barrels. Then I saw him dash his hat to the ground and jump on it in a kind of frenzy that hardly indicated joy and triumph.

The next thing I knew, the little rifle of the lady in green was up. I did not even see the deer. The rifle spoke. The clamoring pack, now almost upon us, began a wild milling. Then they hushed.

"All right," said Maid Marian serenely, "I killed him."

Gentlemen, she spoke the truth, and the stag she killed was the buck with the palmated horns. At sixty yards, in a full run, he had been drilled through the heart. On several occasions I had seen his horns, but I had not dreamed that they were so fine—perfect, ten-point, golden in color, with the palmation a full two inches. A massive and beautiful trophy they were, of a kind that many a good sportsman spends a lifetime seeking, and often spends it in vain.

However, mingled with my pride and satisfaction there was a certain sense of guilt; yet I was trying to justify myself with the noble sentiment, "Women and children first." I had told Steve to drive this buck to my lady in green. He had done it—heaven knows how. He would tell me later. But his plan had worked. But now came the critical phase of the whole proceeding. Standers and drivers began to gather, and afar off I could hear many deep oaths. These, I felt sure, would subside in the presence of Maid Marian. They did, but not the anger and the protests.

There seemed to be one general question, asked in such a way that it would be well for the person referred to to keep his distance. "Where's that driver?" I heard on all sides. "I mean

the big, black, slue-footed driver. I believe you call him Steve.
I had a good mind to shoot him."

"I'd have killed that buck if he hadn't got in the way."

"What was that flag he was waving? Looked to me like he
was trying to turn the buck from us."

"He was coming right on me when that driver jumped out
of a bush and started waving that flag."

"Well, after all, gentlemen," I said, "here's the buck, and
I must say the lady made a grand shot. Wouldn't you rather have
her kill him than do so yourselves?"

Everybody had now gathered but Steve. When questioned,
the other drivers disclaimed all knowledge of his whereabouts or
his peculiar behavior. But they knew perfectly of both. One
artfully sidetracked the whole painful discussion by saying,
"Steve ain't neber been no good deer driver nohow."

Tyler Somerset, a prince of backwoodsmen, drew me aside.
"Say," he said, "I know what went on back there. You can't fool
me. That's the smartest darky I ever did see. More than once
he outran that buck. And he sure can dodge buckshot. I wonder
where he got that red and white flag he used to turn that old
buck?"

We made several other drives that day. Five more stags were
slain. But the buck and the shot of the lady in green remained
the records. On those later drives Steve put in no appearance.

When my friends were safely gone, Steve shambled out of
hiding to claim his just reward. I loaded him down with
Christmas.

"By the way," I said, "some of the standers told me that
you headed that buck with a red and white flag. Where did you
get that?"

Steve grinned with massive shyness, as he does only when
anything feminine comes to mind. "Dat's de biggest chance I
took—wusser dan dodging buckshot. Dat was Amnesia's Sunday
petticoat."

"Huh," I muttered with gloomy foreboding. "If she ever
finds that one out, I'll have to take you to the hospital."

"Cap'n, I done arrange it," he told me—the old schemer!
"I did tore seven holes in it with all that wavin'; but I tole
Amnesia I was ashamed to have my gal wear a raggety petticoat,
and you was gwine give me a dollar, and I was gwine give it to
her to buy a new one for Christmas."

FLORA'S BUCK

One of my sons, his wife, Flora, and their little daughter, Elise, then aged eight, had been with me on the plantation during the month of December. Weather permitting, we were in the woods every day.

On this particular morning we decided to drive the Wambaw Corner, a famous hang-out for bucks. As he was very fast on his feet, I left my son on the road that runs south of the drive. I decided to post his wife on the famous Dogwood Hill, with her little daughter with her. After giving her such directions as an old hunter gives a green stander, I posted Flora on a good pine stump, just the right height. Her little daughter stood beside her. My good colored driver had already gone down the old road with the hounds. I had cautioned Flora to be alert; for often a wary old stag, long before the drive begins, will slip out if he hears the least suspicious sound.

I walked down the road about two hundred yards, and then turned into a dry pond. I thought it might be a likely crossing, though I had never shot there before.

In not more than five minutes I heard Flora shoot twice. Then she let out a series of tearful yells. Leaving my gun, I beat it up the road as fast as I could run. I remember saying to myself, "My God, she must have shot Elise!" But when I got there, little Elise was standing by the stump, as cool as a frosted apple. Flora had laid her gun on the ground; and as I came up, she threw both arms around my neck, wildly weeping—"Oh, Dad," she said, "the biggest buck in all the world, and I missed him!" I tried to comfort my huntress, at the same time asking Elise, "Did Mother really miss him?"

From *The Woods and Wild Things I Remember* (1970).

102

"Oh, yes," she said practically, "she did not touch him. He looked as big as a barn," she added, and "Oh, what horns!"

A few days after this unfortunate adventure, my son and his wife and daughter had to leave me. As we were saying good-bye, Flora drew me aside. "Dad," she said with great earnestness, "please promise me one thing. Some day soon go sit on that same stump and kill that huge buck for me."

Listening to Flora's request, I felt as if she had asked the impossible.

As every hunter will realize, that was a large order, but I promised Flora to try, at least, to fulfill her wish.

After my children left, I waited exactly ten days. An old buck will come home, but you have to give him time. From a week to two weeks would be right.

My good foreman and I again went to the Dogwood Hill, where I perched on the very stump where Flora had been sitting on her bad-luck day. I have, at times, on a stand, indulged the bad habit of reading or smoking. But not this time; I had a promise to fulfill. My gun was loaded; I was alert; I was wide awake before my foreman started to drive. Many a deerhunter will, at times, doze on a crossing. I fear I have committed this sin myself, but not this time.

The woods were still, and my driver had not begun to drive. In the autumn, the Dogwood Hill is a fairly open place. Behind me and to the right and left were some well-spaced pines. Directly in front of me, and facing the drive, there were some tall leafless bushes. This was the only growth nearby that resembled a thicket. And what did I now see gently rising and falling rhythmically above those bare bushes? They were horns, and what horns! On they came, directly for me, with not a thing pushing him. If he kept on coming, he would soon be within gunshot. This just had to be Flora's buck, and I had orders concerning him. My gun was up, and on he came. You know how you feel when you are sure you have a buck in your pocket? I had that foolish thought. But a buck is never yours unless you have him hung up or ready to hang up. It is not only between the cup and the lip that there's many a slip. Every good hunter knows how that is.

I was always a regular nut about the range of a gun or a rifle. It seemed to me essential for every hunter to study *distances*. My .250-3000 rifle would easily kill a buck (if I hit him) at one hundred to one hundred twenty-five yards. But with a shotgun, which, on account of the level nature of the country is the weapon generally used in the South, forty yards is a certain shot (depending on the hunter); fifty yards is a little uncertain. With an old thirty-two inch barrel Westley-Richards, a muzzle-loader, I once killed an eight-point buck at one hundred three yards. He had accommodated me by standing still broadside. I broke his back with one buckshot. Of course, it was pure luck. I once asked a veteran deer hunter what was his favorite shot at a deer. He said, "At thirty yards, standing."

The creature now headed for me on the Dogwood Hill was no ordinary deer. He was *One of Them*. I was hoping for a nice broadside shot at him, and was pretty sure I could handle him if he so presented himself. But you know how it is. At a moment of crisis in the big woods, unexpected things may happen. You may have it all figured out perfectly; then someone may heave a wrench into the machinery. As a hunter of many years, I learned to expect as much bad luck as good, with occasionally a really heart-breaking experience.

Flora's great stag came within fifty yards of me; then he stopped. He was literally wedged between two pines. He suspected something—probably me. He presented me, not his flank, but his brisket. In my long experience the most difficult shot at a deer (at least with a shotgun) is a head-on shot. The second most difficult is the straightaway. The brisket is one of the very toughest parts of a deer.

Well, here was this real monarch of the glen standing between two pines. I had the sight of my gun on breast. If a buck is coming to a crossing and stops, an experienced hunter can tell whether or not the old boy has made him out. Although I was silent and still, I felt that this great creature had identified me. Usually if you do not move and a buck does not wind you, he may run over you and trample you. Very often I had to make some movement to keep a deer from running me down. Depend upon it, a deer will *always* recognize *movement*.

In my position that morning, with Flora's admonition bearing down on me, I had to use fast all the brains God gave me. I knew that if he ever jerked back from between those two pines, and got into that brambly thicket, my chance would likely be gone—and likely gone forever. As I have said, I already had my gun up. I now eased it over until the sight rested squarely on the forefront of the great stag's neck. I then squeezed off the choke barrel. At such a moment I was prepared for something, but not for what happened.

At the blare of the gun in those still woods, I expected all kinds of things, but as is so often the case, not the thing that did happen. Few indeed, are the hunters who can predict the exact result when the trigger of his gun is pulled. At the blast of my gun, Flora's huge stag stood almost straight up, until he seemed to look as tall as one of the pines that surrounded us. Then he fell back with a mighty crash among the dry bushes. I thought for a moment it was all over, but then I saw some of the tops of the bushes shaking. To any good deer hunter that means that his game is down, but not dead. And there can be a great difference between the two.

Among my pack of five hounds there was one named Southwind. While she had no social background, she had a wonderful nose. And in the canine realm, the second gift is far better than the first. Just give me a dog with a good nose, and you can have all the aristocrats.

Southwind had more than a nose. She had a habit of always coming to the sound of a gun. This may have been touching faith in that trait. I at least had found it at times very useful.

For example, I once walked up to a big buck and shot him down in a thicket. When I went up to him, although he was sprawled suspiciously still, I did a very foolish thing—something no real hunter should ever do. Leaning my gun against a pine, I got on the fallen buck's back. Taking hold of one of his big horns in my left hand, I drew my hunting knife with my right. No sooner had the point of the knife touched the old stag's neck than he vaulted up, as if I had caught him napping. His sudden leap made me lose my knife; and there I was riding a wild deer at full speed through the woods. I had him by his big antlers, but that was all I had of him. That was where Southwind came in. A flash of white came around the running buck, and Southwind grabbed him by the nose. The old buck did not have as much steam in him as I thought. Southwind's sudden nose-grip threw him headlong, and by that time, my son, who had been holding a crossing down the road, had run up; so had my good driver and all the hounds. Although the buck was a ten-pointer and a beauty, I had a hard time explaining to my fellow-hunters about my knife and my gun.

Once when I was talking with a Canadian deer-guide about some accidents I had known with wounded bucks, he looked surprised and said, "A wounded buck can kill you. When we get one down, we keep on shooting him until we know he is dead."

Southwind may have saved my life; at least she saved my buck for me.

When she broke across the Dogwood Hill after Flora's tremendous stag I had shot down, little Southwind was running all alone. The other hounds were away on another deer. I was rather dismayed when she kept on running. I did not think the old buck I had shot in the breast could go so far. But, brother, you never know.

Nothing hurts a hunter so much as to have a really great chance and to monk it. Had I done this—and after my promise to tearful Flora? I could hear little Southwind's voice, but growing fainter, so that I knew she was getting farther away. I felt disgraced. Neither my gun nor my shell would afford me an alibi. I knew them too well. My only likely excuse was the buck's heroic size. But was that any real excuse?

A hundred yards from where I had shot, Southwind had taken the old buck across a sandy woods road. There was plenty of blood; moreover, there was a bad blunder. In my experience, a blunder is far more significant than blood. A buck can bleed a good deal and get away; but if he ever falls headlong, he is probably down for good. Indeed, if you shoot at a deer and he *changes his stride,* he is probably hit; if he shows no change of pace, you have probably made a clean miss. Let me add for the comfort of hunters who have had that experience that, at least if the deer is running, its curious undulant gait is such that it is one of the easiest of all game to miss.

Just when my heart had just about reached by boot-soles, Southwind stopped running! I had my record buck after all! But don't count your chickens before they have busted their little eggshells! Here came Southwind back to me, her snowy little coat covered with blood. She was plainly scared to death. Her ears were down, her tail was between her legs, and she was whining rather pitifully. I could see that some of the blood on her was her own. She had been fighting with that monster, and evidently had gotten the worst of it. I tried in every way to get her to take me back to him, but she evidently had had a plenty. She just lay down and whined.

By this time my driver had reached me. The blood trail was easy to follow. Presently, to our surprise, we came to a deep ditch or canal, evidently dug long ago for drainage. Although a deer is usually very deft and canny about jumping ditches, fences, and other similar obstacles, when Flora's buck had reached this canal, too far gone to cross it, he had just plunged headlong into it. True, he had enough life to give Southwind a bad time for a few minutes. When we came to him, his great spirit had fled.

It took my driver and me at least an hour to get him out of that old canal and back to the road. At home we had some very heavy scales on which cotton-bales used to be weighed. This buck weighed three hundred twelve pounds—which is about a record for my part of the country. He was a thirteen-pointer. For of the tines were more than twelve inches high. They were massive, beautiful, and symmetrical. I guess a girl does not often beg a man to do so impossible a thing as to kill a certain huge wild stag. But Flora did. And I somehow managed the feat for her—after some memorable difficulties.

MEMORIES
OF MAGIC MOMENTS

Part III

E very experienced hunter knows magic moments, and
once they have passed he relishes them—those treasured times when fate chooses to smile on his endeavors. Such
moments need not involve killing (or missing) a trophy deer.
They may instead focus on some unusual or unique circumstance, or perhaps one's companion or surroundings give the occurrence a special aura.

Archibald Rutledge knew far more magic moments than
most hunters are privileged to experience. There were several
reasons for this good fortune. For one thing, he spent untold
hours afield. For another, Rutledge did most of his hunting in
the vast Santee River Swamp and adjacent highlands where
whitetails were incredibly abundant. The bulk of his sporting
career falls in an era prior to the onset of deer restoration in
South Carolina (the South Carolina Wildlife and Marine Resources Department launched its restoration program in 1949).
The wild, remote location of Hampton Plantation and Rutledge's
consistent conservation efforts and judicious harvesting of whitetails sustained the quality and population level of the deer herd
at Hampton and in surrounding lands.

Rutledge's expertise as a woodsman also afforded him an
extraordinary number of opportunities as a hunter. He was a man
who spent a lifetime learning from nature, and the knowledge
gained thereby helped him kill deer the average sportsman
would never even have seen. Those same skills placed him in
intimate contact with whitetails and gave him an opportunity,
quite possibly unrivaled in America during the first half of the
twentieth century, to observe them.

By his own carefully maintained records Rutledge reckoned
that he shot 299 bucks during his hunting career. That is a feat

which seems little short of incredible even by today's standards, when deer populations have skyrocketed to all-time highs. He was aware of the fact that this prodigious record of deer slaying was one that some might find troubling, but he defended it in typically straightforward fashion. "I will remind the reader that South Carolina is a good deer state and that some of its zones have the longest season in the United States. A hunter is allowed five bucks a season and I have hunted for seventy-eight years."

Underlying all of these factors, of course, is the man's consuming passion for the animal. Rutledge watched, hunted, and studied whitetails in a fashion which suggests that they had a firm hold on a corner of his soul. He had many remarkable experiences, and he retold them in inimitable fashion. Here is a sampling of some of the most memorable of Flintlock's magic moments.

MY COLONEL'S LAST HUNT

Not only do I admire hunters as a class, but I have learned greatly to love certain woodsmen, and to treasure the details of some of their famous hunts. Such a man was my father, and such a hunt was his last one.

Though my father had, throughout his long and active life, little occasion to consult a doctor, and though he hunted until his eighty-second year, there came a day when it was necessary to call in a physician for the old gentleman, and this heartless and tactless man told my Colonel that his hunting days were over. At the time I was living nearly a thousand miles from home, but I soon got a report of this distressing affair.

> The old idiot [my father wrote me in his usual spirited fashion] says I must hang up my hunting horn and lean my gun in a corner—for keeps. I'll hang him up, or stand him in the corner for keeps before I'll stay out of the woods. I'm only eighty-two, Benjamin. [He always called me that because I was his youngest son.] Why quit so young?

My Colonel, judged by his skill and by his sportsmanship, was the best hunter I ever knew. Not to my knowledge did he ever break a game law; yet, hunting like a gentleman, he killed in the old plantation regions of our home more than six hundred whitetail deer; and his record of thirty double shots on deer (one with each barrel) is, so far as I know, still good in South Carolina.

When the brusque doctor's verdict came to the old huntsman, I was, as I have said, far away; but I knew very well from his letters—and just from knowing him—how he took the thing. He simply wouldn't take it. Give up hunting? Not while he could

From *Hunter's Choice* (1946).

113

draw a breath. Give up life, if the call came, but not the grand sport that he had followed since earliest boyhood!

After the physician left the house, I know my Colonel looked thoughtfully at himself in the glass, and probably admitted the meaning of that silvery hair; yet surely the blue eyes had lost none of their glinting fire. He probably took a rather fierce five-mile walk, just to prove that the doctor was an old mountebank. Again and again he took his beloved shotgun out on the big front porch and sighted it at imaginary deer at various distances. He could still put it on them. Quit the woods? Not he!

But the real test of his age came when he went down to the stable lot to interview his ancient handy man: Will Alston, a Negro of exactly the Colonel's own age, who had faithfully served his master well for more than sixty years. Will was still milking the cows and feeding the stock; and up to that very time, whenever my Colonel felt like taking a turn in the woods, Will had acted as his guide and his deer driver. As he walked down to interview the old darky, my father wondered if the years were telling on his faithful old servant as much as they were on him.

As he approached the dusky figure crouched beside the cow, the Colonel wondered just how he was going to introduce this delicate subject of their relative ages and their fitness for the chase. The cow settled that question. She, a skittish young thing, had just been waiting for some excuse to kick over the bucket, and my father's coming supplied it. She gave it a resounding wham, at the same time jumping away from Will. The old Negro gaily saluted her in the ribs with a double-barreled kick, with a jauntiness that amazed both the cow and the Colonel.

"Why, Will," he said, "you don't seem to feel old."

"No cow ain't gwine tarrigate me," he said defensively.

At this show of mildly defiant spirit, the Colonel felt younger himself. But he doubted that he could have delivered those kicks with the same spontaneous accuracy and vim that Will had used.

"You are pretty sassy with a cow," the Colonel ventured. "How about a deer? You and I have given many a one a ramble. Are you going to be game to hunt this winter, Will?"

"My wife done tole me I mustn't go in the woods no mo'," Will confessed sadly.

"That's what they are telling me too, Will. But we aren't through yet, are we?"

There was an eager pathos to the question.

"As long as a buck grow horns, and we got two feet, we gwine to follow him. Huntin' is all."

As the Colonel returned to the house he was whistling an old ballad.

A gentle rain was falling, but to this he paid no attention. Nature had never hurt him, and he never learned to coddle himself. But his wife and his three daughters met him on the porch—one with a shawl for his shoulders, one with a cup of hot tea, and two with anxious insistency that he sit in his big chair by the fire. With artful strategy he accepted all these ministrations, but his was a wildwood heart, and tea could not tame it. Slippers and a fireside had no allurements when an old stag might even then be bedded up in the Thickhead or the Rattlesnake or some other famous plantation thicket. He might be a ten-pointer; he might run straight for the Double Pine stand. What was a little rain? Damn all doctors! If Will could kick a cow gaily, he could surely drive out a deer branch. A man can't get up an appetite for dinner by drowsing by the fire.

"My dear," he said to his wife a half hour later, "tell Will to come in here. I must see him on important business."

This affair called for ancient strategy. For a man there is no evasion quite so difficult as that of feminine care.

When Will appeared the two old cronies sat by the fire and talked in whispers of the great crime and affair of state about to be committed.

"It isn't raining hard, is it, Will?" asked the Colonel in so pleading a tone that but one answer was possible.

"She gwine hol' up after a while," lied Will encouragingly.

"We can't use the horses, or we'll get caught," my father advised. "Do you think the bushes out in the Thickhead are very wet?"

"No, sah, not as wet as sometimes," replied the incorrigible Negro.

"You hide my gun under your overcoat, and slip out by the stable lot. I'll bring the shells. I am going down by the river, make a circle, and meet you at the gate."

While the feminine members of the family were busy about their domestic affairs, the Colonel tiptoed down the hallway to the back porch, whence, with an air of indifference, he sauntered through the shrubbery toward the river. Once out of sight of the house he made a fast detour, and in ten minutes joined the waiting Will at the edge of the big woods, then dripping and misty under the slow but incessant rain. The two old culprits grinned guiltily but delightedly when they saw each other.

Down the puddly, sandy road they went, making for the deer drive known as the Thickhead, more than a mile from the house. As they approached this famous hangout for deer, a green thicket of myrtles and bays set in the wide and lonely pinelands, the two wily old strategists laid their plans as they had a hundred times before. Only now they had no horses and no hounds; besides, there should be four standers for the Thickhead, and now there was only one.

"Bossman," said Will calculatingly, "is you want me to compass 'um or to focus 'um?"

Translated, this meant simply: Shall I go round the thicket, or shall I come straight through it?

With the deliberation that so momentous a question merited, the Colonel considered long. Finally he said, "Focus it, Will. I am going to stand at the Double Pine. Give me fifteen minutes to get there."

Will waited in the steady rain while the old huntsman, his cherished gun under his coat, made a circuit of the drive—far through the dripping bushes—coming at last to the famous stand where he had killed more than forty deer. A yellow pine stood at the critical place; a pine that forked two feet from the ground, sending two mighty shafts towering into the blue. For more than a generation it had marked the place where deer might emerge from the Thickhead, two hundred yards straight ahead.

But what of the Pond Stand, and the White Stand, and the Opening to the West? These, too, were famous runs. The Colonel, with mingled feelings of guilt and the old excitement of the chase, looked the situation over. There might be no deer in the Thickhead. If there were a buck lying in that dripping sea of greenery, he might run over one of the empty stands; or, since Will had been directed to come straight through, he might easily double back. Bucks, when unpushed, have almost a habit of running round the driver. The Colonel knew also that a deer will almost invariably start out of his bed in the direction toward which his head was pointed when he was couched. It was all a great gamble.

There was not a sign of life in the woods. The pines' mournful, sweet song was hushed in the shower. All the birds were hidden and still. The squirrels were asleep in their holes. My Colonel felt that only two foolish and incorrigible old men were out to get a thorough wetting. What would they say at home when he returned bedraggled and empty-handed? And Martha, Will's ebony consort, would blame my father for the whole sinful escapade.

But Will had begun to drive. The Colonel could hear the old fellow's voice quavering at the far end of the Thickhead. The lone stander broke open his gun carefully and made certain that he had in the right shells. He was all set.

The Thickhead looked so dense and so wet that it seemed incredible that Will would ever start anything from those reeking bushes. On he came, rapping the pines with a club and shouting manfully. There was an ardent and a cheerful quality in Will's shouting that showed that he had in mind sweet venison steaks.

He was now near the very middle of the green wilderness of bays. It was a likely place for a jump. But nothing happened. The Colonel's keenness and tension abated somewhat. Poor old Will! he thought. He must be as drenched as a sponge. But he was making a manful effort. He didn't seem old, and his voice had that old ring. Through the deep thicket the driver came. The stander could see him. Well, they had hunted anyhow, even if they hadn't killed.

But wait. . . . A sudden wild change in Will's voice meant that he had spotted something. Then . . . well, what happened is best told in my father's words, in a letter he wrote me the very day of the Great Affair:

> I had about given up, Benjamin, when old Will sang out, as if he had got religion, or found a jug of liquor. I knew he had seen a deer, but I was not prepared for what followed. You remember that little point of huckleberries that makes out toward the Double Pine? There's a little rosemary pine there not ten feet high, all overrun with smilax. It was under that canopy that this stag was lying. Will heard his first rush, and I saw him come tearing

out—a great monster of a deer—as if he had lighted fire-crackers tied to his tail. When he got within thirty yards I showed myself to make him turn. As he presented his broad-side, I saluted him. The gun kindled and he went down—it was all over. He was a true monarch of the glen—a ten-pointer, and so large an animal that it seemed incredible that he should be found right here in the home woods.

After my shot, I glanced toward the Thickhead, and here came Will, clearing the bushes like a yearling! He got to the deer as soon as I did just as it gave a final, convulsive heave. Over the stag's splendid prostrate form we solemnly shook hands—we two old sinners, we two old down-and-outs whose hunting days were over!

Such was my Colonel's last deer hunt. He died in his eighty-third year.

MY FIRST BUCK

Who can describe the feelings of a bare-footed plantation boy nine years old, who finds himself on his first deer-stand? I had long pleaded with my father to take me out; and when he consented, and I had at last what I had so long desired, I was somewhat overcome by the responsibility. I imagined that if I let a deer get away, the end of the world would be a natural and speedy consequence. The weapon with which I was armed was not designed for the execution of big game: it was a little single-barreled gun, very short in the barrel, with no sight, and with a bend in the barrel itself. One day when crawling after some doves in the cornfield, I had thrust the muzzle in the earth; and, without knowing that it was choked, had fired it, bursting it badly. The plantation blacksmith filed the end smooth, and I had learned, when sighting, to make due allowance for the twist.

As I stood ready on my stand, every sight and sound, every flash and shadow that varies the light of the woodland, was vividly alive to me. I looked so hard at the drive that the trees seemed to come up close to me. I saw tiny warblers, busily searching the bay-bushes for their elfin fare. The joree hopping about and rustling in the dead leaves on the edge of the thicket, the cautious crow, cawing at me persistently from a safe distance, the insolent sharpshinned hawk, circling high above the silent pines, each in turn caught my attention, but failed to hold my interest. I was after deer; but of deer I saw no sign. After what seemed an interminable time, I heard the Negro driver begin to whoop and to whistle to dogs; he had turned them loose, and if there were anything in the bay thicket before me, it would soon

From *Wild Life of the South* (1935).

119

make its appearance. But nothing came. The dogs were voice-less. There was no wind blowing, and the driver's voice sounded sufficiently loud to wake all the sleepers in the woods. At last one hound struck what might have been a mazy fox-trail, and my heart began to pound; but it ceased its pounding when the Negro whistled the dog off. I could now hear the driver crashing through the underbrush, and splashing into pools of water; sev-eral times, far through the woods, I saw the sunlight on the barrels of his gun. I looked over toward a pond in the woods where a great blue heron was standing like a statue in the dark water. I looked back toward the drive—and—three hundred yards away; parting the bay-bushes straight ahead of me, there stood a splendid buck, his great antlers towering and glinting in the winter sunlight. I remembered that his chest looked shaggy and black. A moment later, the dogs opened full cry, and the buck with a single bound cleared the thicket, and now headed for me, disclosing behind him a smaller deer with peg horns.

The chorus of the hounds rose high; the cautious crow left his perch and flew away, cawing harshly. On came the splendid creatures, and I was the only obstacle in their path—I and my little twisted gun. My father had told me never to follow a deer with my gun, but rather to pick an open space between two pines, and to shoot at the deer the moment he darkened it. I levelled my gun on an aperture between two giant short-leaf pines. Suddenly the great buck launched himself in front of my gun. I fired quickly. To my unutterable chagrin, through the smoke I described both deer continuing their flight! The dogs passed me like a living whirlwind. In a few moments the two old hunters came riding up.

"Dat's de grandpa buck, Cap'n," the driver said to me: "I hope you done shot him!"

But there was no hope in his voice. However, he honored me by dismounting and looked for bloodsigns. Suddenly he cried out and fell on his knees in the pine-straw.

"You hit dat grandpa! You hit dat grandpa!" The Negro was sure of it, and his voice was full of triumph. He pointed to the dark drops of blood which he had found.

"Where are the dogs?" I asked suddenly; "I can't hear them."

A still as were the woods, we should have been able to hear them a mile or more away. But there was not a sound. We listened a moment more, almost incredulous, knowing that the silence could only mean that the hounds had overtaken the buck. It was a happy silence for me; and it remained unbroken.

A few minutes later, half a mile from where I had shot, we found the buck lying stone dead, with the hounds standing guard over him. Behind his fore-shoulder were three buckshot-holes, immediately in the region of the heart; yet he had run that distance without any apparent laboring on his part.

TROPHY OF A LIFETIME

From earliest boyhood days the antlers of whitetail deer have had for me a curious and never-failing fascination. Whenever I heard of a fine head of horns, I would go miles to see them. I have twice seen the National Collection of Heads and Horns; and I personally have a collection of some three hundred sets of antlers, most of them taken on my South Carolina plantation, and some of them dating back almost a hundred years.

Not long ago I was showing an especially massive set to some visiting tourists.

"This pair," I said (for I have a record of all these horns), "was taken ninety-three years ago."

"My!" exclaimed one of the ladies. "You surely have hunted a long time!"

It is a strange thing that while two of my sons have killed what might be termed Great Heads, I had never, until lately, taken one. Irvine shot, at the Kinlock Club, a superb and stately stag that for years had been called "Sebastian." Middleton, on Rice Hope Plantation, shot a great buck that was dubbed "The Emperor" by the fifty hunters who saw him on that memorable day. And, while I have killed a great many seven, eight, and nine-pointers (about three hundred deer in all), what the English call a "hart royal" had just never come my way. In fact, in a lifetime of hunting, I have seen only two or three of these regal old boys, whose magnificence sets them apart from all other bucks.

It's often strange how great endings follow little beginnings. On Christmas Day, 1942, the wife of my Negro foreman, Prince

From *Those Were the Days* (1955).

Alston, presented him with his first-born son. Because of the general domestic excitement we did not hunt on Christmas Day, but early the next morning I said to my foreman: "Prince, we ought to go in the woods to celebrate the boy's birthday."

As he is a man to whom deer hunting is wine, women, and song, there was no delay about our starting. The day was calm, warm, and shimmering with dew. We went into the Wambaw Corner, a famous drive for bucks; and as I was the only stander, I selected a place where a good many runs converge. Three hundred yards behind me was a wide road, but I was careful not to stand on that; for old stags have a most disconcerting way of running for a road, stopping to reconnoiter, and then turning back or turning aside. I really was a good distance inside the drive.

Deer hunting in the South in midwinter is very unlike the same sport in the North. I have tried both. In the North, one associates it with bare woods, snow, and often bitter cold. When I sat down on a pine stump that morning, the air was balmy, birds were singing, and the dewy bays, myrtles, and pines scented the air. It was very still—a most important factor in deer hunting, at least for me. I depend on my ears as much as my eyes; and on a very windy day I had just as soon stay home.

Prince took my two hounds, Red and Queenie, more than a mile down an old lumber road in front of me. He would put them in, far back by the river, and come out toward me. In such a situation it pays the hunter to be alert from the moment he takes his stand. He should not be off his guard just because the drive has not begun. As often as not, a wary old buck will hear or scent a driver going toward the starting point, and will attempt to slip out before the real performance begins. I have known many a man to lose a chance a few minutes after he had taken his stand, by failing to be on guard—even by neglecting to load his gun—thinking he had plenty of time. Depend on a buck to do what you don't expect him to do; while you are thinking he will not be along for an hour, if at all, he may be on you the next minute.

Well, here I was, with my gun loaded, waiting cautiously, with every condition favorable, except perhaps that while I was on a slight elevation, there were heavy thickets within sixty yards on each side of me. For twenty minutes I waited. Nothing happened. All was silence, serenity, with the quiet woods stretching away boundlessly on all sides. Then, down in the edge of the deep river swamp I heard Prince begin to drive. Almost immediately the hounds started to trail, although I could hear them but faintly.

Then it happened. Suddenly, silently, spectrally, out of the thick woods before me, there appeared the buck for which I had waited fifty years. (I killed my first when I was nine; and I am now verging on sixty.) He was in front of me, to my left; and as he was coming up a slight incline toward me, I could see nothing but his horns. I knew at once that—for me—he had a record head, a twelve or fourteen-pointer; the height of the tines was spectacular. There were some troublesome bushes between us, but he kept coming. At fifty yards he stopped, almost concealed; but he did not discover me. On the second I had first seen the tips of his antlers I had raised my gun. On he came, straight for me from the left quarter. At exactly thirty-two yards (a distance that I carefully measured later) he stopped again, facing me. He had literally wedged himself between two big pines, so that nothing but his breast, his neck, and his grand head showed. As I was sitting practically in the open, I thought, "Now or never." With the utmost deliberation I laid the sight of my gun on his lower neck, in front of his heart, and touched the trigger of the left barrel, which is full choke. I was shooting a high-base express shell, chambering twelve buckshot, a load that I have long found to be deadly.

As was to be expected, at the roar of the gun things happened. That great stag—and he was huge of body—stood almost upright, and then plunged backward. His gigantic struggles beat anything I had ever seen. But I was so certain that these were his death throes that I never left the stump on which I was sitting—never thought of shooting him again. Finally he righted himself, though he was down at the stern, like a vast sinking battleship, but even then I just watched him, sure that he could not go ten yards. Then in a few seconds, it seemed to me, he gained headway, and while I was trying to get up my gun to give him the second barrel, he had vanished into a dense thicket. Even then I was not much disturbed, for I knew he was mortally shot. But when I tried to follow him, my concern grew apace. I found little blood, but I have never counted much on a blood trail. Some of the clearest of such trails I ever saw were thrown out by deer that got clean away; whereas I once shot an old buck through and through with eleven buckshot, and he ran a mile before he fell, while I never saw a drop of blood that he lost.

As I fought my way through the vines and dense bushes, I kept looking for that kingly crown. But none appeared. I knew I could not have missed him; for a deer that is clean missed may give evidence of being startled by the report of the gun or the rifle; but he will never fall and struggle on the ground.

As it is a wise plan to let a wounded deer lie down, I returned to my stand, chagrined, but still not without hope. I carefully examined the two pines between which the buck had been standing. In the one on the right there were no buckshot. In the one on the left were three, inches from where his neck had been, and at exactly the right height. Nine were unaccounted for, and I felt that he carried them.

The hounds had meanwhile jumped another deer, and had taken him back toward the river. Leaving my stand, I walked down the old road, blowing my horn for Prince. It was perhaps an hour before I collected him and Red and Queenie. We took them to the spit of my rendezvous, and they took the trail with little hesitation. It may seem surprising, but hounds seem to run a fresh trail with more enthusiasm than they do a blood trail that is getting cold. Telling Prince to follow the dogs, I got back to the main road as fast as I could, as it was toward that point that they were heading. With heavy misgiving, I heard them keep on running, and in a few minutes they had crossed the road. How could that old buck have run three hundred yards with nine buckshot in his breast? But at that, one of the most amazing features of all nature is the wild vitality of the whitetail deer. By the time I got to the big road, the dogs had gone some distance beyond it, and Prince was standing there in massive black discomfiture. I joined him, ashamed of myself, and we listened to the hounds. At such a time you can tell much by their behavior.

Their full-running cry was suddenly hushed; then they began a sharp, yelping bay, as though they had come on the wounded stag. It may appear strange, but few hounds will close with a wounded buck. They will stand off and bay him, but as a rule they will not go in on him. I have even seen them turn tail and run the minute he turned on them. Indeed, a wounded buck is a fearsome creature to behold, with his hair standing out, his head lowered, and savagery in his aspect.

"They got him," said Prince, a relieved gleam lighting his eyes.

But before we could take a step forward, Red, who is small and timid, came running back to us, plainly scared and apologetic. Nor could we persuade her to take the trail again. To our chagrin, we heard Queenie running once more, bearing toward a vast, marshy rice field that fringes the river, about as howling a wilderness as you will ever find. We hurried after her, but soon could hear her no more. Had she run out of hearing? Was the buck down, and she lying calmly beside him, as is her custom? To follow the trail was impossible through the gross jungles that lay ahead of us.

Three times we tried to get Red to retake the trail, but she shook her wise little head, saying, "Nay, nay; I'm a deerhound. I'm not gong to run afoul of any brontosaurus again."

So there my Negro driver stood in the woods, pretty helpless, as you can imagine. Finally we decided to separate, each of us following half the rim of the old rice field, in the hope of picking up the track in the soft mud. I had gone perhaps a quarter mile when, from the very center of that wild morass, I heard Prince let loose a jubilant whoop. Somehow through that fearful jungle I got to him, after sinking over my boot tops in muck and water. Prone on the edge of an old bank that spans the field lay my "lifetime" buck. And he was stone dead.

Beside him Queenie was contentedly curled up. In the buck's neck were nine buckshot holes. Prince told me that he had picked up the trail not long after leaving me, and that he had followed it through the bog without difficulty. The buck was so heavy that we could not manage him by ourselves, and had to get help from a near-by Negro settlement.

When we finally got him home, and I had a fair chance to look him over, I knew that he was by far the largest buck I had ever killed, and perhaps the largest I had ever seen. In this region of the Carolina coast there are three distinct types of the whitetail: the deer of the coastal islands are invariably small, and their antlers always have a curious upward pitch; the pineland bucks are long and rangy, and their antlers are usually slender. The deer of the river swamps are burly, short-legged, and dark in color. And this stag was one of their oldest veterans.

Well, I got a great deal of pleasure in entering his antler measurements in my records: apparently they are a record for

South Carolina. The spread between beams is twenty-five inches, the circumference of beam at the base, five inches, and the number of points, thirteen. Two of the tines measure eighteen inches and two, seventeen. The antlers are remarkable for their beautiful chestnut color, their heavy beading, and their almost perfect symmetry.

Perhaps never again shall I have another such experience. But really it paid me to wait for fifty years for a stag like that. And I hope you'll get a chance some day at one just like him.

A SHOT I REALLY REMEMBER

When a man lives in the wilderness, and has hunted all his life, it is natural that of all the shots at wild game that he has made, most will be ordinary, and some will be memorable. There are certain shots that, regardless of the lapse of years, a hunter cannot forget. Probably the nature of the circumstances accounts for our long remembrance of our more eventful shots.

As some of these seem worth recording, and as each has a real reason for having been eventful, I shall tell in simple fashion of a few of the more memorable shots I have made.

One Christmas—it was far back in 1904—I had spent two weeks vacation at my Carolina plantation. Of course, I enjoyed my visit; but as my last day approached, it looked as if one great object of my trip would not be accomplished: I wanted to kill a fine buck. Day after day my faithful Negro foreman, Prince Alston, and I had ranged the wild pinelands and the melancholy moss-hung swamps in quest of an antlered monarch of the chase. But all our questing had been vain. One cause of our failure was the fact that it was the very end of the long Carolina deer-season—and at such a time bucks have developed an excessive wariness.

I was compelled to leave on a Saturday; and the evening before, my good Prince and I planned a last drive for the following morning. But, deep in the night, I was wakened by a wild wind lashing a heavy rain against the windows. When day broke, it was still blowing and raining. Without any hope of being able to get into the woods on such a day, I got dressed and went into the kitchen to see if Martha had the coffee ready. To my surprise,

From *Those Were the Days* (1955). Reprinted here is the first section of the story entitled "Shots I Really Remember."

there was Prince, hugging the stove. I lamented to him the fact that we had no chance for a buck on such a day. But he gave me the kind of rebuke that only an old-time Negro can give a white man.

"One thing is certain sure," he said: "We ain't never gwine to kill no buck in this kitchen."

So that was that.

"My mind tells me that an old buck will be lying in the Little Corner on a morning like this," he said.

Because of Prince's hardihood and his stubborn hope, we went out into that bleak winter rain. The tall longleaf pines were rocking in the northwest wind. I viewed without enthusiasm a prospect that looked futile. But I acquired a little confidence when, as we were almost swimming out the plantation avenue, my driver explained his strategy to me.

"You must go to the Pond Stand," he said, "at the head of the drive. You leave the rest to me. I b'lieve I'se gwine to drive a buck to you."

Two miles I sloshed through the rainy woods, looking strange and veiled and mysterious. Reaching the Pond Stand, I stood against a big pine, my back to the rain and wind. I can still feel that pine rocking against my body.

The open pinelands before me were rolling, and that was why the deer I saw coming straight for me disappeared from sight in a hollow. I could not yet tell whether it was a doe or a buck. For a steadier shot, I went down on one knee, and got my gun to my shoulder. Suddenly, topping the rise about a hundred yards ahead of me I saw a craggy rack. Then the whole tawny buck came into view. Prince must have given him quite a scare, for he was really making time. I believe he winded me, for he quartered to the right, giving me a broadside shot at thirty yards. I killed him dead; and hardly had I reached him when Prince, hat in hand, came running up. We forgot all about the wind and rain in rejoicing over this splendid eleven-pointer.

As Prince was leaving me to return home to get the wagon to haul in our prize, he said, "We must call this one 'The Last Chance Buck'." I guess that name explains why that shot is one I shall always remember.

THE SURPRISE OF MY LIFE

There are two or three deer drives on my Carolina plantation that I usually save for special friends. One of these, the famous Wambaw Corner, is about as certain a place for an old buck as any I know; and when a friend of mine is badly in need of slaying a stag, I usually take him there. But one should not make the mistake of supposing that the laying low of one of these rough-shod veterans is merely a matter of killing a deer. Its consequences are likely to be far-reaching. I have known a beautiful, wavering girl to marry a man for having proved his woodland valor by bringing home a twelve-point buck, and I have known many a husband to emerge from the domestic dog house when he filled the ice-box with venison.

Of course, to assure a friend a shot at a big buck is one of the hardest of all promises to fulfill. In the first place, the buck doesn't want to cooperate, even if the plan were made clear to him. Then, time and again, he will run to a stander to whom killing a deer is an old story. Finally, an old buck is full of strata-gems of his own, and you can't kill him mathematically. I mean, he is a highly intelligent big-game animal, a born dodger and skulker; and what he is going to do is usually unpredictable.

During last Christmas holidays, two of my sons were hunt-ing with me. As I had already killed four bucks that season (our limit is five) and as they had not had a shot, I naturally was eager to give them some sport. They had only a few days at home, and we had to hunt intelligently if we were to do something.

Early one morning we started for the Wambaw Corner, a

From *Those Were the Days* (1955).

long peninsula with deep water on three sides of it. Our plan
was to send the drivers far down toward the river and drive it
out to the road. At the head of this drive, on the old, broad,
sandy country road, there are really only two stands, and both
of them are buck stands. You know, every drive has its stands,
but some of them cover favorite buck runs. Does and fawns will
come out to any stand, and often to no stands at all; but a buck,
true to his warier nature, has his decided preferences every time.

It has been my experience that when a buck goes into a
corner such as the one we were about to drive he is likely to
come out exactly where he went in. I once knew a buck to enter
such a drive by going under a bridge over the road; I know he
did because I saw his tracks on a sand-bar under the bridge. Not
believing that when he came out, with drivers and hounds in full
pursuit, he would go under the bridge again, I stood on a rise
some distance away, a rise on which there is a regular crossing.
But that deer sailed right under the bridge and got clean away!

My drivers with the hounds had gone silently deep into
Wambaw Corner, and I then proceeded to post my sons on the
two famous crossings known as the Ground Bridge and the Dogwood Twins. At the latter stand I saw where a master buck had
walked in over this place the night before. He wore a number
sixteen shoe. Here I posted my youngest son, Irvine; my son
Middleton I put at the Bridge.

Then I wandered off into the drive, but clear of the run-
ways, so that the boys could shoot. I was not ahead of them, but
off to one side. On the slope of a little hill about a half mile from
where they were standing I sat down on a pine stump just to
wait until the bombardment was over. The drive was off to my
right. The hill on which I was sitting sloped downward toward
the drive and then upward for a long distance; but, like all so-
called hills in my part of the country, the rise was gentle. Over
this long slope the woods were open, with just a few big pines
standing here and there. I could see for a long way.

Possibly I had been on my stand for fifteen minutes when
things began to happen. I had not heard a sound from the drivers
or the hounds, but as I looked far ahead and to my right I saw
something coming. During the course of forty-nine years of deer
hunting I have seen thousands of deer in the woods, and most
of them were running; but never before had I seen a truly great

buck running for so long a distance within plain view. From the time he first came into sight until he disappeared toward the standers on the road, he must have run a full half mile.

Motionless on my stump, I watched him. He had been startled, but he did not seem worried; he was not running hard, but was steadily covering the ground with a kind of cautious haste. When he was broadside, he was within a hundred and fifty yards of me. That distance is no good for a shotgun; it would have been a perfect rifle shot. But I did not want the chance. I was only too happy that he was heading straight for my boys. I barely turned my head to watch him pass, and not until he was out of sight did I move around on the stump to locate the sound of the gun so that I would know which son had killed him.

Whoever got him would, I knew, have a prize, for rarely have I seen in the woods so burly a buck—a true swamp stag, with short, heavy legs, barrel-like body, and massive and craggy horns. Indeed, as I watched him pass me a slight feeling of relief came to me, and I was glad that the responsibility of laying him down was not mine. A buck as big as that one, running in that masterly fashion, makes a man lose a little faith in his gun's ability.

As I had been able to see the buck until he was within three hundred yards of the road, I fully expected to hear a gun within three or four minutes. Beyond the road is a famous swamp known as Deertown; it was toward this that he was heading. And he simply had to cross the road at one of the two stands. I listened, I heard no gun, but from the direction from which the sound of the gun should have come I thought I heard laughter. The road is not much traveled; but occasionally Negroes pass along it, and when they do they are always bantering one another. I wondered if what I heard had really been laughter; and if so, if it would be enough to upset all my carefully laid plans.

As you come to understand buck nature, two of his characteristics will impress you as almost paradoxical. One is that he is one of the hardest animals in the world to turn. I mean that if he has really made up his mind that he is going to a certain place, why, that's where he's going. My Negroes put it succinctly when they say, "He gwine where he gwine."

On the other hand, if a buck is "feeling" his way out of a drive, nothing else in the world is so easy to turn. This buck that had passed me had some definite sanctuary in mind, but he had not fully committed himself to the course he was taking. A buck that hasn't gone all out for a certain run is the old boy you have to watch. The slightest hint of danger ahead will suffice to make him change his course radically and suddenly.

Well, here I was sitting on that stump, waiting for somebody's gun and for somebody's wild war-whoop of triumph. But I heard nothing.

"The old devil has stopped short of the road," I said. "Those boys aren't expecting anything, but I hope they aren't moving."

The very best way to fail to get a shot at a buck is to move around when you are covering a crossing. The motionless, self-effacing hunter is the one who gets the big chances. Even to smoke or to fidget on a stand may be fatal. Do what you please when it's all over; but as long as you are the guardian of a crossing, be as still as King Tut, who has been dead three thousand years, I believe. Not only that your approaching buck will infallibly see movement of any kind, but you can't listen properly if you are restless.

Often a moment's warning is enough to afford the deer hunter a chance to get ready, and he is not likely to hear that warning unless he is still and listening. What I mean by a warning is that shuffling of the dead leaves, that stealthy cracking of a dry twig—any sound not in consonance with the prevailing sounds of the forest. A hunter, and sometimes a good hunter, is likely to miss a deer if it takes him completely by surprise. Always surprise your buck; try never to let him surprise you.

So there I sat on a stump, facing the standers and facing the place where I had last seen the buck, which was running straight for them. As they had not shot, I felt certain that he had stopped to reconnoiter. Unless a deer is hard pushed, he is almost sure to do that very same thing when he comes to a road. My gun lay across my knees. It was not my old long deer gun, either. That being temporarily out of commission, I had borrowed this one, and my faith in it was none too strong.

When I had last seen the stag, he was disappearing into a dense growth of sweet-bay and myrtle that fringed the road deeply. Now I saw some of those bushes jarred into movement. Something was not going through them, but was coming through them! The old buck was heading back my way. There was no time to consider just why had had so radically changed his course;

my immediate business was to shoot him. He was not coming straight for me, but was coursing off to my right, to pass me at about sixty yards. Making for the river, he was running through bushes that almost hid him. Honestly, he looked so big that the gun in my hands felt insignificant.

I didn't move, letting him come as close as he would. When first he had been roused from his bed and had made that long run to the road, he was decidedly uneasy; he was getting out of that country. But now he was really scared. I have seen deer run faster, but never with more purpose and power. Just as he came in sight, I heard the hounds take his trail from his bed, nearly a mile away in the drive.

Considering his speed, the distance he was away from me and the angle, I gave him the choke barrel, drawing six inches in front of his burly neck. At the crack of the gun he literally tore the thicket open. He got away so fast and so low that I had no chance for a second shot. The last I saw of him was just the tips of his great chestnut horns sliding through the bush-tops. While I was satisfied that I had hit him, I never hoped to see him again. Neither coming to me, nor going from me, had he had his tail up.

Some hunters claim that if a buck is running with his flag up, and you hit him, he will flatten it down. Yet I have seen mortally wounded bucks sail off with their tails as high as they could get them. But there is one infallible sign of a wounded buck; if at your shot he changes his stride, you have done something to him; how much will remain to be seen. In the case of this buck I had no chance of seeing a change in stride; but from the way he ripped out, he was evidently aware of something more than the sound of the gun.

On came the hounds in full run. Soon they were in sight, running my buck's trail. They went almost to the road, just as he had done. Now they came back toward me. When they struck the place where I had shot at his old man of the woods, their clamor suddenly increased.

"That means blood," I said to myself.

Within a minute their wild chase ceased, and I could distinctly hear Red Liquor growling. He claims every dead deer for his own.

I walked over where they were, and there lay my buck, and I mean he was truly one of them. He had gone only sixty or seventy yards; and if the woods had been open, I could have seen him fall. I had put only three buckshot in him; my own gun would have put about seven. But one of these three had gone through his heart.

There was then a happy gathering of drivers and dogs and standers about his fallen monarch of the deep river swamps. An idea of his size may be had when I say that when fully dressed, with hide and head off, he weighed 178 pounds.

"Boys," I asked of my sons, "who was that laughing in the road? That laugh cost one of you this chance."

They told me that, not thinking the drive had even begun, they had been joking with an old Negro who happened to wander by.

I felt less selfish later that same day when my son Middleton killed a fine stag, and my son Irvine killed two great bucks in the same drive. A dad likes to accomplish things in the wilds, but I guess he gets more real pleasure out of having his sons accomplish what he knows is not so easy to do.

THAT CHRISTMAS EVE STAG

Nearly all hunting in the Northern States closes before the middle of December. Having been abroad on several zero days near the end of the season, I have heartily wished that it had closed earlier. But in the South some seasons for hunting are open until late in the winter; and on the great plantations venison and wild turkey for Christmas and New Year are standard fare. Not to have a stag hanging up on Christmas Eve is to confess a certain degree of enfeebled manhood—almost a social disgrace.

When I met my Negro driver Prince on the morning of that famous Christmas Eve, I could tell from his mien and general attitude that something was heavy on his mind. A thought of any kind on a Negro's mind—barring the joyous fundamentals of eating and sleeping—is likely to be depressing.

"What's the matter, Prince?" I asked. "Did you tie your horse last night with a slip-knot round his neck?"

"Not this time," the good Negro assured me. "But I was just thinkin', Cap'n, that all these years we been huntin' deer together we ain't neber yet done hang up a buck on a Christmas Eve."

"Well, let's do it to-day."

"We can try, Cap'n. But my wife done say we ought to be gwine to church 'stead of hunt."

"I see," I said, understanding his difficulty. "You think we are on the downgrade when we hunt on Christmas Eve?"

A gleam of humor came into Prince's eyes. "Cap'n, it ain't that; but we must use this day to show my woman that Christmas is a good time to hunt. If we can't bring nothin' back to-night, she gwine say, 'Ain't I done tole you, you triflin' sinner?'"

From *An American Hunter* (1937).

Prince had put it over to me that we must prove our moral soundness by bringing home a buck. I had never hunted deer before for this especial reason; but as I intended hunting anyway, I didn't mind that reason tagging along with me. Yet so long and so well had Prince hunted with me that whatever affected him had its influence on me. And as that day in the woods advanced, the taunt of Prince's wife seemed to have more and more in it. Eleven deer we started—six of them full-antlered bucks—but my three boys and I didn't get a single shot. It was a day on which all breaks broke the other way. Perhaps the most extraordinary escape of a stag is a matter worth recording.

For several seasons we had seen a huge creature that we had christened the Blackhorn Buck. He was one of those oversize men of the woods, and his antlers were massive, craggy and swarthy. The buck seemed to have a body as big as a swell-front barrel.

Well, after posting us at Fox Bay, Prince was riding back to the tail of the drive when he rode up this old monster. Of course, the deer headed the wrong way. Mounted on a fleet and sure-footed pony, Prince undertook to race the stag to turn him. Helped somewhat by a header that the old buck took over a fallen log, the Negro actually got ahead of the deer. Both stopped, some twenty feet apart, horse panting and buck panting, looking at each other curiously.

But it's a darn hard thing to make a deer right-about-face, especially if he has a notion that he is the object of herding tactics. The Blackhorn estimated his chances, saw a stretch of fallen timber marking the wake of a summer storm, and lithely rocked away over the obstructions. The horse could not follow.

"If I done had a rope," Prince declared to me, his honest face glistening with the perspiration of his effort to give us sport, "or jest a sling-shot, we might've had him."

"Or if it hadn't been Christmas Eve," I reminded him soberly.

By the time this deer escaped us, the sun was burning low in the crests of the yellow pines, and we knew that we might as well turn homeward. Our party divided. Some took a short cut through the woods to the house; but my two older boys, Prince and I traveled the road.

Now I'm ready to tell you about this Christmas Eve buck. We got into the highway by the Brick Church. Before us lay a straight stretch of broad road three miles long—a stretch that was used as a race-track in Revolutionary days. The last rays of the setting sun were glinting in the forest, and the wildwoods as far as we could see were suffused with a rosy light. But despite the beauty of it all, our hearts were dejected. We were going home on Christmas Eve without a thing to show for our long day's hunt.

We had come a half mile down the road in our complaining little car, with Prince's walking horse almost able to keep up with us. I saw something skulk across the road about two hundred yards ahead of us, heading for Montgomery Branch, a dense thicket of pine and bays just off the road to the right.

"Turkeys!" I said, jamming on the brakes so suddenly that the tiny car tried to stand on her nose.

Violently I waved for Prince to come up. The three of us piled out of the car and began loading our guns with turkey-shot.

Prince was with us in a moment. In another he had the whole situation straight. "I'll ride ahead and around," he said.

"You go across the branch. Put one boy in the thicket and leave the other on this side. Christmas Eve ain't done over yet!" he added with twinkling eyes.

I left my Gunnerman, as I call my second boy, in a tiny patch of bays a hundred yards on the near side of Montgomery— just half-way between the road and the branch. My eldest boy I posted in the branch itself, while I stole quickly forward into the open country beyond.

Just as I was emerging from the fringes of the dewy thicket, I heard a sound ahead. Then I saw a tall white flag! If I hadn't had turkey-shot in my gun, I might have let drive at him. In a moment he was lost in a thicket of young pines.

Creeping forward, I took a stand for the turkeys. At any moment they might come through the broomsedge in their swift, jerky fashion. But nary a turkey did I see or hear. The sun set. The woods seemed full of shadows. I could hear Prince riding down the thicket toward us. There seemed to be no game in front of him. When it comes to giving the hunter the slip, wild turkeys must always be given an A No. 1 rating.

I turned back toward the thicket, and was half-way through it when I heard my eldest son call out. All I could catch was "A buck!" At the same moment I heard something split the bay-bushes wide open. I dashed forward to get into the open for a shot, at the same time changing my turkey-shot for buckshot. By the time I had cleared the branch, the buck had done the same thing.

The scene that followed is imprinted on my memory as vividly as any recollection I have of the wildwoods during nearly forty years of roaming in them. The buck broke the thicket about seventy yards to my right, running as if he had just turned into the home stretch of a quarter mile Olympic race. Directly ahead of me stood my little Gunner. He had heard his brother call. He saw what I saw.

I was afraid to shout to him; besides, he appeared to be taking in the situation. Yet he was in acute distress. His gun was in his left hand, unbreeched. He had the turkey-shot shells out. His right hand was jammed in the tight pocket of his corduroy trousers, from which he was trying to pull out the buckshot shells. He could get his hand out, but not his hand and the shells too.

Meanwhile the buck, running on a curious arc, was coming for him, apparently gaining momentum at every leap. I have seen many a deer run in my time, and certainly they have showed me some breezy capers. But I do not think I ever saw a deer run like this one. I believe that deer feel unusually frisky at twilight, and they often frolic then just for the fun of the thing. Are they not limbering themselves after a long day's rest, and do they not feel the glamour of the twilight, just as we do—or at least to some degree?

I remember roaming the pinelands after sunset one January day and coming upon a stag that had just begun to feed. He did some fancy jumping that I have never seen another deer do— cavorting over high bushes, blowing through his nose, and then making a few more spectacular leaps, just like a pony that plays with you and won't let you catch him.

But the deer that was headed for my Gunner was not putting on any flourishes. He was just plain scared, and was running as a ringneck does when he means to get away and doesn't care to take wing. Wildly this buck ran, low to the ground, skimming over the bushes and the logs like an incredibly swift hurdler doing his stuff. He seemed to glimmer between the trees. The fading light emphasized the speed at which he was going. Prob-

ably he knew that he was in the same fix as were the chargers
of the Light Brigade, who, as we learned back yonder in school
days, had

> Cannon to right of them,
> Cannon to left of them.

When he thinks he is cornered, that is the time a deer is
going to show you how to get out of a corner in a hurry. Indeed,
in one sense, you can't corner a deer.

I could see from the course he was taking that the buck
would run about thirty yards from my boy, crossing his front. I
could see that the stander now had the breech of his gun closed.
He was awaiting the moment. Between him and the deer, as the
fugitive got directly in front of him, there would be a tiny pine
about four feet high—a young yellow pine with a bushy top. I
wondered how the Gunner would manage that obstruction. I
didn't have long to wonder. The twilight hurricane was upon
him. The buck looked very curious. His tail was down, his head
and neck far outstretched. He was in the utmost extremity of
speed.

Up went the gun with steady precision. A second later came
one barrel. I saw two things distinctly: the top of the little pine
was shot away, and the stag flinched, changing his stride. Such
a bit of behavior is said to indicate that a deer is certainly hit.
But it seems to me that a deer will sometimes flinch from the
sound of a gun, if it is close to him—just as he will sometimes
execute a dodging maneuver after the first shot has been fired at
him. Many a hunter has claimed to have shot down a deer, when,
as a matter of fact, the crafty stag has only dodged.

Whether struck or not, this buck gave no evidence of having
any difficulty in getting away. I wondered why my Gunner did
not salute him with the second barrel. Straight toward the sunset
ran the stag, far through the rosy woods—a beautiful but heart-
breaking sight. My chief feeling was one of pity for my Gunner.
I knew how he would mind this. Yet that flinching of the deer.
Had he really been missed?

A full three hundred yards I watched the fleeing stag. Then
he vanished in a tall growth of weeds by an old abandoned
sawmill.

In another moment I was with my boy. "I think you struck him," I said. "How about the second barrel?"

"My pocket was so tight," he said, "that I couldn't pull out both shells at once, and I didn't have time to pull them out one by one."

He looked peaked and miserable, as a hunter will look after missing a fair shot at a stag.

With my hand on his shoulder, he and I started to look for any signs of blood, but the light was so bad that we couldn't see a thing to encourage us. My elder boy meanwhile came up, and Prince rode up expectantly. What he saw in my face confirmed the superstition that had haunted us both all day.

"'Bout five turkey done fly up and gone back," he announced.

"Well," I told him, "at least one buck flew by here and has gone ahead."

The dusk of Christmas Eve was fast settling down—on the world and in our hearts.

"Prince," I said, "this deer flinched at the crack of the gun."

He grinned good-humoredly. "If anybody would shoot at me, Cap'n, I would flinch too. He was so close," he went on, taking on the tone of the professional hunter, "he would sure have come down."

"Well, anyhow," I told him, "ride down yonder by the old camp and see if you can see any sign at all."

My boys searched about disconsolately for blood-signs while Prince rode down the glimmering ridge. He was out of my mind for a few moments until I heard the whoop of whoops. Looking toward the far-off camp, I could barely see him, his hand raised high in ecstatic triumph, while the wildwoods rang with his superb shouts of victory.

"Gunner," I said to my young huntsman, "you killed that buck. Prince has him now."

Together the three of us ran through the darkening woods. When we came to the place, the Negro was on the ground beside the fallen stag. A beauty he was—in his prime, with good antlers. He lay just within the shelter of the tall dead weeds into which I had seen him vanish.

A joyous home-coming we had that Christmas Eve. On the plantation the Negroes take the killing of a fine deer as an occasion for much festive hilarity, and certainly the white hunter has in his heart rejoicings of his own. In state we hung up the Gunner's buck, and then went into a wild turkey dinner and an hour of perfect peace, yarning before the great open fireside.

I must add that when the stag was dressed we found that one of the three buckshots that struck him had passed straight through his heart. Yet he had run nearly a quarter of a mile at top speed without a hesitation or a blunder. The vitality of wild game is a thing almost incredible.

After a day that ended so happily, I had to have a little talk with Prince before saying good-night to him. "Well," I asked, "what does your wife have to say now about our hunting on Christmas Eve? Doesn't this deer prove to her that she was wrong?"

"Cap'n," said Prince soberly, "I ain't never can't prove nothin' to a woman what she ain't want to believe. She done say this luck was a acci-*dent*."

And the more I think of Sue's description of our good fortune, the more inclined am I to believe that she was right.

THAT CHRISTMAS BUCK

When I am at large in deer country there is no need for friends to try to lure me off the fascinating following of the whitetail by promises of more abundant sport with smaller game. Quail and ducks and woodcock and the like do not look very good when a man feels that an old buck with majestic antlers is waiting in the woods for some one to talk business to him. I admit that the game of deer hunting is sometimes tedious and the shooting of the occasional variety; yet my experience has been that the great chance does come to the faithful, and that to make good on it is to drink one of Life's rarest juleps, the memory of whose flavor is a delight for years.

It may be that this love of deer hunting was not only born in me—the men of my family always having been sportsmen—but was made ingrowing by a curious happening that occurred when I was not a year old. One day I was left alone in a large room in the plantation house where first I saw the light of day. Lying thus in my crib, what should come roaming in but a pet buck that we had. My mother, in the greatest dismay, found him bending over me, while, if we may believe the account, I had hold of the old boy's horns and was crowing with delight. I have always felt sure that the old stag (since he knew that his own hide was safe) passed me the mystic word concerning the rarest sport on earth. He put it across to me, all right; and I am going to do my best here to hand on the glad tidings. I want to tell about a deer hunt we had one Christmas not long past.

Things on the plantation had been going badly with me. There were plenty of deer about, and a most unusual number

From *Plantation Game Trails* (1921).

of very large bucks; but our hunting party had achieved nothing of a nature worth recording. We had been at the business nearly a week, and we were still eating pork instead of venison. That's humiliating; indeed, in a sense, degrading. On a certain Wednesday (we had begun to hunt on the Thursday previous) I took our Negro driver aside. It was just after we had made three unsuccessful drives, and just after some of the hunters had given me a look that, interpreted, seemed to mean that I could easily be sold to a sideshow as the only real fakir in captivity. In the lee of a great pine I addressed my partner in crime.

"Prince," I said, drawing a flask from my pocket, "as deer hunters you and I aren't worth a Continental damn." (This term, as my readers know, is a good one, sound and true, having been the name of a coin minted before the Revolution.)

"Dat's so, sah, suttinly so," Prince admitted, his eyes glued to the flask, his tongue moistening his lips.

"Now," I went on, "we are going to drive this Little Horseshoe. Tell me where to stand so that we can quit this fooling."

The flask sobered Prince marvelously, as I knew it would. To a Negro there is no tragedy like seeing a drink without getting it; and the possibility of such a disaster made the good-natured Prince grave.

"Dis summer," he said, "I done see where an able buck done used to navigate regular by the little gum-tree pond. Dat must be he social walk," he further explained; "and dat may be he regular run. You stop there, Cap'n, and if he is home, you will bline he eye."

That sounded good to me. Therefore, the calamity that Prince dreaded might happen did not occur; for we parted in high spirits, and with high spirits in at least one of us. But there must have been a prohibition jinx prowling about, for what happened shortly thereafter appeared like the work of an evil fate.

As I was posting the three standers, the man who had already missed four deer took a fancy to the stand by the gum-tree pond. I tried politely to suggest that there was a far better place, for him, but he remained obdurate. I therefore let him stay at what Prince had described as the critical place. And it was not five minutes later that Prince's far-resounding shout told me that a stag was afoot. Feeling sure that the buck would run for the pond, I stood up on a log, and from that elevation I watched him do it. He was a bright, cherry-red buck, and his horns would have made an armchair for ex-President Taft. He

ran as if he had it in his crafty mind to run over the stander by
the pond and trample him. He, poor fellow, missed the buck
with both barrels. His roaring ten-gauge gun made enough noise
to have stunned the buck; but the red-coated monarch serenely
continued his march. All this happened near sundown, and it
was the end of a perfectly doleful day. Prince laid the blame for
the bull on me when he said, in mild rebuke:

"How, Cap'n, make you didn't put a true gunnerman to the
critical place?"

The next day—the seventh straight that we had been hunting—it was an uncle of mine who got the shot. And this thing
happened not a quarter of a mile from where the other business
had come off. My uncle and I were hardly a hundred yards apart
in the open, level, sunshiny pine-woods. Before us was a wide
thicket of bays about five feet high. The whole stretch covered
about ten acres. Prince was riding through it, whistling on the
hounds. Suddenly I heard a great bound in the bays. Prince's
voice rang out—but a second shout was stifled by him designedly.
A splendid buck had been roused. He made just about three
bounds and then stopped. He knew very well that he was cornered, and he was evidently wondering how to cut the corners.
The deer was broadside to my uncle and only about fifty yards
off. I saw him carefully level his gun. At the shot the buck, tall
antlers and all, collapsed under the bay-bushes.

Then the lucky hunter, though he is a good woodsman, did
a wrong thing. Leaning his gun against a pine, he began to run
forward toward his quarry dragging out his hunting-knife as he
ran. When he was within ten yards of the buck the thing happened. The stunned stag (tall horns and all) leaped clear of danger, and away he went rocking through the pine-lands. Believing
that the wound might be a fatal one we followed the buck a long
way. Finally, meeting a Negro woodsman who declared that the
buck had passed him "running like the wind," we abandoned
the chase. A buckshot had probably struck the animal on the
spine, at the base of the skull, or on a horn. Perhaps the buck
simply dodged under cover at the shot; I have known a deer so
to sink into tall broomsedge.

That night our hunting-party broke up. Only Prince and I
were left on the plantation. Before we parted that evening I said:

"You and I are going out to-morrow. And we'll take one
hound. We'll walk it."

The next day, to our astonishment, we found a light snow

on the ground—a rare phenomenon in the Carolina woods. We knew that it would hardly last for the day; but it might help us for a while.

In the first thicket that we walked through a buck fawn came my way. He was a handsome little fellow, dark in color and chunky in build. It is possible to distinguish the sex of a fawn even when the lithe creature is on the fly, for the doe invariably has a longer and sharper head and gives evidences of a slenderer, more delicate build. I told the bucklet that I would revisit him when he had something manly on his head.

Prince and I next circled Fawn Pond, a peculiar pond fringed by bays. Our hound seemed to think that somebody was at home here. And we did see tracks in the snow that entered the thicket; however, on the farther side we discerned them departing. But they looked so big and so fresh that we decided to follow them. Though the snow was melting fast I thought the tracks looked as if two bucks had made them. Deer in our part of Carolina are so unused to snow that its presence makes them very uncomfortable, and they do much wandering about in daylight when it is on the ground.

Distant from Fawn Pond a quarter of a mile through the open woods was Black Tongue Branch, a splendid thicket, so named because once there had been found on its borders a great buck that had died of that plague of the deer family—the black tongue, or anthrax. Deciding to stay on the windward side (for a roused deer loves to run up the wind) I sent Prince down to the borders of the branch, telling him to cross it, when together the two of us would flank it out. The tracks of the deer seemed to lead toward Black Tongue, but we lost them before we came to the place itself. While I waited for Prince and the leashed hound to cross the end of the narrow thicket, I sat on a pine-log and wondered whether our luck that day was to change. Suddenly, from the green edges of the bay I was aware of Prince beckoning violently for me to come to him. I sprang up. But we were too slow. From a deep head of bays and myrtles, not twenty steps from where the Negro was standing, out there rocked into the open woods as splendid a buck as it has ever been my fortune to see. He had no sooner cleared the bushes than he was followed by his companion, a creature fit to be his mate. They were two old comrades of many a danger. Their haunches looked as broad as the tops of hogsheads. Their flags were spectacular. They were just about two hundred yards from me, and, of course, out of gunshot.

Had I been with Prince at that moment (as I had been up to that fatal time) I should have had a grand chance—a chance such as does not come even to a hardened hunter more than a few times in a hundred years or so. The bucks held a steady course straight away from me; and their pace was a rocking, rhythmic, leisurely one. Speechless I watched them go for half a mile; my heart was pretty nearly broken. As for Prince—when I came up to him, I found him quite miserable and unnerved.

"Oh, Cap'n, if you had only been where I been jest now!" was all he could say.

From the direction that the two great animals had taken the Negro and I thought that we knew just where they were going. Telling him to hold the hound for about fifteen minutes I took a long circle in the woods, passing several fine thickets where the old boys might well have paused, and came at last to a famous stand on a lonely road. Soon I heard the lone hound open on the track, and you can imagine with what eagerness I awaited the coming of what was before me. The dog came straight for me; but when he broke through the last screen of bays he was alone. The deer had gone on. It was not hard to find where they had crossed the road some ten yards from where I had been standing. Judging from the easy way in which they were running they were not in the least worried. And from that crossing onward they had a perfect right not to be concerned; for beyond the old road lay a wild region of swamp and morass into which the hunter can with no wisdom or profit go.

I did not stop the dog, deciding that by mere chance the bucks might, if run right, dodge back and forth, and so give me the opportunity for which I was looking. The old hound did his best; and the wary antlered creatures, never pushed hard, did some cunning dodging before him. Once again I saw them far away through the woodlands, but a glimpse of their distant beauty was all the comfort afforded me. After a two-hour chase the hound gave them up. Prince and I had to confess that we had been outwitted, and in a crestfallen mood we quitted the hunt for the day.

The next day was my last one at home; and every hunter is surely familiar with the feeling of the man who, up until the last day, has not brought his coveted game to bag. I felt that we should have luck on our side or else be beaten. I told Prince as much, and he promised to be on hand at daybreak.

Before dawn I was awakened by the sound of a steady winter rain softly roaring on the shingle roof of the old plantation house. It was discouraging, to be sure; but I did not forget that the rain ushered in my last day. By the time I was dressed Prince had come up. He was wet and cold. He reported that the wind was blowing from the northeast. Conditions were anything but promising. However, we had hot coffee, corncakes deftly turned by Prince, and a cheering smoke. After such reinforcement weather can be hanged. By the time that the dim day had broadened we ventured forth into the stormy pinelands, where the towering trees were rocking continuously, and where the rain seemed able to search us out, however we tried to keep to the leeward of every sheltering object. The two dogs that we had compelled to come with us were wet and discouraged. Their heads, I knew, were full of happy visions of the warm plantation fireside that they had been forced to leave. Besides, it was by no means their last day, and their spirit was utterly lacking in all the elements of enthusiasm.

After about four barren drives, when Prince and I were soaked quite through and were beginning to shiver despite precautions that we took (in Southern deer hunting a "precaution" means only one thing), I said:

"Now, Hunterman, this next drive is our last. We'll try the Little Corner, and hope for the best."

Two miles through the rainy woods I plodded to take up my stand. All the while I took to do this Prince waited, his back against a pine, and with the sharp, cold rain searching him out. The wind made the great pines rock and sigh. Even if the dogs should break into full chorus I thought I could never hear them coming. At last I reached my stand. A lonely place it was, four miles from home, and in a region of virgin forest. So much of this wide woodland through which I had come looked so identical that it hardly seemed reasonable to believe that a deer, jumped two miles back in a thicket, would run to this particular place. But men who know deer nature know what a deer will do. I backed up against an old sweet-gum tree, waiting in that solitary, almost savage place. I thought that in about a half-hour my good driver, bedraggled and weary, would come into sight, and that then we two disillusioned ones would go home sloshing through the drizzle.

But wonderful things happen to men in the big woods. Their apparently insane faith is not infrequently rewarded. Hardly had I settled myself against the big tree for shelter when, far off, in a momentary lulling of the grieving wind, I heard the voice of a hound. One of the dogs had a deep bass note, and it was this that I heard. Sweet music it was to my ears, you may well believe! From where I was standing I could see a good half-mile toward the thickets whence had come the hound's mellow, rain-softened note. And now, as I looked searchingly in that direction, I saw the deer, heading my way, and coming at a wild and breakneck pace. At that distance I took the fugitive for a doe. It was running desperately, with head low, and lithe, powerful legs eating up the pine-land spaces. If it held its course it would pass fifty yards to the left of me. I turned and ran crouchingly until I thought I had reached a place directly in the oncoming deer's pathway. I was in a slight hollow; and the easy rise of ground in front of me hid for a few moments the approaching racer. I fully expected a big doe to bound over the rise and to run slightly on my left. I had a slight suspicion that the deer might be an old buck, with small, poor horns that on my first and distant view had not been visible. But it was not so.

Hardly had I reached my new stand when over the gentle swell of ground, grown in low broomgrass, there came a mighty rack of horns forty yards away to my right. Then the whole buck came full into view. There were a good many fallen logs just there, and these he was maneuvering with a certainty and a grace and a strength that it was a sight to behold. But I was there for more than just "for to admire."

As he was clearing a high obstruction I gave him the right barrel. I distinctly saw two buckshot strike him high up—too high. He never winced or broke his stride. Throwing the gun for his shoulder, I fired. This brought him down—but by no means headlong, though, as I afterwards ascertained that twelve buckshot from the choke barrel had gone home. The buck seemed crouching on the ground, his grand crowned head held high, and never in wild nature have I seen a more anciently crafty expression than that on his face. I think he had not seen me before I shot; and even now he turned his head warily from side to side, his mighty horns rocking with the motion. He was looking for his enemy. I have had a good many experiences with the behavior of wounded bucks; therefore I reloaded my gun and with some circumspection approached the fallen monarch. But my caution was needless. The old chieftain's last race was over. By the time I reached him that proud head was lowered and the fight was done.

Mingled were my feelings as I stood looking down on that perfect specimen of the deer family. He was in his full prime. Though somewhat lean and rangy because this was toward the close of the mating season, his condition was splendid. The hair on his neck and about the back of his haunches was thick and long and dark. His hoofs were very large, but as yet unbroken. His antlers were, considering all points of excellence, very fine. They bore ten points.

My short reverie was interrupted by the clamorous arrival of the two hounds. These I caught and tied up. Looking back toward the drive I saw Prince coming, running full speed. The dogs had not had much on him in the race. When he came up and saw what had happened, wide was the happy smile that broke like dawn on his dusky face.

"Did you see him in the drive, Prince?" I asked. "He surely is a beauty."

"See him?" the Negro ejaculated in joyous excitement. "Cap'n, dat ole thing been lyin' so close that when he done jump up he throw sand in my eye! I done reach for he big tail to ketch him! But I done know," he ended, "dat somebody else been waitin' to ketch him."

I sent Prince home for a horse on which we could get the buck out of the woods. While he was gone I had a good chance to look over the prone monarch. He satisfied me. And the chief element in that satisfaction was the feeling that, after weary days, mayhap, and after adverse experiences, the great chance will come. For my part that Christmas hunt taught me that it is worth while to spend some empty days for a day brimmed with sport. And one of the lasting memories of my life is the recollection of that cold, rainy day in the Southern pinelands—my last day for that hunting trip—and my best.

MY 250TH BUCK

No matter how many deer a man has killed, he never forgets the first one. I was excited and shaky and filled with suspense, as who isn't! Moreover, I had a slightly unusual handicap to overcome, for the barrel of my shotgun was both sawed off and bent, so that I had to make a special allowance for this when shooting. But the old gun and I managed to drop a fine eight-pointer.

I was eleven years old that December of 1894.

Fifty-six years had passed when I set out to hunt another buck last December, the white-tail that would bring my score to 250. I would still be excited but not, I hoped, shaky. The taking of so many deer—begun at a time when there were no seasons— does have a steadying effect although one can't always be sure, what with the mystery of a swamp and the heady music of coursing hounds.

My hunting nowadays is mostly in the Santee Basin country of South Carolina, a state which still permits the taking of five deer in a season that lasts four and a half months. While I have killed a good many whitetails with my .250-3000 rifle, a shotgun is my usual weapon because of terrain conditions. Ordinary stalking is not possible among the jungle-like swamps of the Carolina coastal plains, where the deer are strictly nocturnal and are rarely seen by daylight unless they have been disturbed. A rifle would be dangerous in such flat country.

As in much of the South, we run deer with hounds. Aside from the absolute necessity of using hounds in level country where the woods are prevailingly dense, there is considerable

From *Those Were the Days* (1955).

excitement in hunting deer this way. It is a sport of ancient lineage, and honorable as well, and there is a fascination in the sorcery of the trailing hound that cannot fail to appeal to any man who loves dogs and really understands the miracles of their performance.

So-called deerhounds are really foxhounds, as a rule. Walkers or redbones. But I have used beagles with great success, and I killed two of my very finest bucks in front of a cocker spaniel. Once I was hunting quail, my gun loaded with No. 7½ shot, when my old English setter, following a covey to the dense green borders of a damp thicket of little pines and sweet bays, came to a stand. I edged in to flush the birds. But my dog had been pointing a buck. As he ripped up very close to me, I killed him with the 7½s.

Where conditions are favorable, it is no uncommon thing for a bird dog to point a couched deer. But I believe the dog must come to him upwind, and the deer must be so hidden in his bed that he cannot see the dog.

Few experiences are more thrilling to an understanding hunter than to see and to hear a good hound in action on a buck. A whitetail deer has six powerful scent glands. One is in the cleft of each hoof. These leave the scent on the ground. On the inside of each knee on the back legs, surrounded by heavy tufts of hair, is another gland, which deposits scent on tall grasses and low bushes. A good hound, I believe, hardly knows the meaning of a track, but he follows the ground scent. And when he is on a cold trail, you will see him running his nose up and down grass stems and over the leaves on bushes. He knows, moreover, which way the deer has gone. A really experienced hound will not run a back track. Once when I took two hound puppies out with their wise old mother, they began to trail a deer the wrong way. The old hound knowingly ran around them, turned them back, and made them head in the proper direction. I have owned two hounds that would run a buck only.

If a morning is very cold, I believe deer scent will be frozen in the ground, and is released as the snow or frost melts. For this reason, in using hounds on deer, it is wiser to wait until the sun has had time to thaw out the scent.

One great advantage in using hounds on deer is that a badly wounded buck rarely escapes. It is curious, but most hounds, while they will go wild on a buck's trail, will not go in on him when he comes to bay. A hound is not naturally a "ketch" dog. The best dog for that should have a strain of mongrel in him.

But back to my choice of a weapon.

The great marksman Bogardus said of a shotgun, "After forty yards uncertainty begins." I once killed a buck at 102 yards with an old Westley-Richards muzzle-loader, having thirty-two-inch barrels. A single buckshot did the work. On the other hand, at thirty-five yards, I drove eleven buckshot clear through an old stag. The hounds caught him nearly two miles away. The shells I use chamber No. 1 buckshot. With that load, if the aim is true, a hunter should kill a buck at fifty, or even sixty, yards.

The most consistently successful hunter, aside from those who may have some freakish luck, is the man who best understands the nature of the game he is after. This is especially true in deer hunting. The whitetail has acute hearing, but that does not mean that he will leave his bed when he hears a noise. Like a rabbit, he will often sit tight, thinking to be passed by. Repeatedly I have walked up deer that let me come plenty close enough to shoot them when they get up. Yet they must have heard me coming a long way off. Deer seem to ignore sounds made by cars, wagons, and even by dogs, if the dogs are not actually after them. Dogs, by the way, rarely press a deer to any extreme speed. A master of the subtle arts of dodging and skulking, he plays in front of a pack of hounds.

I had a pet buck that would deliberately taunt my dogs until they would give him a chase. They would have a great time racing over plantation fields and fences. Then the buck would lead the clamoring pack back to the yard, and the whole thing would be over. It was just a game. Once a cousin of mine brought in his dog, and he joined my pack in this frolic. But he did not understand that it was all in fun. When the buck returned to the yard and all my dogs stopped chasing him, this strange dog kept right on. The leader of my pack, a wise old veteran named Rowley, taking a short cut, intercepted the rude intruder, caught hold of him, and manhandled him. That was about the smartest thing I ever saw a deerhound do.

A deer's eyesight is keen to detect movement, but if he does not wind you, and you remain motionless, he may almost run you down and trample you. One of these very close shots can be a difficult one. A long shot may seem like a hard one, but if you have to get out of a deer's way before you shoot, don't be surprised if you miss. One of the most difficult of all shots to make successfully is one at a buck that is coming head-on for you. And the shot straightaway is not easy. Of course, I am thinking of deer on the run as they nearly always are when hunted with hounds.

Once when I was loaded with No. 9 shot, gunning for woodcock, I roused a fine old stag. I would have risked a shot at him with buckshot, but as he was fifty yards off there was no need of my burning him with the mustard seed I had in my gun. Just the same, I jumped up on a fallen log just to watch him go. I had unbreeched my gun in the momentary thought that I could slip in a buckshot shell in time. I was on the log with my gun open when the bushes cracked behind me. Before I knew what was happening, a second buck sailed over the log within two feet of me. I almost lost my footing from surprise, but, slamming my gun shut, I shot him when he was not more that fifteen feet away from me. The whole load, at that close range, went like a bullet, killing him instantly.

An experienced deer hunter can nearly always tell by the actions of a deer when he has made a successful shot. If the shot is followed by a blunder, a wild rush, or even a change in stride, the shot have found their target. I have often heard it said that a buck will slap his tail down if he is badly hit. This I have not found to be true. Sometimes a deer will put his tail down for no reason of which we can be sure—perhaps the crack of the gun has suddenly decided him to be wary and less spectacular in showing all that topsail. On the other hand, I have repeatedly seen a buck, mortally wounded, go off with his tail high, even nonchalant and jaunty.

Last year I shot a buck, and he fell heavily. But then he got up and began to walk away. He was in pines so thick that I did not shoot again; nor did I think it necessary, as I believed he was shot through the heart. As long as he was in sight, his snowy flag was high. I found him dead 200 yards away. One buckshot had gone through his heart. At least when using the shotgun, I have not found that a deer's bleeding necessarily indicates a fatal shot. If an artery or vein is severed, a buck may bleed heavily; but sometimes a mortally wounded deer gives out no blood. If the deer throws out frothy blood, a lung shot is indicated. This is about as fatal as a heart shot.

In my part of the country, a deer hunt can be the most exciting of all sports. Drivers who handle hounds are usually plantation Negroes, and when a Negro is a good woodsman, he is as good an an Indian. There is the thrill that comes from recognizing the voice of each trailing hound, then there is the grand chorus when they start the stag. With a pack after him, a buck, unless he slips warily out far ahead of the dogs, will come out in high gear, and his strange undulant gait does not present an easy target. He may look big, but he can readily be missed. In swift motion, a deer is a deceptive big game animal to shoot at. And sometimes at a critical moment, a buck will execute a fast maneuver that will throw a hunter completely off balance.

Of course, I have learned not greatly to regret the escape of a fine stag, for such a wild creature has the power to invest the woods with mystery and wonder. If he is gone, they go too. And it is not as if an old buck is a casual visitor in a certain place. In the mating season one of these old boys may wander far in search of amorous adventures, but as a rule he has a pretty definite home. He loves the place, and though you may run him out repeatedly, he is certain to return. And, depend upon it, although you may own the woods in which he lives, he knows them far better than you do.

It may seem strange, but wherever the whitetail deer is found, he is prone to run to specific crossings or stands, not only in hill or mountain country, where runs are determined by the character of the terrain, but in country that is dead level; and though the aspect of the woods may be changed by the opening up of new roads and the cutting of timber, the runs remain the same. I know from family sporting history that deer have been running to the same stands on my plantation since long before the Revolution. I might add that I live on a place that has been with my people since 1686. In the plantation house are more than 400 sets of whitetail antlers, taken on the place. The largest is an eighteen-pointer, with tremendously heavy palmated beams. The largest buck I ever killed was a twelve-pointer. He was a giant, weighing 305 pounds.

Our deer of the river swamps invariably are larger and carry more massive racks than those of the open pinelands. The swamp deer are darker in color and shorter in the legs. In the lonely marshes of the great deltas of the southern rivers, the deer have nearly all the hair trimmed off the legs by the sharp blades of the marsh, and from having to travel on boggy ground. These deer develop an astonishing spatulation of the hoofs.

Once, at twilight, I walked up to a buck standing in the brush on the edge of a field. I was in an old sandy road, and was either not visible to him or else he counted on my passing him by. A direct approach is what usually scares game. When I shot, I was chagrined to see a white flag bobbing away into the dusky woods. However, when I went to where the buck had been standing, there lay an eight-pointer, dead. Just out of curiosity, I followed the other one a short distance.

A snowy object beside a cypress attracted me. There lay a second, a nine-pointer. They must have been standing together, and I inadvertently got them both with one shot.

I have also killed what might be called the wrong buck. The hounds were running, when out of a dense myrtle thicket about forty yards away a fine stag broke cover. Then he stopped, though poised for flight. Before I could get my gun up, he made a violent swerving rush into a thicket. I shot where he had been. I went over to where he had been standing, and there lay another buck, dead. One must have stopped just behind the other. The sudden dodge of the first exposed the second to my shot. I am not sure that a man should be proud over killing a buck at which he did not even shoot.

In my long life as a hunter of the whitetail, I have missed very few deer. But I am not paying a tribute to myself as an expert marksman. I have killed my last 116 deer straight. This is simply because I will not shoot at a buck unless the chances are in my favor of killing him. I have learned to judge distances in the woods, and I never call on my old 12-gauge, 30-inch Parker gun to do the impossible, or even the unlikely. I have used this gun since 1904. Those shots I have missed have been the easy ones instead of the difficult ones. The hardest shot I ever made was on a grand stag at sixty-five yards, going like a projectile through brush so heavy that I could see nothing but his great antlers and the dark line of his back. I believe that a buck, a natural pauser, skulker and dodger, never runs like that unless hounds are hard on him, as they were in this case. There are probably many experienced deer hunters who have never seen a buck "low-grading," as my Negroes say.

I once timed the speed of a buck, running parallel to the

road I was driving. He was in an old field beyond a fence, and he chose to run the line of the fence. My speedometer showed thirty-five, forty, forty-five, forty-seven miles an hour before he turned aside, and just stood there, looking. He did not seem to be winded, and I am not at all sure that he might not have been capable of greater speed, at least for a certain distance.

I guess it is about time now for me to come to that 250th buck. After I had killed 249, for some reason I thought the next one might be something special. He was, and the circumstances of his fall are worth recording.

On December 3, 1950, my oldest son and I took to the woods. We had with us Prince Alston, my Negro plantation foreman and deer driver; and we had our hounds, Bugle and Music, Borer and Burn, Red Liquor and Ringwood. We decided to drive Peachtree Plantation, formerly the property of Thomas Lynch, Jr., next to the youngest signer of the Declaration of Independence. This plantation, now deserted, is an ideal place for deer. As the weather had been bitterly cold, most of the deciduous leaves were down and the woods were fairly open. However, a forest fire had passed through that tract last March, leaving a wilderness of burned bushes; then, following the fire, an exceptionally tall growth of broomsedge had come on. A deer, especially if he is sneaking, can make himself almost invisible in broomsedge and burned bushes. Nor can one ever count on hearing a deer's approach. Even when in full flight ahead of hounds, it is remarkable how eerily silent these creatures can be.

I was standing on a slight elevation, with a dense swamp to my left and in front of me. Off to my right was an avenue of live oaks, marking the site of the house where the parish preacher used to live long ago. My son was at a crossing beyond the oaks. Under those great evergreen trees I had left my car.

I had not been on my stand more than twenty minutes when I heard the hounds begin to tune up, then my good Negro driver let out a squall as if he were leading a revival meeting. I knew a buck had been started; later, I learned that there had been two.

In hunting with hounds, it is possible to tell the direction a deer is taking, but he is usually so far ahead and he is liable to change his course so often that you can never be certain of the angle of a deer's approach until you actually see him.

The hounds were heading far to my right, and I expected

my son to shoot. But when the two deer almost ran into my car, they separated, each flaring in a different direction. One passed my son too far away for a shot. I saw the other under the oaks, heading my way at a tangent. If he held his course, he would run behind me. I swung around on the stump on which I had been sitting but lost him as he dipped out of sight in a little watercourse.

Then he reappeared, running low and fast through the burnt bushes and the broomsedge. A big buck, and running hard, he did not make a sound. I had my gun up in an opening that was just ahead of him. As he reached it, I gave him the choke barrel at forty-five yards.

He went down at the shot and was dead when I reached him—a fine deer with sporty rather than a massive eight-point rack.

I plan to kill other bucks—and I'll miss others—but even after those 249 before me, there seems something special about Number 250.

JOYS
OF THE QUEST

––––––––––––– Part IV –––––––––––––

D edicated deer hunters recognize that their sport involves a great deal more than killing. Indeed, the act of pulling the trigger is often almost anticlimactic, the concluding scene in an unfolding drama which may have involved countless hours of patient preparation. Perhaps that is why the consummating act, a successful shot, tinges the instant when a whitetail is taken with bittersweetness. Still, amid the whirlwind of emotions which engulfs even the most experienced sportsman at such moments, the hunter's dominant feeling is likely to be one of triumph.

We are not so far removed from our primordial roots as to have fully shed from our emotive cloak the sensations killing game held for prehistoric man. Rutledge recognized as much and, more important, he was honest enough to say so in print. He had little use for those opposed to deer hunting, terming them "pantywaists" or dismissing them as "parlor naturalists and lollypop sentimentalists" who were "incapable of understanding that it is far less cruel to kill wild deer than it is to poleax a defenseless ox in a stall." For him, there was no "hunting achievement quite equal to out-guessing an old white tail," and every time he succeeded in doing so he rejoiced in the feat.

By the same token, Rutledge was acutely attuned to the wider ramifications and to the most subtle nuances of sport. He cherished the heady smell of gun oil and the acrid aroma of burnt gunpowder. To him the feel of the well-worn walnut stock of his beloved Parker double-barrel brought warm comfort. The cacophony of sounds produced by hounds hot on a stag's trail was music to his ears, and his love for the taste of venison is obvious from his frequent allusions to the hunter's repast.

In short, Rutledge was titillated by those sensations which

161

collectively comprise the hunt, and his love for the sport never palled. The word *romance* is used repeatedly in his writings on whitetails, including the title of one of the selections printed here, and certainly there is no doubting Flintlock's romantic attachment to the totality of the deer hunting experience. He felt it gave "a man a sense of balance, a sanity, a comprehension of the true values of life."

THAT HUNT AT JASPER HILL

When you are hunting in the old plantation region of South Carolina, you are sure to encounter many names that antedate the Revolution; names such as Brewton Hall, Essex Place, Medway, and Jasper. I have been told that this last place took its name from the fact that long, long ago there had been found, on the bluff overlooking the glamorous wide reaches of the lower Santee, a jasper arrowhead of exquisite workmanship, wrought by the craft of the Santees in those days when this delightful wilderness was theirs. But I don't hunt arrowheads on Jasper Hill; I hunt stags. And the plantation is of such a nature that I have seldom been disappointed in a visit to that wild and romantic deserted estate.

During the last days of December just passed. I had just about run all the deer off my own place, having with me a party of eager hunters who were fast-goers though not great executors. I was casting about in my mind for a neighboring place on which I might amiably trespass—the owner probably living in Richmond or Baltimore or some other Northern city. While in this frame of mind, who should come shambling up the road but Old Testament himself, the watchman of Jasper Hill—an ancient Negro of religious air and bootleg habits. I could not be sure but that he was coming to try to drum up a little business with my guests. It is getting harder all the time for a man to get out of the Santee country without being more or less innocently burdened with some of the fruit-juices of that lost Eden.

"Well, you old muscadine murderer," I began, "have you hid the demijohns near the gate?"

From *Those Were the Days* (1955).

163

Old Testament laughed behind the back of his hand.

"You mustn't let my little secret slip," he laughed. But at once he sobered up.

"Ain't dat dis time," he protested. "I want you gen'mens to come down to Jasper Hill and kill some of dem big able buck. Gettin' so I can hardly navigate after dark for the deer."

"I suppose you're afraid they'll eat up all the mash," I suggested.

"They eat up all my crop last summer, and they is jest waitin' for me to plant again. Ain't you gen'mens can help me?"

"We sure can," I told the venerable pleader. "I wish a man could stay good as easy as he can come to Jasper Hill to hunt a buck."

"I don't care if you shoot de whole gang, dem deer have me so tarrigate and worrigate dat I can't live reg-lar."

"Old Testament," I told him "this war is going to begin no later than this morning. And you might as well put on your pot."

Five of us hunters, each mounted, three Negro drivers, all walking, and eleven dogs composed our party. The dogs were walking too. High hope was in our hearts, and in our hands were weapons supposed to be deadly for deer. But it's one thing to hunt a stag, and it's another thing entirely to bring him safely to bag. I do not know a hunting achievement quite equal to outguessing an old whitetail.

Jasper Hill lay four miles to the south of us, down the river, and this distance we traversed in an hour. I had repeated to my comrades what Old Testament had told me; but while they accepted the story at its face value, I was by no means so sure of the entire truth of it. Sadly from experience have I learned that it is the buck that is cornered and just waiting for you to point-blank him which usually gets away. Deer hunting is just as much a matter of speculation as marriage.

In the Santee country, deer are hunted as they have been hunted in England since time immemorial; and as they have been hunted in that wild region since the first English and Huguenot settlements toward the end of the seventeenth century. We use horses and hounds. In other parts of the country dogs are forbidden, and for very good reasons; but where the cover is dense even in midwinter, and where the swamps are impenetrable, and the trails mazy and obscure, hounds are essential. Moreover, one has the feeling that their use is legitimate; and, feeling thus, the sport certainly is enhanced by the music of a good pack. With Smut and Smoke, Check and Mate, Ringwood, Drum and Fife, and other dogs of less high-sounding appellations and certainly less noble heritage, we invaded Jasper Hill. The five of us took stands on the old plantation road, now little more than a grassgrown trail, while the Negro drivers took the pack into the sweet wilderness adjacent to the river.

It was the kind of morning that makes the midwinter of the South the most delightful season of the year. The frost of the night before had been melted away by the genial sun. Aromatic airs breathed from the towering yellow pines, from the needles of which the dew-drops slipped sparkling to the ground. Towhees rustled in the leaves under the shadowy copses. A Carolina wren was singing his free and joyous song. High in the morning heavens flocks of teal and mallards sped on their way to their feeding grounds in the marshes of the delta. The fragrant forest glimmered away on all sides, awakening, radiant, roseate, brimming with a nameless enchantment. As far as the day was concerned, it was perfect. But what would the harvest of our hunt be?

When the deer of the southern pinelands are roused by hounds and drivers from their daytime drowsing in thickets and sunny sanctuaries of broomsedge amid old logs and stumps, they are far more likely, unless they are suddenly pressed, to use their old craft of skulking than they are to flee wildly before pursuers. When it comes to the matter of achieving the honor of sneaking out of a drive noncommittally, hang the costliest medal on a wary old stag.

I could hear our drivers whooping, whistling, beating their clubs against pines. Now and then I heard a dog give a yelp as if he had information that he had the track of some kind of game. But really nothing happened until the drivers were almost within sight; and I had begun to have in my heart some feelings derogatory to the reputation of Old Testament, when this business began. How shall I ever forget those dramatic moments at Jasper Hill? A deer hunter may forget to go to church; he may forget whether he married Grace or Glorianna; he may kiss the door and slam his secretary; but he cannot forget a big time in the woods—down to the last detail. If he does, order the crepe.

The driver nearest me, Steve Boykin, had begun to abate his shouting; and I saw him assault a pine very negligently with his huge club. He was so close that I could see that he was muttering—probably assailing the pedigree of Old Testament. Between Steve and me was a little pond not a quarter of an acre in extent. Hunters of the Santee country know that a buck loves a pond. A whitetail seems to me most at home close to water. This pond was fringed by baybushes and sweet myrtles. A single cypress spired from its placid bosom far into the placid sky. Toward it Steve came, remembering my injunction to be particular about ponds. Now Steve was singing. You should have seen him and have heard him. His mouth was such that when it opened there wasn't much chance left of seeing Steve. He was gloomily warbling about God's gattling gun that shot all sinners at the rising of the sun. Dramatically this song changed.

"Great guns, Cap'n!" he yelled, as if seventeen devils had set upon him, "look out for de ole man. . . . Oh, don't miss de old man!" he wailed.

Out of the thin fringe of bushes on the edge of the quiet little pond the great buck sailed. He had been there all the time I had been standing in the road—not a hundred yards from me. One giant leap carried him clear of the bushes; another one shot him about thirty feet father into some breast-high golden broomsedge. There, to my amazement, with Steve, close on him, yelling as if he had found salvation or a watermelon or something like that, the splendid stag came to a full stop. With almost any kind of a rifle I would have been afforded a beautiful shot. But in such hunting, in those level woods, it is an unwritten law that every man must use a shotgun.

There stood the magnificent stag, "reading his book," as the Negroes say, to determine "where do we go from here?" In deadliest peril a deer can be deliberate. He is too intelligent to run anywhere incontinently, like a sheep, just because he happens to be startled. As he now stood, he was going to run parallel to all standers, at about the same distance that he was from me. He might run back, or he might come my way. It is exceedingly hard to drive a deer toward danger when he has been driven toward danger before.

I was afraid to shout to Steve to get around him for fear that I would throw sand in the bearings. Here was Big News in sight, but would any of us ever be able to tell it?

For a full minute the stately wildwood creature estimated his chances. For me, I think, the moment was as dramatic as it was for him. The scene is indelibly photographed on my memory. Clearly out of the past comes that scene, with the magnificent stag, his eyes gleaming with attentive light, standing almost within gunshot, paying not the slightest attention to Steve yelling behind him. Of course deer get so used to seeing Negroes and to hearing them shout in the turpentine woods in which these dusky persons toil from tree to tree all summer, that I have frequently been persuaded that deer pay less attention to Negro rovers of the woods than they do to white men. Nor would this be unnatural; for it is a law of the caste system of the South that Negroes shall not kill deer.

I suppose that the other standers had guessed from the outcry of Steve that something was afoot. All the hounds, however, were silent, having followed the other drivers, and having struck no trail.

For a moment the fate of our hunt hung in the balance; then the buck made his decision. He leaped quartering out of the drive to my right, his course bringing him within eighty yards of me. That distance is a very unsatisfactory one for buckshot, and it is especially so when a man thinks that, by taking a long chance, he may spoil a much better shot for one of his friends. I have known many a hunter to take such a chance; then, having botched the whole business, to declare that he had merely shot to "turn the deer," imputing to himself a generous motive that had never been his.

It was now my turn to decide; the stag had played his card. I decided not to shoot, but to show myself, turning the buck in toward Weston, the next stander. I did now know that Weston, having seen the drivers and dogs approaching him listlessly, had let his stand and had gone forward to meet them. His stand was wide open.

My maneuver had the effect of making the old stag run a stately curve over the next stand. Seeing him take the right course, I just waited to hear the shot. Steve, meanwhile, was whooping as if a hant had him.

Straight over the stand went the great buck; he might have run over and trampled Weston had he been at the spot. I stooped down to see if I could catch a sight of the stander actually shooting the buck. But Weston was farther from the fugitive than I was. Apparently the tormentor of Old Testament's crops was heading for the open woods, with nothing ahead to stop him. But a green hunter sometimes does a lucky thing. Ashmead, the man next to Weston, had likewise left his stand, having gone behind it some distance to try to get a shot at a fox squirrel. Now, with both barrels loaded with duckshot, he suddenly become aware of the apparition of the great stag coming head-on for him. He was in the right spot, but he had the wrong load. He must have jumped with he saw the deer, for the deer saw him; and deer do not usually see anything except what moves. I mean that their power of recognition is not good.

The Jasper Hill stag, thinking himself clear, and suddenly confronted by an enemy, just reversed himself completely and came rushing back to the place whence he had just come. Ashmead meanwhile brushed off both haunches with loads of number 4's at a long distance, the only effect of which was to make the old stag speed up. The sound of the gun having made us alert, we now saw the old buck coming back straight for us.

At such a time it seems to me slightly better not to shoot a friend than to kill a deer; and I called to the gunners to be careful. All of us except Ashmead were close together; and with us were the drivers and lolling hounds. And this was as strange a situation as a hunter will ever encounter.

Here were four guns, a crowd of dogs, a bunch of drivers; and here was a beautiful buck, heavy-racked, coming straight for us on about seven of his eight cylinders. You would think he was hunting us. Then I saw what a man seldom sees unless he is dealing with a badly wounded deer: the buck, seeing the hounds but apparently not aware of us, lowered his head and charged straight through the whole pack of waiting dogs. And they were so amazed that they dodged, skulked, and ran. We, too, made way. Here, then, was the singular spectacle of a stag scattering dogs and men before him. The whole thing awoke in the drivers emotions of superstitious nature.

"Dat's a token," I heard Steve mutter, meaning one of these supernatural goin's-on.

In a moment the stag had passed us, entering a pine thicket beyond the road. As he was vanishing, four guns blared out, giving him an especial salute of honor of eight barrels, speeding after his broad white tail about a hundred and fifty buckshot. I saw the tops of several little pines jump off. But so did the deer. As far as I could see, he was heading for the tangled wilds of Jasper Hill, and for freedom. To make matters worse, the demoralized drivers let the dogs get away, and in a moment they were yowling merrily on the buck's trail. From the way they were going, our shots had merely encouraged the buck in his flight.

"Great guns," lamented Steve, "but he got a ham same like the top of a barrel."

"And the horns," said Ashmead, who breathlessly joined us, "did you ever see such antlers?"

"I ought to done knock him in the head with my stick when he passed me," Steve muttered inconsolably, and with no especial compliment to our shooting.

"Hold on," said Weston suddenly, "I can't hear the dogs."

When a pack of hounds after a wounded deer suddenly "shuts up," there is a practical certainty that the deer has been overhauled.

Away we thronged through the woods; and a half-mile from where we had done the shooting we came upon the great Jasper Hill stag, stretched on the forest-floor, the hounds ranged around him.

"I dunno whether it was de shootin' or de scarin' what done make him fall," said Steve, "but here he is anyway."

Five of us had shot at him; but Ashmead had only dusted him. Of the four of us who poured two barrels apiece after his fleeing form, which one had held true? Not each one of us, certainly, for there were only two buckshot in him.

At any rate, the stag was ours. We had raided Old Testament's Jasper Hill domain; and while we hadn't interfered with stills or other treasurers, we carried away what I think was the chief prize of that old plantation.

THE GHOST POINT BUCK

After some rather steady and strenuous work on the public roads, for the duties of which position the State of South Carolina had supplied him with a nice striped suit, my Negro Steve at length returned to my plantation. For several months he had been doing time for having failed to make sure that the hog he had killed had been his own. But because he and I have hunted so long together, I just can't hold anything against him. He wasn't a freed convict—just good old Steve.

It was late in December when he hove to; and as both the deer and the turkey seasons were open, we decided to try immediately a combination hunt—one of these exploring operations, more to get a line on things than to do any execution. I thought the wildwoods would go a long way toward getting the taste of the chain-gang out of Steve's cavernous mouth.

In this inauspicious way began the most remarkable experience I have ever had with a whitetail buck; and I have hunted deer for fifty years. You know well how it is: every encounter with an old buck gives you an entirely different story to tell. So it was with this one; and some of the circumstances attending it afford a pretty good idea of the behavior of a wild stag. It is well for each one of us to pass on to the rest of the boys whatever we have learned in the woods.

It was rather late in the afternoon when Steve and I got to where we were going; and to tell the truth, Steve has no great relish for that place, for it is named Ghost Point. Many years ago I killed an albino buck near that spot; hence its name. But Steve

From *Those Were the Days* (1955).

170

didn't want to have anything at all to do with ghosts. I compromised by telling him that I would stay at Ghost Point while he went a mile down the river and then came back toward me.

In the country that I am describing, this is a good way to get a shot at a wild turkey or a deer. Steve is especially good at this sort of thing. For some reason, game does not mind him. It will move on ahead of him, but is never very scared of him.

After he had left me to make his little round, I selected my stand; and I want to give the exact details here because they will help you to understand the nature of the fireworks soon to follow. To begin with, I was in the deep wilderness. It was near sundown. The woods were perfectly still. To my left, and within gunshot, was a swamp full of water, dully gleaming in the late afternoon sunlight.

I was in a kind of arena, open and level, with a thicket behind me and a very dense one in front of me. Off to my right and down a little slope was a series of ponds, along the edges of which deer love to run. I almost decided to take my stand there, but something told me to stay where I was. I sat on a big pine stump, looked the whole situation over carefully, and then relaxed to wait for Steve or any wild game that might come.

Because the chance at a deer was a little better than at a turkey, I had both barrels of my gun loaded with buckshot; the long shells I was using chambered twelve of these heavy shot. As I had told Steve not to whoop, I knew that if I heard any noise before I heard the slewing of his huge feet through the leaves it would likely be game. I listened intently. Nor did I have long to wit. Behind the thicket ahead of me, yet in the water of the swamp, I heard something. It didn't sound any heavier than a rabbit.

About that time, over on the pond edges to my right and out of sight from me, I heard a deer running. It ran like a doe. For a moment I was tempted to move over there. The buck might soon follow her. But what if it happened to be the buck I heard in the water? If it were, he was coming right up to my stand.

In a moment I heard whatever it was come ashore. The minute it got on the dry leaves I knew it was not a turkey, for a turkey walks just like a man. Because of his four feet, you never get a deer's footfalls so distinctly. For a moment I was half afraid it might be nothing but a wild hog. But then I knew it could never be. No hog ever walked in water or on land with so much delicate secrecy.

Although as yet I could see nothing. I knew the creature was coming along the edge of the swamp on my left. I got my gun up, laying it in the only opening between the dense thicket and the water. I even had my sight at the proper height from the ground for a buck. Then suddenly I saw him!

Old-timers, regardless of how many bucks you may have killed, doesn't the sight of one always somehow surprise you? This one amazed me, for while he was in the opening through which I had felt certain he would come he was almost flat on the ground! Also, he stopped—which was a bad sign. According to later measurements, he was at this time exactly thirty-four yards from me. But I could not see him. I saw his huge rack, the brow-tines of which were broadly palmated; I saw his face. While the back of his neck was almost on the ground, his black muzzle was higher, and tilted upward. That was another bad sign, especially since a slight wind was moving from me to him. Of his body I had not a glimpse.

Well, here was my chance. Or did I have any chance? Lowering my gun until the sight was right in the buck's fore-head, I touched the trigger of the choke barrel. I took the shot when I did because, from the utter wariness and wildness of his look, I was satisfied that he was about to make a bolt backward toward whence he had come. No doubt he had been with the doe, and no doubt he was on his way to rejoin her. But while he may not actually have made me out, there was something about the set-up not to his liking; and, believe me, a buck knows what to do when even the faintest suspicion assails him.

I remember thinking, just before I shot, that if he got away, and I found him later, it would be easy to identify that noble rack. After I shot, I saw absolutely nothing on account of the dense intervening thicket. But I heard a-plenty, and I judged the effect of the shot by the sounds I heard. On his first leap backward he fell headlong. Then I heard long, heavy breathing. Another jump, and he fell again. In fact, I heard him fall four times. Then utter silence followed.

I thought: "He is shot through the lungs, and probably one of his hind legs is broken. If I try to run in on him, he may make a clean get-away with his fast-ebbing strength. If I stay where I am, he will die where he is. I'd better wait right here until Steve comes."

But Steve never hurries. The sun went down. Twilight began to gather. The woods began to get dusky. In the dense thicket into which the buck had gone it was pretty dark. At last came the Negro.

"Steve," I asked, when at last he reached me, "did you see what I saw?"

Immediately his eyes bulged, and he looked warily about, his mind on ghosts.

"Is you done shoot?" he questioned, and I knew he felt like expressing the hope that I had not fired on a spirit.

"The old man himself," I said, "with one of the biggest racks I ever saw. I think he's right here."

I took him to where I had shot the buck, and, to my chagrin, we could see neither blood nor the sign of any special blundering. I told him about the gasping and the falling.

But as our search continued in that eerie thicket, and we came upon absolutely nothing, not even a hopeful sigh, Steve said, "Cap'n, is you sure dat was a real sho'-nuf deer?"

"You aren't scared, are you?" I asked.

"On, no, I ain't scared; but I know my way home better'n I know my way about in dis place."

To tell the truth, it was nearly dark, and we were a long way from home. And while I did not share Steve's superstition, I realized that there was good sense in what he said.

"Early tomorrow," I said, "we'll bring all the hounds. He's a dead deer."

At daybreak the next morning, which was calm and warm, we hied us back to the spot, and this time we had plenty of help. I had not only Steve himself, but I had Prince, Sam, Will, Joe and Precinct; and for hounds I had Sailor, Bing, my beagle, Blue, and Queenie. The latter is not a good looker, and she is crippled; but she has more nose than all of the other hounds, and she'll never notice anything but a deer. Bing is also a good deer dog, but she just can't pass up a bunny.

I decided to stay where I had made my shot, sending the boys about half a mile ahead and around, to come back toward me. The one great danger about hunting for a wounded or a dead deer with hounds is that they are very liable to jump another deer; and if you don't happen to see him, you don't know what to think.

After a while I heard the boys coming my way, whooping a bit to encourage the dogs. When within about four hundred yards of me, Queenie sang out. Then both packs, canine and African, made the woods ring with their wild melody. I was certain they had started the wounded buck and were about to pull him down. Unfortunately they did not head for me, but took a tangent off to my right and around me. I was afraid they were after another deer, yet their progress was so unnaturally slow that I knew they might be on the buck.

I had time to get ahead of them, but a long pond with gloomy waters of unknown depth barred my way. They passed me, and then bore directly behind me, making for the river. Not over three hundred yards from where I was standing, in the heart of a fearful thicket on the rise of a low hill, the whole pack suddenly quit; and by the time the boys got to me, the dogs had also returned.

Not one of the Negroes had seen the deer. I knew it was a deer, or Queenie would never have run him. We held a brief council and decided that it could not have been the buck. In the first place, I thought that if we did find him he would be either dead or too mortally wounded to run anywhere. We decided in a half-hearted way to go up toward the thicket where the hounds had stopped; but they took no trail, and we saw nothing. With a rather heavy heart I gave up the whole thing. I'd always rather make a clean miss than to wound a wild thing and have it die in the wilderness.

Next day, telling Steve that our bad luck had been due to our fooling around a place like Ghost Point, I suggested that we try our chances again. This time I would stay on an old road, and he would amble up the river toward me. If he roused a deer or a turkey, I knew the stand where it would cross.

It so happened that in coming toward me he passed through the very thicket in which the hounds had quit their race. The woods were silent until I heard Steve let out a most clamorous yell, and that was not all—he kept on yelling. Then he began to blow his hunting horn. Under the circumstances that was not so good, for he was blowing three times, and that meant I must come to him. I was afraid he had fallen and hurt himself, or perhaps run afoul of a diamondback rattler. When I first heard him yell, I got ready to shoot at a whole herd of bucks; but when he blew the horn, I gave up that idea and headed for him as fast as I could make it. He never let up on his yelling and his blowing.

When I got near enough for him to hear me, I called to ask him what was the matter.

"I done fin' de big buck!" he shouted.

When I reached good old Steve, he was well-nigh unnerved from excitement. He told me that he had been afraid to stay where he was, but more afraid that, if he once left the place, he could never find it again. And it was easy to believe him, for here was as dense a thicket of myrtles, young pines and gallberries as I have every seen anywhere.

With a trembling forefinger Steve pointed into the dimness of the thicket. I saw horns. There lay my buck, dead. As I approached him, I recognized him immediately by his size and the palmation of his antlers. He was a real monarch of the wilds. Here the hounds had run him and here he had fallen. Any ordinary hound, you know, is not interested in a dead deer; and when the dogs had found him, they just suddenly lost interest in the whole proceeding.

I examined the buck for wounds. He had one shot in the chest, and his left hind leg was broken at the knee. These wounds, of course, accounted for his loud gaspings and for his heavy falling. A deer with a front leg broken is likely to get away; but one with a hind leg smashed finds the going tough, at least at first. They apparently get used to such a handicap, for I have seen a deer with a hind leg sloughed off at the knee, and healed over, get along very well in the woods.

"Well, Steve," I said, "I did not lie to you about this being a real deer and about my hitting him."

Steve's answer was surprising. "Cap'n," he said, "we is hard to beat if you do de shootin' and I do de lyin'."

"It wasn't anything of a shot," I told him. "I simply mean that I tell you the truth."

I could see that Steve had something on his mind. "You always tell it to me, Cap'n," he said; "but if I steal another hog, don't tell it to the judge. Truth is all right," he muttered darkly, "but sometimes you must keep it to yourself."

This was a strange parley to hold over a fallen stag. Yet so it was, and hence I record it.

I have nearly three (?) hundred sets of whitetail antlers. In my dining room I have six of the very finest sets, and of these the horns of the great Ghost Point buck are the largest and the heaviest. As you can well imagine, when I glance up at them, all the vivid details of this strangest of deer hunting adventures come back to me.

THE ROMANCE OF DEER STANDS

In my Carolina coastal country, where the land is as flat as a poet's pocketbook, deer stands, as they are here called, have a very remarkable history, and about them have grown up a lot of truth, legend and folklore. Some of the boys call them crossings. They are one and the same, except that "crossing" is more appropriate for hill country, and "stand" for the level woods.

To me the most wonderful thing about a real stand is that all the changes incident to road building, timber cutting and the like have not altered the habitual runs of the wild deer. In most instances they take the same courses today that they took in 1670, when my part of the world was first opened to the white man. And this consistency of theirs is not hard to explain. Unless we have an earthquake or a tidal wave or a W.P.A. project, the great fundamental features of any wild deer-supporting forest do not greatly change with the centuries. They may seem to change, but in reality they do not.

Here, for example, is a bushy-edged swamp where bucks like to drowse through the day. A couple of miles off yonder is a morass that is a perfect sanctuary for a deer that is pursued. Let us say that these two features of the landscape do not vary. Well, jump a buck today on that swamp-edge, and he will likely take his ancestors' course for the morass. He will do what his fathers have done before him. There is no mystery about it. Yet there is always a fascination about attempting to figure out these runs.

In my baliwick deer runs didn't have to be figured. Our

From *The Woods and Wild Things I Remember* (1970).

fathers did so long ago, and named the stands picturesquely, so that when I was hunting with friends who knew a particular drive I did not have to take them to their stands. In some cases the object that gave the stand its name (as the three giant yellow pines that were the Three Sisters), had long since disappeared. It made no difference. Deer kept right on coming there.

I remember hunting a strange place one day. The man who was to post me was careless. In deer hunting, putting a man at the critical spot should have all the scrupulous care of a religious rite. He said to me, "Cross that swamp, go a hundred yards, and stand by the pond there."

Following his instructions, I found not one pond but three. They were remarkably alike, in a straight line, and some two hundred yards apart. As soon as I saw this layout I had a sinking feeling, and I recalled what I had once heard an old woodsman growl at a hunter who happened to take up a wrong position. "If you don't get on the stand," he said, "you better stay home." Such was my feeling. But, having to do something, I elected to stand by the second or central pond. I had the optimistic idea that this might afford me a triple chance.

Before long a ten-point buck appeared, running easily. But he was not coming to me. He passed me beyond the first pond; and as he was out of range, I just had to watch him, which is not very satisfactory if you love venison and fine antlers.

Later, when I chided my friend about his failure to get me properly located, he looked very much surprised. I told him my difficulty and where I had stood. Then he laughed.

"No buck," he told me, "has run where you stood since a hatchet was a hammer. The stand is by the first pond by the big cypress. You should have been there."

Actually, instead of telling me, he should have taken me there.

I remember posting a friend of mine, a fine friend, but a poor hunter, on a famous crossing. I showed him how a buck was likely to approach. After I had walked away from him I turned and walked back. He was excited enough as it was, and my return almost unnerved him.

"By the way," I said, "we usually run into some wild turkeys in this drive. You had better keep your eyes open for one."

"What does a wild turkey look like?" he asked. And his question was not so dumb as it sounds, for many a hunter is slow to identify wild game in its natural surroundings. I have had a Harvard graduate and a plantation owner take two bucks for "two fine cattle," as he called them.

Before answering my friend's question I looked over the country ahead of him. A wild turkey looks very different in different places. Here was an open, level stretch of woods with scattered big pines that towered high and a low growth of huckleberries on the ground.

"Of course," I said, "you would recognize one in the air if he came flying out, as he is likely to do. But if he comes running out through those huckleberry bushes look for a long black snakelike head and neck above the bushes."

A wild turkey's head is blue, almost indigo; there's also some red about it, and the neck is not black if you examine it in a laboratory. But I was talking of the way a wild bird would look in the woods and at some distance.

Feeling virtuous over the thorough-going way in which I had explained everything, I went about two hundred yards farther, to my own stand. Hardly had I reached the place when I heard him shoot. It is painful to relate, but he had shot at an idly wheeling turkey buzzard, supposing it to be a wild turkey, and had missed it at that. For some reason the drivers and the hounds did not seem to be stirring up much in that drive. I heard some indifferent trailing, but nothing more. Yet once again my friend's gun suddenly blared forth. This blast was followed by a mighty yowling. Against all the laws of deer hunting, I left my stand and strolled toward the place of commotion. My friend met me, more accusing than apologetic.

"You said," he told me, "that if I saw a black snakelike head and neck above those bushes it would be a wild turkey. I'm afraid I shot at the tail of a black hound."

There was no doubt of it. As the dog come up to me I saw that his tail had been broken by buckshot. I promptly christened that place the Broken Tail Stand, and so it remains to this day—a grand deer crossing.

It often happened that a hunter, especially in the old days, was partial to a particular stand—probably because it was the best in the drive. I know one called Dr. Cordes' Stand, one called Old L. P.'s Stand, and one named Morgan's Stand.

The names are sometimes derived from the nature of some memorable encounter that took place there, connoting triumph or disaster. Thus we find the Shirttail Stand, the Doeboy Stand, the Handkerchief Stand and the Six-Master Stand. The first took its name, of course, from a major miss executed there; the second from the slaying of a doe by an overeager hunter; the third from an incident that happened some fifty years ago.

As a little boy I was posted near a very near-sighted old gentleman. I heard the drive advancing, and then I saw two beautiful bucks going straight to him. When the two stags, which he did not see, were within thirty yards of him and coming head on, he decided that would be a good time to clean his glasses. Deliberately taking a huge white handkerchief out of his pocket, he shook out its folds, thereby making a great display. He literally shook it in the faces of the oncoming bucks. They don't like that kind of thing. They swerved widely and passed him without his ever having seen them.

Really great deer heads are, I think, rare anywhere; at least I know many a lifelong deer hunter who has never had a chance at one. The Six-Master Stand took its name from a huge twelve-point buck that was killed at that place a hundred years ago.

Stands are sometimes named from the nature of the places themselves. Among the best I know are the Log Landing, a regular place for deer to take off to swim the river by my house; the Jamb Stand, which is the focal point of several converging runs; the White Stand, a crossing on a road at a point where the sand is always deep and snowy; the Haulover Stand, which is on a river bank at a place where duck shooters haul their boats over; the Savanna Stand, a name that explains itself.

I have hunted deer in the mountains with a rifle and I have hunted them with a shotgun in level country. Always, it seems to me, the problem of choosing a crossing, when one is not known, is the same: the buck is going to take the easiest way from here to there, though perhaps not the most direct. An exception must be made of the badly-scared buck. Give him time, and he will surely make for a crossing. But if he has a right to think that the devil is behind him, he's getting out of there as fast and as straight as he can.

All deer hunters know that in hills and mountains a buck will rarely go straight up a ridge. He knows all about grades. An official of the Pennsylvania Railroad told me that when that road's difficult line was surveyed over the Alleghenies, to achieve the proper rise and descents, the railroad men did not have to vary two feet from the trails made ages ago by the buffalo that then roamed the mountains of our East. And the deer is as good an engineer as the buffalo.

Once, in the Pennsylvania mountains, from high on the crest of a ridge, I saw a whole herd of deer coming my way, unaware of danger. There were eight or ten, led by a tremendous buck. When I first saw them, they seemed to be heading directly up the side of the ridge; I was about three hundred yards off to one side. What I did was to drop behind the ridge and crawl over, so as to place myself directly in the path of their march. I was young then; and while I don't know much now, I knew less then.

Ten minutes later, all ready for my shot of the ages, I peered over the brow of the ridge. Not a deer was in sight. Then I looked back to the place from which I had come. There they were, crossing the very place I had just left! As I might have guessed they would do, they had ascended the slope on an incline. They were zigging while I was zagging, and that is how I lost my shot. Later, when I went back to where I originally had been, I found a distinct deer trail crossing the ridge at that point—a thing I had failed to notice in the first place.

When I say that deer will run for stands, I mean that deer that inhabit a regular range have favorite crossings. But if a deer is a stranger, he may run anywhere. I know a plantation owner who introduced a huge buck from Michigan to try to improve the strain of his native deer. He just turned him loose in his woods, and for years, although regular deer hunts were staged, that old buck survived. He didn't know enough to come to a stand!

Once when hunting in the pinelands during a time of great flood in the river, I saw a most remarkable sight. Between me and the next stander, and out of range from each of us, a herd of twenty-six deer crossed the road. They were strangers, routed from their delta haunts by the high waters. What saved at least some of them was their ignorance.

When a deer crossing is well established where the contour of the land almost compels a buck to run the identical course every time, I always found it wise to take a position a little to the right of the actual crossing. A head-on shot is one of the most difficult of all shots to make on a moving deer, and there are few experiences in the woods more disconcerting to a hunter than to have a big buck come straight for him, as if to run him down and trample him. If you let him cross on your left, you have him where you ought to have him.

A DAY IN THE PINELAND WILDS

To be again in one's boyhood home; to be forty-two miles from a telephone; to stretch one's self in a big armchair before a great fire of pine and live-oak, and to discover, just before dinner, that the plantation had not as yet heard the name of Volstead! Any one of these things should be enough to make a man feel that life was handing him out something pretty fine. But these things were not all, for I had the promise of a long day on the morrow with my brother in the wilds of the Carolina pinelands. It was this prospect more than the distance from city distractions, the genial fire, or the magical bottle of Old '89, that made me feel as carefree and as light-hearted as a lad. It's a good feeling after a man's hair is graying.

It was about six o'clock the next morning when I set forth into the woods. Most deer hunters of the South like to ride, and occasionally I do the same, but it is so long since I have been abe to get a sensible horse for shooting that I prefer walking. In riding up deer, the fact that he is mounted may work against a man; and after a rider has been thrown once or twice, or—worse yet—slammed in the face by the tossed head of a gun-frightened horse, he is going to take a lasting fancy to walking. An all-day walk in the pinelands is not hard; the going is easy, and usually dry; the country is level; and of course a hunter always does a certain amount of still-hunting, which means, in this case, just sitting down and resting, watching and waiting.

My brother and I, when we reached the plantation gateway, unslung our horns and gave a little sunrise serenade. This was

From *Days Off in Dixie* (1925).

to summon Prince, our Negro henchman, who lives a mile across the ricefield from the plantation house. We seldom hunt without Prince. He manages the hounds, helps us decide where to hunt, drives out the small bays and thickets for us, is willing to grin, even at the end of a hard-luck day, and helps us bring the bacon home and dress it. When we blow for him he leaves his cabin and we always meet by the outer plantation gate. There we hold a regular political conference before beginning the great work of the day.

I shall never forget my feelings that morning. For two days I had been cooped in a dusty, musty sleeper, and I had been looking out on a dismal winter landscape as the train carried me Southward. Now, at last, I was at home. The day was fair, warm, and calm. The air was delicious: it was full of all those spicy and aromatic odors that one gets in October in the North when out after ruffed grouse. As my brother and I walked down the sandy, pine-trashed plantation road thickets of holly, myrtle, scrub oak, and pine flanked us on either hand. Everything was hung with dew that glinted in the light of the rising sun. The thickets were full of birds of all kinds—singing, rustling the dead leaves, and flitting happily here and there. I think a migrant's life is an ideal affair.

"Look here," said my brother, pausing and pointing to the gray sand that had been slightly packed by a shower of the previous afternoon, "I have been telling you that they are here. Tracks don't lie."

I counted them. Four deer had crossed the road in the night. This was not half a mile from the house.

"Don't let's fool with them," my brother said. "They've been here all summer and fall. I have seen them: an old buck, a peg-horn, and two does. There are two fawns, too—born right over there in the big myrtle thicket by the ricefield. But they were not along on this party last night. We ought to keep a few near the house like this—just to give the puppies practice."

We now came into the big road a mile from the house, and there the good Negro Prince met us. He is an unassuming, intelligent, genial darky, and when it comes to deer hunting, I hardly know his equal for the particular part that he plays.

"I done already see two this morning," he announced. "Come here, Trigger!" he suddenly yelled at a hound. "I bet I will teach you and Hammer for learn a lesson 'bout huntin'!"

"You saw two, Prince?" I asked.

"Yes, sah, 'bout dayclean, going across the ricefield."

"The two fawns I was telling you about," Tom said.

"What about these two dogs?" I asked, eyeing with a little misgiving the two creatures that Prince had brought with him.

"They will run," my brother said; "but they aren't choicy about the kind of game: rabbits, 'coons, deer, sheep, hogs, people, cattle, turkeys, wood-rats—anything that happens along."

"We ought to get one of those varied bags you read about," I said. Again I looked appraisingly at the dogs. I am careful not to call them hounds. Centuries ago, indeed, a hound may have crossed the trail of one of their ancestors, but these two woolly, lean, foxy-faced, savage, suspicious creatures were what in the Santee country we call just plain nigger dogs. As such, I am sure that they were full blooded. Prince smiled upon them broadly and tolerantly.

"Dis one," said Prince, indicating Trigger, "he done get me in trouble no later than last Sunday."

"How so?" Tom asked.

Prince laughed loudly.

"Dat preacher," he explained, "he done was coming over home to talk to me 'bout my sins; dis dog here 'most done eat up the preacher."

"Did he really hurt him?" I inquired.

"He done tear he pants off," Prince explained with exactness; "and all dem gals done been lookin' on."

"Well, said my brother, "we want to see him tear the pants off one of these old men of the woods to-day."

"Let's go down here to Fairfield Hill," I suggested; "we can tell whether anything walked there last night."

Between our gate and Fairfield we counted many fresh deer tracks, but we had an idea that there was a special show waiting for us down the road on the crest of the big white sandhill. It was so. My brother come upon them first. I heard his low whistle of surprise.

"I didn't know that there were so many of this kind left," he said as Prince and I came up. "Just look here. Six crossed here early this morning; and from their blunt hoofs I know that every one is a buck. They are all fine deer."

"Yes," I agreed, just then seeing what Tom had not seen; "six deer and one ox. Look at this track."

There was a huge imprint beyond the others; deep and wide it was, and as it was some distance from the others, I considered it a lone track.

"One of those old solitary swamp-bucks," said my brother. "Prince," he suggested, "see if your coyotes will take his track."

Trigger and Hammer were brought to bear on the plain trail, that in the damp sand looked remarkably fresh, but they gave it no particular notice.

"They have to see something to run it," I mildly remarked to Prince.

"Dey is pretty good on the hot scent, Cap'n," the Negro replied.

"Specially on a preacher's," Tom put in.

But all this," I said, "reminds me of what old Jake Henderson said a few years ago when he came here from Berkeley County to hunt deer. We had been showing him a lot of signs, and had been bragging of the number of deer we had. 'Well,' he drawled, 'but I ain't lookin' for signs; I'm lookin' for deer.' Let's go after some of these seven."

We struck off to the right through the fragrant pinelands on the calm December morning. The only air that moved was a faint aromatic breeze high up that gently moved the crests of the towering pines. Half a mile off the road we came within sight of a bay-fringed pond. My brother did not speak; but in sign language he told Prince what to do. Then Tom and I tiptoed round to the windward of the dense little piece of cover. In about two minutes, after a few preliminary whistles and shouts, Prince squalled. His voice hits high C whenever he sees a whitetail flaunt before him. In this instance he had jumped two deer, a buck and a doe, and the dogs were almost upon them before they left their cover. I hardly had time to slide my safety up before I saw something coming my way. Unfortunately, I had done a foolish thing in taking my stand. Selecting a pine stump for shelter, I had sat down in the broomgrass behind it, with my legs stretched out in the warm sunshine. Now, it is all right for a man to sit on a log, or on some kind of slight elevation. But when a man is sitting flat down and two deer come tearing along straight for him, with two hounds running almost under them, he is awkwardly placed. Many an old deer hunter of my acquaintance believes that the steadiest shot at a running deer is made from the knee. How often have I seen a real hunter who, running down a road to cut off a deer, when he reached what he chose as the place to stop, would drop to one knee and a moment later salute correctly the road-jumping cyclone with horns! But I wasn't fixed at all; and I was afraid to move for fear of violently turning the two deer. On they came—a beautiful sight in the dewy morning woods. Their course was straight for me; I was positively embarrassed. I felt as if I ought to get out of the way. And I am telling a true thing when I say that if I had not been directly behind the big stump, some ten feet high, the deer would probably have jumped over me. As it was they made a slight swerve in deference to the stump, and rushed past me at a distance of about four feet. The buck was in the lead by a yard. I killed him as he was passing me. But it was a crude and boyish shot; and because of my cramped position, and of the fact that I was busily blaming myself for taking it, the shot came near being a miss. However, the male of the species was tumbled over, and in a few minutes my brother and Prince had joined me, and we viewed with satisfaction the fallen stag. He was not a remarkable deer, but he was a fine piece of venison and he was ours. We carried him back to the pond where he had jumped and there hung him on a stout tree-bay. We got him well off the ground, for in those pinelands there are razorbacks that like nothing so well as a deer that you leave carelessly where they can get hold of it. And you haven't seen a thing properly torn to pieces until you have seen what is left when a gang of these brutes gets through with a deer.

We now struck off westward through the day-brightened pinelands. We were in a tract of virgin timber, and as far as we could see in every direction the huge shafts of yellow pines towered into the blue sky. In walking along through this magnificent stretch of timber we separated; Prince and the dogs took the middle, and my brother and I were about a hundred yards respectively on either side of him. There was little undergrowth, but the broomsedge was tall, and in this on sunny, still days in winter deer are very fond of bedding. We struck no deer in this stretch, although the three of us counted eleven fresh beds. But I was very much surprised and pleased to see the number of coveys of quail that we flushed just walking along casually. We saw seven coveys in this one reach of the pinelands. These were strictly birds of the woods, and they fly very much farther than quail of cultivated lands. Moreover, it is their habit to make for some swamp or heavy bay when molested. I am sure that, as far as human hunters are concerned, they can take very good care of themselves.

Leaving the big timber we began to cross a ragged strip of woods that had been logged only two years before. It was full of old pine-tops, tangled vines that had grown over fallen trees, and heavy patches here and there of scrub-oak and young long-leaf pine.

"Better deer country," said my brother to me, "than what we have just been through. A buck loves a pine-top. Let me tell you what Jim Morrison told me the other day: he said that he was lumbering near Wambaw Swamp not long ago, and toward the end of a certain day his men cut down a monster of a short-leaf pine, whose big top he admired very much. The very next morning when he returned to the place he went up to the fallen pine, when out of the dense crest there jumped a fine old buck. He had chosen it for his bed on the first night that it was on the ground."

We decided to let Prince drive out some little pine thickets for us, and Tom and I took up stands with which we have been familiar since boyhood. I had just located myself when I heard one of the hounds give an opening yelp.

"Warm trail," I said to myself; "something's been here since daylight. Of course, it may not be a deer, but they love this place."

About two hundred yards off to my left I heard a wild turkey give one querulous note. I looked over. It was my brother signalling to me to be on the lookout.

Of course, every sportsman has his own ideas of what is the most thrilling moment in the great game of hunting. And an interesting chapter could be written on these various exciting situations, but to me that moment in life is most interesting when, on a deer-stand in good country, I hear a dog open, and, if I am fortunate, have my brother signal to me to be watchful.

I listened keenly, but no further sounds came from the dogs. That is what comes from not using real hounds. If I had had a good trailer he would have been singing the Song of Songs. The next sound I heard was an astonishing one. In a pine thicket on a small sandy hill about two hundred yards form me four big deer got up, and they got up flying. I believe that Trigger and Hammer had nosed them out of their beds. I never heard so much floundering and so much tumultuous muffled racket. But they did not come our way. Deer have a habit of disappointing one in that respect. As soon as I guessed that they were headed away from my brother and me, I stood on a pine log and watched the four splendid creatures make off through the pinelands. It was a great sight, and it was unusual in that I was permitted to watch them so far. For almost a mile I could see their stiffly erect tails go glimmering off into the distance. But somehow there is less beauty to a hunter in one of these vanishing flags than there is flaunting defiance.

I motioned to Tom, and he came quickly over and joined me.

"There were four," I explained, "and they ran for Boggy Bay. The dogs are after them now."

"Let's go over to where they got up," he said. "Prince must be there now."

Forthwith we entered the little pine thicket, and within a few minutes came upon Prince.

"How close were you?" I asked.

"Been on dem," he said, his disappointment showing in his honest face. "Oh, look out!" he suddenly cried.

I caught in the corner of my left eye the flash of a white tail. It was not thirty yards off, but the thicket was dense. Running to the edge of it I saw two more deer making off. These six had been lying up there together. and those two had probably jumped up with the first four; but they had not decamped until we obliged them to.

By this time the two so-called dogs returned.

"They probably lost sight of the deer," my brother suggested with mild sarcasm. "These two other deer were plenty close enough for us to shoot if we had had clear woods."

"I think they have gone into the Briar Bed," I said. "Why not let Prince go round by the Rattlesnake Branch, while we take up the two stands on the road?"

To this plan we agreed; whistling to the dogs we made off through the woods to the westward. Our way led through the timber slashing, which is unlike similar places in the North and West in that no wilderness of sprouts succeeds the removal of the big timber. We saw deer signs innumerable, and we saw more than mere signs, for once, a hundred yards form us, an old doe and her yet unweaned fawn rocked out of a patch of huckleberries. It was a pretty sight to see them going.

My brother paused by a stout scrub oak tree under which the ground was bare to show me something.

"I think he was here last night," he said; "see where this old buck has raked and pawed this ground. This is a sure sign that he is still running. The fact is, I am sure, that our deer continue to mate until January is nearly gone."

When we came out into the big road on which we were to stand, Prince left us to take a big circle in the wildwoods beyond us known as the Briar Bed. He would return to us, bringing, we hoped, something in front of him. My brother and I walked down the sunny road which stretched for many a mile straight through the glimmering pinewoods. We were the only people on that lonely road, and perhaps a week might pass without another human being passing that way. But it is a road over which deer cross by the hundreds every day and night. The largest number ever recorded as having crossed it as a herd was twenty-five. This phenomenal sight occurred about twenty years ago, at a time when the Santee River was in flood, and when doubtless many swamp deer had joined their fellows of the open woods.

We came to a gurgling wood-stream that flowed under a wooden bridge spanning the road. As we were within easy reach of our stands, we sat down on the bridge to eat our lunch and to talk of the old days of our boyhood, when we had many a time hunted in these very same drives near this bridge. I recalled having had a bunch of thirty-five wild turkeys walk out to me on the stand just beyond the watercourse, and Tom remembered the ensuing bombardment. Those turkeys were so bewildered that I actually got seven shots before they cleared themselves. But don't imagine that I got seven turkeys. My brother reminded me of the double that he had made on bucks near a small pond visible from where we were sitting. He shot both down, whereupon each one got up and sailed away in a discouragingly sprightly fashion. But we overhauled them. One had been shot through the heart, and one across the spine.

We had been on the bridge half an hour before we heard Prince. He was as yet far off, and he had roused nothing, but he was coming toward us; therefore we separated and took up our stands. I sat on an old pine log and drank in the sunshine; any man can stand the grind of office life if he has the memory or the prospect of a few days a year of sunshine-drinking.

When Prince was half a mile immediately in front of me I suddenly heard him squall. It meant that he had started deer. Then I heard the alleged dogs, but they were going in the wrong direction. I was sorry, for I wanted Tom to shoot. He must have wished to accommodate me because off to my left beyond the watercourse and the bridge I heard his gun—one barrel and then another.

"Two barrels from him call for two deer," I said, quitting my stand to join him.

When I came up he was standing in the road. But I saw no deer.

"It's all right," he said, not in the least excited. "A big peg-horn tried to pass me on my left here. It was about a seventy-five yard shot, but we'll get him. I saw him change his stride; you know what that means."

"I know what black blood means, too," I told him, pointing to the trail of it crossing the white sand of the road.

"Let him lie down," my brother advised. "When Prince comes with the dogs we can get him."

Within five minutes the Negro appeared, and to him we explained the situation. The dogs actually seemed to want to take the trail; it was because of the blood. I took a circle in the woods; Tom and Prince then turned the dogs loose. Within three minutes they bounced the buck, and in half as many more he was down. When we examined him we found that two buckshot had struck him, one in the paunch and one in the neck—either one fatal.

We now had two deer, and the afternoon sun was slanting. I looked inquiringly at my brother.

"Home for to-day," he said; "by the time we get these two dressed it will be dark."

We knew a Negro living near, and we borrowed his horse and wagon to take the deer home; the second one we picked up as we neared the bounds of the plantation. One further incident enlivened the closing day. Just outside the plantation gateway Trigger suddenly swerved to the left toward a small branch grown densely to sweet bays. On the edge of it he jumped three beautiful deer—an old buck and two does. They were hardly a hundred yards from the road and in full sight. They started head-on for the road; then they checked up and did a little flirtation dance; pressed by Trigger, who had not been joined by Hammer, they whirled broadside and did some spectacular jumping—fake jumping, I call it. They turned for the road again, and again they shied. I never saw deer play so prettily and so jauntily. Both Tom and I had our guns ready, but something restrained us. The shot would have been a long one, and then, we already had two bucks for that day. For at least five minutes the deer played with the dogs; then the buck must have spied us clearly, or else winded us. He whirled, laid his great head back on his broad shoulders, and went tearing in earnest through the bay-thicket. His two consorts followed him with graceful speed. We saw them once more when they emerged from the covert and crossed an open pine ridge.

"It's good to see them, isn't it?" Tom asked; "it's almost as good as bagging them."

"Yes, Cap'n," Prince said; "but it ain't so good to see one gittin' away if you ain't got none to 'company you home."

THE GRAY STAG OF
BOWMAN'S BANK

This title sounds as if a story is to follow; and I suppose this narrative might be dignified by calling it a story. But distinctly it is not fiction. It is just a matter-of-fact account of a rather unusual deer hunt that I was fortunate enough to enjoy during the Christmas season of 1919. The circumstances surrounding it were somewhat romantic, perhaps; and there was a coincidence involved that seldom occurs, even in the big woods, where almost anything unexpected is likely to happen.

The time was the 31st of December, and the place the pinelands near the mouth of the Santee. I had been at home on the plantation for a week and had had some successful hunting, but most of my time had been spent in fighting a far-reaching forest fire that threatened destruction to everything inflammable in the great coastal plain of Carolina. I know for a fact that this fire burned over a territory forty miles deep by more than a hundred miles long. Of course, here and there it was cut off; but for the most part it made a clean sweep. The wild life of the countryside suffered less in this conflagration than might have been expected; and more than once I saw deer which seemed not in the least dismayed by the roaring flames near them. Finally the fire passed us, and then I took to the woods as usual with my gun.

On several successive trips I hunted deer near a place called Bowman's Bank, a wild and solitary stretch of swampy country about four miles from home. In the old sandy road that dipped down from the wild pinelands, I had seen a track that showed

From *Plantation Game Trails* (1921).

the maker to be a stag worth following. It was, indeed, I suspected, the track of a very old friend of mine—one who on a
certain occasion had played me a kind of a mean trick. He got
the thing off in the manner I now describe.

Early one October morning, two years before this, a party
of us had been hunting near Bowman's Bank. In the big main
road we had come upon a track so large and so fresh that we had
decided to let the hounds take it; but before we slipped them
from the leash, four of us tiptoed a half-mile through the dewy
morning woods and took up the well-known stands at the head
of the bank. Within a few minutes we heard the dogs open as
they were loosed, and they lost no time in coming our way. From
the manner in which they kept bearing hard toward the left, I
felt sure that the buck would come out to me. The hounds
surely were bringing glad tidings in my direction. They clamored
through the deep bay-thicket ahead of me; they were so close
that I saw them. But no deer appeared. He must have dodged,
thought I, and I listened for the gun of one of my partners.
Suddenly the hounds broke out of the branch and headed straight
up the easy hill toward me. They came flying on the trail, and
straight at me; yet not a sign of what they were running could I
see. With some difficulty I stopped them and tied them up.
Then I examined the ground. A big running track had come
head-on over my stand. The buck must have heard us coming,
and made off over my crossing about a minute before I reached
it! The thing hurt me, for I had the crazy idea that a hunter
sometimes gets that a certain old stag belongs to him by rights,
despite a clever getaway and other significant facts. I felt no
better when our party had gathered and when the stander next
to me said:

"I saw the deer. I was up on a little ridge when you were
in a hollow, Arch; and he went out about a hundred yards ahead
of you. He surely was a beauty—and a peculiar-looking buck,
too. He seemed an iron-gray color to me; and his horns were
enough to give him the headache."

Well, ever since that day I had had a leaning toward Bowman's Bank which was nothing but my hankering after another
sight of the gray stag that had played me so heartless a trick.
And the track that I had begun to pick up in the vicinity of the
bank gave me reasonable hope that my wish might be fulfilled.
Although several expeditions into that section of the woods had

yielded me only a spike buck, I had a feeling that something else was waiting for me there. That instinct in hunting is not a bad thing to follow; for while I have small faith in premonitions and the like, I do believe in anything that exacts patience from a hunter. In fact, it has been my experience that a man in the woods gets the chance he wants if he keeps in the game long enough.

One afternoon after dinner, which on a Southern plantation means about three o'clock, I got on a horse and turned his head toward the Bowman Bank region. In many places in the pine forest the woods were still smouldering, and as the afternoon was still and warm, the smoke hung low. Occasionally a smoking mass of débris of some kind would suddenly burst into flame. So prevalent was the smoke that I saw myself coming home within an hour or two with nothing to show for my afternoon's ride.

Turning off from the main road I made my horse circle a small pond fringed with bays. From the farther side of the pond I was suddenly aware of a deer slipping silently out. It was too far for a shot; and it melted with astonishing quickness into the haze that now was hanging everywhere. Had I been on foot I might have come much closer on that deer, I thought. Therefore I dismounted and tied my horse on a strip of burnt ground, where, I knew, whatever fire happened to spring up near him could not cross to reach him. I went forward then on foot toward Bowman's Bank, taking the identical route that I had followed that October morning two years before when the gray stag had outwitted me. The sun was now taking a last red and glaring look through the smoke. The aspect of the forest was weird and anything but inviting. But in hunting, a man has to take the rough with the easy; and not infrequently it is the poor-looking chance which yields the luck.

On account of the smoke, and because the sun was now going down, I knew that I had but a short while in which to do what I was going to do. There would be no long and dewy twilight, with an afterglow in which a man can see to shoot. Night and the pall of smoke would soon shut out the world from human vision. Prospects were discouraging, but I trudged onward.

Perhaps it will not be amiss for me to say that the kind of deer hunting I was now doing is of the type that I have long

enjoyed and found successful. Because the pinelands are inter-
laced at almost regular intervals with narrow bay-branches, which
are small watercourses grown to low underbrush, it is possible
for a man to walk these out and get about as many and as sporty
chances at deer as he can have in any other way. It approaches
stalking as nearly as any hunting in the Southern woods can
approach it. I sometimes go thus alone, and sometimes with a
friend; and I have had as much luck hunting without a hound as
with one. A man gets his money's worth when, in this type of
still-hunting, he bounces an old stag out of his bed, and has to
hail him for business reasons within the range commanded by a
shotgun. I find that a Parker twelve-gauge, with thirty-inch barrels, gives good results when loaded with this shell, which is the
best I have ever seen used on deer: U.M.C. steel-lined Arrow,
high-base; two and three-fourths inches long; twenty-eight grains
Infallible smokeless; one and one-eighth ounces of buckshot.
The second size of buckshot is preferred to the big ones, the
very best being those that chamber sixteen to a shell. I was
loaded with two of these shells on that smoky twilight that will
live in my memory as long as memory and such things last.

About halfway I had come to a certain wide arm of swampy growth that
stretched out from the dim sanctuary of Bowman's Bank, and
was undecided as to whether I should cross it or pass round its
edges. I decided on the former course. My way was none too
easy. Smoke worried my eyes. A fire of some four years previous
had left the swamp full of black snags. There were slippery
hummocks of sphagnum moss and sudden pools of black water.
It is a hard thing for a man to watch his footing when he is intent
on looking for something else. Yet his footing is a vital matter;
for if he misses it at the critical moment, his chance may be
gone.

About halfway across the melancholy morass into which I
had ventured I felt as if I might just as well turn back. If anything
did get up, there was hardly enough light for a shot—certainly
not enough light for a decent chance. Besides, off to the left a
terrible fire had suddenly begun to rage, and it appeared unreasonable to suppose that any wild life would be lying serenely so
close to that withering sweep of destruction. But strange are the
ways of nature, and strange are the things that sometimes happen
to a woodsman.

As I was toiling on in a half-hearted way, suddenly above

the dull roar and the sharp crackle of the fire I heard a familiar sound. It was the "rip" of a deer out of bay-bushes. I located the sound before I saw the deer. A buck with big antlers had jumped some thirty yards ahead of me, a little to my right. He had been lying on the very edge of the swampy arm, and on the farther side from the point at which I had entered it. I saw his horns first, and they were good to look upon. They gleamed high in the smoke. For the first twenty yards or so he ran like a fiend, in one of those peculiar crouching runs that a buck assumes when he wants to make a speedy start. He hardly had his tail up at all. My gun was at my shoulder, but because of a dense screen of black gum and tupelo trees, I had no chance to put anything on him. And he was getting away on all six cylinders! But he was bearing a little to the left—to run over the regular stand. It was the identical stand where the buck had escaped me before. Into the gap between two trees I threw my sight. By the time the stag reached it, he thought he was clear; for the rabbit-like contortions through which he had gone at his start had given place now to regulation long leaps, with a great show of snowy tail. Indeed, that tail was the thing on which I laid my gun. But the shot seemed hopelessly far. Just beyond the stand that the buck was about to cross was a thicket of young pines. I must shoot before he reached that. Holding on the regimental flag as accurately as I could, I fired. The second barrel was ready to let go, but not a sign of a deer could be seen. "He is gone," thought I; "he's gone into that pine-thicket. It was too far, and too smoky."

I crossed the remaining part of the swamp and made my way slowly up the sandy hill. A huge pine marks the stand there. To my amazement, stretched beside the pine lay the stag, stone dead. He lay exactly where I had stood two years before. And he was iron-gray in color! Had I been one of the ouija-board people, I suppose I should have run. But I just stood there in the twilight admiring the splendid old stag, and wondering over my absolutely dumb luck in getting him, and over the strange coincidence that I had killed him precisely where he had once escaped me. For there was no doubt in my mind that this was the same old buck. Every hunter knows how a stag will take possession of a certain territory and remain in it for many years. As to his color, I suppose that he had some strain of albinism in him. I have seen other gray deer in that part of the country; and, within twenty miles, several pure albinos have been killed.

That my luck was extraordinary I did not fully appreciate until the buck was dressed, when I discovered that the buckshot had struck him in a peculiarly vital manner. Two shots only reached him. Both of these entered the small of the back just forward of the left haunch, and ranged forward through the body, through the neck, and lodged behind the jaw. It was no wonder that he came down without any preliminary flourishes. Had he not been going up a slight rise from me those shots probably would have taken him in the haunches and he might have kept right on. More than once I have taken old buckshot out of a deer's haunches, and the deer themselves appeared to be in prime condition.

Leaving the stag, I walked down into the swamp, carefully pacing off the distance. This I found to be eighty-nine steps. It was too long a shot; but the break had come my way. The question now was how to get my stag out of the woods. But here, too, luck favored me.

I walked toward the main road, hoping to meet a Negro. To meet a Negro in the pinelands is the easiest thing a man has to do. I met one within a few hundred yards. He and I managed to get the old buck out to the road. It happened that two sisters of mine had driven down in a spring wagon for the mail, the post-office being some five miles from home. As I reached the road, I saw the wagon approach in the dusk.

"Have you much mail?" I asked my sisters; "I have a little package here I'd like you to take home for me."

CATCHING THEM ON THE DEW

"If them there ole bucks don't run to the regular stands, why don't you go a-jumpin' of 'em? But you must catch 'em on the dew."

"All right, Ned," I answered, "but you'll have to give me a word of direction about this kind of deer hunting."

"Walk or ride," said Ned, in his slow fashion, always speaking gravely and deliberately when discussing a sportsman's question. And I listened with all my listeners, for Ned Fort has killed upward of seven hundred and fifty deer, and he has taken all of them fairly. "If you ride," he continued, "you ought to have a horse that won't pitch you if you shoot. I favors walkin', for then I has just one critter to steady—and that's myself. Even the gentlest horse is a-goin' to fidget if a buck rips under its nose. Lordy!" he ejaculated softly, his eyes lighting with reminiscent pleasure, "but I have burnt 'em a-jumpin'! But don't ride a mule," he cautioned emphatically; "not unless you want the seat of your pants slammed up to where you wears your hat."

That was the end of our conversation, yet those few words from one of the famous deer hunters of the Southern pinelands led me to take up a new kind of deer hunting that has afforded me days of the most thrilling sport imaginable. To give an idea of the nature of this sport, I can best do so by telling just how I went about it and by recording the results of my experiments.

I had long hunted deer on and near my old plantation home on the coast of South Carolina. The country is comparatively level, and for the most part it is a piney-wood wilderness. Along the rivers are gross swamps of big timber, while the pineland

From *Plantation Game Trails* (1921).

reaches are broken by innumerable bays and the like. These are like little green watercourses in winter woods. Of course, in this kind of a forest much greenery prevails, even in mid-winter, and the broomgrass, while yellowed, is still standing straight, in contrast to what happens to similar growths in the North.

Formerly I had hunted deer according to the usual custom in the South. Several of us would take stands at the heads of bays, then the driver would put the dogs in the foot of the thicket. I had, in other years, killed many in that way, but for some reason the sport had fallen off. Consequently, when Ned Fort, the greatest deer-slayer of my acquaintance, advised me to "jump them on the dew" I was receptive to his plan.

I happened to be the only hunter on the plantation that December; therefore what was to be done had to be done single-handed. Of course, I had hounds, but for this particular work I decided to use one only, and that the slowest dog in the pack. But Blue, though slow, was possessed of a notably cold nose. To summarize my hunting equipment it consisted of the following: One hunter, one hound, one twelve-gauge Parker shotgun, with thirty-inch barrels that know how to reach them at eighty yards, and a sufficient number of buckshot and turkey-shot shells. I usually hunt in a tan-colored sweater, carrying my buckshot in my right-hand pocket and my turkey-shot in the left. In a small pocket high up I carry two shells from which all the shot charge except two buckshot has been drawn. These are for instant use in an emergency; to finish a buck cleanly that does not need a whole load, but which does need something more than a careless approach with a hunting-knife. I have long since learned not to monkey with a wounded buck.

Having gathered this equipment I left the plantation house at six-thirty of a winter's morning. I was walking. The hound, Blue, I led with a rawhide strap. There had been a rain the afternoon before; consequently I knew that all the tracks I should see crossing the sandy pineland roads would be fresh. The morning was clear and cool. There was hardly a breeze stirring. The woods were as fragrant as Northern forests are in October. The conditions were ideal for me to jump them on the dew.

A half-mile from the plantation gate, while still in the main road, I came upon the track of a fine buck. It was so fresh that it looked warm. It smelled warm, too, according to Blue's opinion. He almost broke away from me. I pulled him back, tried to smother his long-drawn yowl, and considered the situation. The buck had not been gone more than an hour. He was heading through the open pine-woods for a pond known as Fawn Pond, which, being surrounded by a dense growth of bays, was a favorite place for deer to lie in the daytime. It looked like my chance to sample Ned Fort's brand of deer hunting. I therefore decided to loose Blue and to follow him closely. That he would jump the buck was a foregone conclusion. The question was, would I be close enough for a shot? "Close enough" with a shotgun means any distance up to eighty yards. I have killed a deer at one hundred and eight measured yards, but that was pure chance. "After forty yards uncertainty begins," is a tried maxim. With all conditions right I should put the limit of uncertainty at fifty. A man can sometimes kill cleanly at eighty yards, but between fifty and eighty the chances are against his doing so.

As soon as I loosed Blue he did a characteristic thing: he smelled at the tracks voraciously, his tail waving exultantly. Then he turned completely around with a waltz motion, sat down on his haunches, threw his head up, and gave vent to a marvelous note. It sounded as if yards and yards of canvas were being musically torn. As the Negroes in that part of the country would say, Blue's feelings were "sweeted." The buck's scent thrilled him so that he had to express his emotions with some degree of ceremony. Having thus relieved himself of some of his keenest feeling, he began to follow the track, slowly and certainly, giving at irregular intervals his glorious music. Nearly every time he would turn around, and he continued his sitting down until by mischance in his fervor he sat on a sharp pine-knot. But he made up that lapse in ceremony by holding his tail higher.

As we advanced through the woods and as the trail became hotter, Blue's bark became shorter, and he no longer turned around. I didn't have to tramp his heels either; the best I could do was to keep up with him. By his change of tone and by his increasing speed I knew that we were drawing in very close. As the morning was warm and still the buck might be lying down in the broomgrass in the open woods. But as the day promised to be a bright one I thought it likelier that the crafty creature had hidden himself in the dense sweet bays and gallberries which surrounded Fawn Pond. But wherever he was I was ready for a sight of him.

Unless a deer happens to be standing, the easiest shot at

him is afforded if he is going straightaway. That, at least, has been my experience. The broadsides and the quartering shots (especially those on the right) are difficult. And what is true in this respect of the shotgun is likewise true of the rifle. I do not use a rifle in this hunting, but my brother does, and he tells me that his hardest shot is a right-hand quartering. A head-on shot isn't easy either; one thing that makes it hard probably being the inevitable excitement that a hunter feels if a buck turns and comes straight for him at close quarters. I find that the peculiar rocking motion of a deer's gait is liable to confuse the aim. To offset this I never "follow" a running deer with my gun trying to get the bead on him. To shoot at a deer in this way usually results in the deer's having a tickled tail or possibly a punctured paunch. The gun must be thrown in ahead of the deer. Then, when he jumps into the vision, nail him. There is a knack in it, and hunters following these directions might miss. As a man said indignantly to me one day: "I did just what you told me. I let him come into the sights, but he just jumped over the shot." I heard an old deer hunter describe one of his best long shots in this way: "He came riding the briars. As he darkened I kindled, and as I kindled he courtesied."

But to return to this other lordly creature I was after and which I was expecting to jump any minute. On coming within gunshot of Fawn Pond I left Blue to work out his end of the business while I tiptoed over to the windward side of the pond. My eyes were not taken off the place. I went on the windward side because I knew the buck would jump into the wind, even if he did get a scent of me. There before me lay the round green bay, the whole thing not a half-acre in extent. Was anybody at home? The green bay-leaves shimmered in the light of the rising sun. A pair of towhees rustled in the edges of the thicket. On the limb of a big cypress that grew in the pond I saw a black fox squirrel crouched craftily. I wondered what else besides a man and a hound he might be seeing. Perhaps he saw a beam of fresh sunlight penetrating the bays and myrtles and gleaming on polished antlers.

By this time Blue had entered the edge of the pond. There for a moment he was silent—evidently baffled. Then there came a great outcry from him, and forthwith out bounded a beautiful buck. He had jumped straight into the wind, his course bringing him within forty yards of me. I shot him dead.

"Well, Blue," I said to the eager hound as I hung the buck on a cypress by the pond, "we surely caught that fellow on the dew. How about another one?"

Blue was game, so on we headed through the piney-wood wilderness. It happened to be the end of a very long dry season. In other deer woods such a circumstance would have rendered still-hunting conditions impossible, making anything like a stealthy approach out of the question. But in those Southern woods much of the ground over which I traveled is normally under water. Now, however, the water had disappeared, leaving a springy footing of damp sphagnum moss. I believe there is no footing in the world that can be as absolutely soundless as this. Such moss appears to absorb sound as it does water. Some of my success undoubtedly was due to the stealth of my approach. Indeed, what happened next never could have occurred under normal conditions.

Neglecting to follow Blue on a little side trail that I believed amounted to nothing, he jumped a deer out of gunshot from me and took it flying away through the woods. I decided to bide my time in the neighborhood, knowing well that both deer and dog would soon come back. My experience has been that when a deer is started, especially by one slow dog, it will play in front of its pursuer, dodging, mazing the trail and doubling, frequently returning to the place whence it was jumped. While waiting I "cruised" about craftily, examining signs. Where I was the deer-paths were as numerous and as well defined as sheep-paths in a pasture or hog-paths in a "crawl."

My immediate environment consisted of a wide amphitheater, level, grown with gallberry and huckleberry bushes, and surrounded by swampy thickets grown to heavy timber. I was then only about four miles from the plantation house, yet it was a region so primeval that, as far as traces of his visits or occupancy were concerned, man might never have seen the place. There is a vast difference in appearance and in spirit between natural wildness and the desolate wildness that sometimes marks the track of man. This region where I now found myself was wild, romantic, lonely, beautiful, and full of a brooding quiet and mystery. As I walked on over beds of gay-colored moss I wondered how long it had been since a human being had hunted there. I stooped to pick up a huge stag's antler, bleached by sun and rain. Suddenly, not six feet from where I stood a doe bounded up. She made a couple of regular jumps and then a super-bound. My gun was on her, but I had a heart. She stopped broadside at fifty yards, her beautiful face full of puzzled wonder as she gazed back at me curiously. As I stood motionless I think she had a hard time making me out. In any event, she watched me for a full minute before she took some stealthy little rabbit-jumps into a thicket. I doubt if she really recognized me. Just as she was disappearing a second doe threw herself out of her bed and rocked off lithely. I had it on her, too, but even though it is legal to do so, killing a doe never gives me any sport.

The beds that the two deer had just left were examined. Evidently to a deer a bed is what a "squat" is to a rabbit. A buck prefers to lie down where his antlers have some play, but a doe delights to creep into bed, selecting the coziest places. One of these beds was in a natural hollow on damp, bare ground, the little nook being overhung with gallberry bushes. The other was in a clump of thick bushes against the base of a great pine. It was evident to me, from the deep foot-tracks in the beds themselves, that these deer had bounded from where they lay. I had always been of the opinion that deer could do that, but its truth had never before been so clearly demonstrated.

Farther on a second antler was found, this one being from another buck. On the sandy ridge spanning the huckleberry savannah there were deer signs innumerable. Turkeys had been there, too. It was the kind of place to make a sportsman happy.

Presently the voice of Blue, which had passed far out of my hearing, was heard returning. Knowing that the deer would be far ahead of him (not in actual distance, but in time, since the dog would have to unravel the dodging trail), I sat down on a pine-log. Inside of five minutes here came the deer—hopping along, then walking with head down, skulking it through, for all the world like a rabbit. He was only forty yards away and he did not see me. But from all the signs that were thereabout I felt sure that there must be something for me of a more respectable size. That spike buck will never know how close a call he had. When Blue, toiling on the mazy track, came up, I put the strap on him, led him away from the trail, and persuaded him to lie down for a while.

By the time we recommenced our hunt it was well on toward ten o'clock. Most of the winter morning's dew was gone. But having denied myself three pot-hunter, pot-shot chances, it seemed not unreasonable to hope that the gods of sport would let the bearer of a brush-heap come my way. I communicated my thoughts to Blue, and he agreed that more sport was ahead for us.

Following the sandy ridge for half a mile, making sure that Blue would not run foul of the many fresh doe tracks that had been made in my presence, we turned into a thicket of pines that were permanently dwarfed. They were not over five feet high, and the group of them covered several acres. I knew this to be good buck ground, for a buck loves a place from which he can clear himself (antlers included) with no loss of time. As we were following one of the paths, my attention was attracted by torn places in the thick sphagnum moss. They were the tracks of a great buck and they looked fresh. As soon as the hound got to them, he said that they were. I knew, of course, that in a place so remote and secret, deer would walk later in the morning than they would if they were close to civilization. This meant that my buck might be standing in the young pines or might be lying down near me serenely chewing his cud.

"Find him, Blue," I whispered, slipping the strap.

As I stood up and as the hound tore off his first grand-opera note, out from a dense clump of young pines there flashed a tail that looked to me as broad as a regimental flag. I fired. Down he came, and when Blue and I reached him he was dead. A magnificent creature he was, a twelve-pointer, with a very unusual spread of antlers. I looked at my watch. It was ten-fifteen.

"Blue," I said, "catching them on the dew is the thing."

Hanging up this buck I returned to the plantation, rode back leading a second horse, and so got the venison safely home.

A few days later, using the same methods, I shot two more deer, besides passing up four easy chances. It all led me to the conclusion that this kind of deer hunting has less tediousness in it than any which I have ever enjoyed, and the excitement when it came was about all with which I could conveniently get away.

OLD FIVE-MASTER

I have told about enjoying a hunt after an exceedingly varied lot of game. Sometimes a hunter goes after one particular individual; and the more of a personality that creature possesses, the less likelihood there is that the sportsman's design will be achieved. This is natural; for certain individuals develop a wariness so acute and a shadowy avoidance so perfect in its technique that they not only save their lives but they become almost legendary because of their sagacity.

Every real deer hunter knows well that certain stags have earned a right to special names; their wariness, their acute intelligence, their way of escaping by doing the unexpected—these and other qualities lead to their christening. And I have little doubt that there is hardly a deer camp in America, or a deer region, where tales of these famous old bucks are not told. To me they are among the most interesting of all wild life legends. Some may be exaggerated, but all have enough truth to make them worth preserving.

Since boyhood days I have taken a great interest in stories of this kind, and I have followed a good many of these elusive old stags myself. I killed the famous Crippled Buck of St. James Parish, in Carolina, after following him for six years. Although he was a cripple, his speed was in no way impaired, and his keenness seemed to be positively increased because of his injury. But it is of a more celebrated stag that I want to tell my fellow sportsmen. It is of Old Five-Master, who earned his singular name because of his habit of skulking and dodging and running rings around the standers only to terminate the chase by swim-

From *An American Hunter* (1937).

206

ming the broad yellow reaches of the Santee, escaping to the immense delta country beyond, a wilderness of reedy bogs into which it is vain for the hunter to venture.

One day this buck performed his usual maneuver. One of my friends climbed a cypress tree in a field bordering the river to see if he could make out the fugitive. Well I remember what he called down to me.

"I see the old rascal!" he said. "And he's nearly across. And his horns make him look like a five-masted schooner." From that time we never called this buck anything but Old Five-Master.

He would not stay on the delta. After lingering in that semitropical morass for a week or so, he would return to the mainland, and of course we would again take up his pursuit.

The sagacity of this great deer illustrates so well the deep intelligence of the whitetail, wherever he is found, that all who have followed this prince of American game animals will be willing to credit the following anecdotes relative to his wildwood smartness.

On one occasion a friend of mine, having determined to waylay Old Five-Master on one of his return trips from the delta to the mainland, haunted the western edges of the river for a period of full ten days, staying until complete darkness had fallen, and taking up his vigil again at the crack of dawn. The buck would usually cross the river just after sundown.

At last the watcher's long wait was rewarded. From the high bluff of Fairfield Plantation he saw, just as the sun had dipped below the towering yellow pines in the west, the wary old fugitive emerge from the distant wilderness of the delta and enter the water. The man had plenty of time to place himself at a point on the bank exactly in front of where the stag would land. This happened to be at the very base of the sandy bluff, there about sixty feet high. It was brimming high tide at the time, so that the hunter did not have to make any allowance for the natural flow of the river taking the deer off his course.

There was a brilliant afterglow; the river was calm. The eager hunter could hardly await the moment when the great stag would come within range. Having imagination, the man even went so far as to fancy to himself that the deed had been accomplished, and that he was telling his friends about it, and that they had begun to call him the Slayer of Old Five-Master.

Along its lower reaches, the Santee is full of shallows; and

when the swimming buck came to one of these, about two hundred yards from shore, he waded out on it and stood there in the
gleaming afterglow. What a shot for a rifle! But in that part of
the world, on account of the level nature of the country, only
the shotgun is ever used on big game. And within a certain range
(say, sixty yards) it is entirely effective.

The hunter waited nervously. The deer seemed to be in no
hurry, and the light was losing its rosy hue and was taking on its
gray tinge. The man was by no means certain that he could
discern the deer when he landed on the dusky beach. The contour of the bluff was such that when the stag came ashore, he
could not turn to the right and climb that toppling sand wall into
the forest. Though there was a growth of vines on the face of
the bluff opposite his landing-place, he was, the hunter felt sure,
heading for his ancient haunts in the forest. But to the left of
the beach there was a depression in the bluff, through which ran
a game trail. What Old Five-Master would do when he came
ashore would be to take the gentle incline of that trail into the
woods.

Reasoning the business out this way, the man left his post
on the high bluff and stole down to a thicket of myrtle that
bordered the trail. From this position he could see the deer on
the sandbank, but he could not see his landing place. Yet, having
landed, the splendid old fugitive would surely come walking up
the dim path. There was really nothing else for him to do.

But that hunter learned what every hunter learns: That
there are always more things for a cornered deer to do than a
man imagines there are.

There in the twilight the man in ambush waited. When last
he saw Old Five-Master, the great buck was swimming boldly
for shore, and was then about eighty yards away. He must have
come straight to land. Yet deep evening fell, and no deer came
up the pathway to the woods. At last, when it was all but too
dark to shoot, the hunter stole down on the beach. In the faint
starlight it was lonely and bare. The buck had vanished. The
glimmering river lay silent. The great bluff towered in eerie
quiet.

The next morning the man made up his mind that he had
to know what had really happened the night before. Returning
to the place he easily found where the wily deer had come
ashore; then to his astonishment, he discovered that Old Five-

Master, probably detecting the dreaded man-scent, and expecting to be waylaid along the obvious pathway into the forest, had climbed the face of the bank for some forty feet, and there had laid down among the thick jasmine and periwinkle vines. Later in the night he had climbed straight up the bank and had made his way safely into the dim wilds that he loved so well.

This same stag played a trick on me that I shall never forget. Like all the other hunters of my neighborhood, I coveted his superb antlers; and his character was such that to outwit him would seem no ordinary triumph. One day, without having Old Five-Master particularly in mind, I drove out one of my plantation roads alone, to do some still hunting. As the deer of the Southern woods rarely move about by daylight, as the places where they lie are usually very dense, and as the stalker does not have the advantages afforded by a hilly or mountainous country, still hunting there means nothing more than walking them up—an exciting and a legitimate sport, for when an old stag storms out of his bed, free-wheeling away at cyclone speed, it takes a steady nerve and eye to stop him. I have found that under these circumstances the hunter's best chance lies in his letting the buck get a few wild jumps out of his system before shooting.

I parked my car in a little blind road and started to walk down a sandy trail toward a famous stretch of bushes where I had often before walked up and killed deer. My car was directly behind me; to my left was a low growth of bays and broomgrass. When I was about fifty yards from my machine, and was in the act of loading my gun, I heard a deer get up behind me to my left. I turned quickly for a shot; and instead of one I saw five deer—three of them bucks, and one of them Old Five-Master himself. The four ordinary deer raced away in standard fashion. But the wary old veteran did nothing so crude and obvious. To my amazement, he dashed straight for my car, dodged behind it, and then, having put that obstruction between us, he rocked away mockingly. Now, some people may say that that performance was accidental. I do not believe it. A ruffed grouse will execute the same kind of maneuver, and this stag is wiser than a generation of grouse.

Every old deer hunter knows that as a buck develops in wariness, it becomes increasingly hard to drive him to standers. He is very likely to skulk, to dodge, and to slip out at the side or to run straight back. This kind of sagacious maneuver I saw Old Five-Master beautifully illustrate one day when I had a party of eight men in the woods with me, every one crazy for a shot. Moreover, I had seen the veteran's fresh track entering the drive, so that I was pretty sure that we would start him. I counted little on his doubling that morning, for we had a pack of nine fast hounds. With more than ordinary caution I posted the standers, telling them at the same time that Old Five-Master would likely be jumped, and it was for us to prove that he did not bear a charmed life. I stood at one point of our halfmoon of standers that covered the head of the drive.

From my position I commanded a wide view of the famous deer-drive before me; there was little cover of the impossibly dense sort, but here and there under the majestic yellow pines were swampy patches of sweet-bay, clumps of gallberries, stretches of broomsedge and of huckleberry bushes—all plenty thick enough to harbor a buck. In fact, it has been my experience during a lifetime of hunting the whitetail in the South, that a stag, in the hunting season, is not usually fond of a very thick place. To hide too closely is to permit an enemy to approach unobserved. A buck loves to bed down on the fringes of a thicket, or in low bushes or tall grass, or just behind an old log in the sun. On a cold windy day more deer will be jumped from the shelter of old logs than from any other kind of place. It was thrilling to stand there looking into the drive out of which I was practically certain that Old Five-Master would soon come. I want to repeat that we had eight men carefully posted; we had nine veteran hounds swarming out through the drive; and we had five Negro drivers controlling the pack. I began to feel positively sorry for the buck we had hunted so long. Surely this must be the end.

A mile and a half to the east of us, at the tail of the long drive, I heard the Negroes begin their work. They used to whoop, but I have taught them to sing while driving. They are born musicians, and their voices are always in harmony with the wind in the pines and birds singing in the sunny thickets. I could hear them begin, "There's a little w'eel a-turnin' in my heart," and at the same time I heard old Ranter, who carries the coldest nose of the pack, bawl out glad tidings. I glanced to the right down the long line of standers, and of those that I could see, all were alert.

Another dog and yet another joined Ranter. They were on the old master's trail, and they were coming pretty fast. The Negroes, too, were quickstepping to keep up with the pack, and Steve, my head driver, who was riding a rangy white mule, was now in sight—Steve, whose wife, Amnesia, had warned him that morning that he might just as well stay in the woods that night if he didn't bring home any venison.

There often comes to men in the big woods a sense that something is about to happen. It may be a kind of an instinct that our ancestors had to a high degree, and even now it awakens in those who spend their lives close to our ancient Mother Nature.

About two hundred yards from me, in the open woods, which here and there showed only a stately yellow pine soaring into the sky, there was a small patch of huckleberry bushes, not over two feet high in any place. I remember how the sun glinted on the bronzed foliage, and for some reason the tiny arena held my gaze for a moment. I just sensed that things were going to happen. At that time drivers and dogs were about as far beyond the bushes as I was in front of them. Suddenly Old Five-Master himself rose from his bed in the tiny copse. He didn't jump up. He just eased himself up and stood as still as a stone. The hounds had his track all right, but the Negroes did not see him. With a rifle I might have had a perfect shot but for the oncoming drivers. However, in that level country only the shotgun is ever used.

The stag was directly ahead of me, and he stood facing me. He did not see me because I did not move. He did not wind me because the gentle air that was stirring was coming from him to me. But this business of instinct is not given to men alone. Animals have it perhaps in a far higher degree. This old veteran probably knew the details of this game of deer hunting as well as we did. And as a stag gets older and more experienced, it becomes increasingly difficult to drive him. Yet now, with my Negroes and other hounds halfmooned behind him, and almost on him; with my eight standers halfmooned in front of him, the two groups almost completing a circle, I did not see how he could do anything but come on. I slipped my safety up, at the same time experiencing a certain kind of misgiving over putting an end to so noble an animal.

Then, to my amazement, I became witness to a daring and masterly maneuver. Old Five-Master, having made up his mind what to do, deliberately turned toward the hounds and the drivers and, putting on steam, he made a spectacular and bewildering race straight through the center of both packs almost before dogs or darkies knew what was happening. I heard a wild babel of yelps and yowls, much shouting from the dusky boys, especially from Steve, whose honor, as head driver, was at stake, and whose welcome home was at stake also. I could see the buck's immense white flag, stiffly erect and jerked from side to side as he fled straight at his enemies. As nearly as I could judge, he almost ran over and trampled Steve—white mule and all. I knew where that deer was going. Two miles away lay the broad reaches of the Santee River. He might stop to skulk and reconnoiter before taking a swim, but he meant to put that water between himself and his pursuers. And so he did, as we discovered by setting the hounds on his trail.

"Now, Steve," I asked, "why didn't you do something? Why didn't you turn him?"

Steve's answer appealed to me as classic.

"Some creeters, Cap'n," he said soberly, "ain't meant to turn."

Sammy, another of my African pack, began to chuckle.

"What Amnesia gwine to say to you, Steve? You done let de dinner gitway."

A little later I killed a small buck, which saved the domestic crisis for long-suffering Steve.

I saw this famous stag last season, and his massive crown of antlers seemed finer than ever. And he was up to his old tricks again. I was roaming the plantation woods early one morning when I heard a single hound trailing. I took up a stand on an old road and awaited developments. Running parallel to the road was the wreck of an old fence; nothing was standing but the posts and a single strand of wire not more than twenty inches from the ground. On came the hound, and after a little while I detected a slight movement in a bay thicket. The deer was coming to cross the road. In a few moments he stepped out into it— the old master of the wilds. He was evidently just easing along in front of his pursuer. He was just too far for a shot. Coming to the fence on the farther side of the road, he neither jumped nor stepped over it. To avoid doing the least thing that would make him betrayingly spectacular, he suddenly got down on his knees and gently insinuated himself (tall horns and all) under the wire.

In another moment he had vanished into the fastness of the pine thicket.

A deer loves home, and when not disturbed, if the food supply be adequate, he will not wander far. Even if driven off in the hunting season, he will inevitably return to his old haunts. No doubt I shall see him again on the plantation during the coming season. For he still roams the deep pine woods and the swamps that are familiar to him, and have been so since fawn-hood. I love to think of that incomparable old stag enjoying life in his own forests, for to them he really has a more inalienable right than I have. And if he ever comes to my stand, though I am an incurable deer hunter, I am likely to pass him up. He has become so much a part of the romance of the woods that I love that his absence would change their meaning. If he were gone, they would never again be quite the same.

A Hunt at the Kinloch Club

While some States find it essential to restock with game their fields and forests every year, in other States nothing of the kind is ever done; and usually it is not done because it is not necessary. Game's chance against hunters depends mainly on two things: the number of hunters, and the character of the country. Where the number is very great, and where the wild land is not very wild, restocking is going to be necessary. I might add that where a season is short, so that a dreadful concentration of hunting occurs, there will be little game left. Deer have never been brought into Carolina—except one or two old Michigan bucks, introduced on private estates in an attempt to improve the size of the stock. The number of hunters is moderate; the deer country is shaggily wild—a true wilderness, in which wild things fare far better than men who pursue them. But certain styles of hunting will bring the deer out of these apparently inviolate sanctuaries.

In the deep South, at many of the great hunting clubs, there is a yearly celebration on the last day of the deer season. This is always a spirited, neighborly, and very picturesque affair. Plantation owners and their friends for many miles around are invited to the hunt; every man is invited to bring his own hounds and his Negro drivers; and it is no unusual thing for fifty sportsmen to gather at one of these festive affairs. On January 1, 1933, at the invitation of Eugene DuPont, of Wilmington, Delaware, my three sons and I enjoyed a rather spectacular deer hunt at Mr. DuPont's great game preserve at the Kinloch Club, in Georgetown County, South Carolina. As the sport was of an unusual

From *An American Hunter* (1937).

sort, and as the hunting itself was of a type rather different from that usually experienced while after the elusive whitetail, I believe some account of it might interest my fellow sportsmen.

For the difference in the hunting I have no apology to make. Every region has its own type of hunting and long years of experience have proved that for the conditions of that region that style is probably best. I love to still-hunt deer in mountains, but in the Carolinas and the Gulf States a sportsman really has no chance still-hunting. The cover is too dense, even in mid-winter, and the areas are so vast that there is never an army of other hunters abroad to keep the bucks moving. It is essential to use dogs after the ancient and honorable English fashion. Moreover, the high-power rifle is practically forbidden for the standers are posted at close range, the woods are thick, and the country dead-level. I have hunted in the South with a great many Northern sportsmen who, while they would use nothing but a rifle in Maine, Michigan, or Canada, cheerfully resort to the shotgun in the Carolinas. New Jersey and Massachusetts have now adopted the shotgun for deer, and Pennsylvania is on the verge of doing so. I have never known one hunter to kill another with buckshot; whereas, where the rifle is used, casualties in a single state of more than a hundred in a season of two weeks have of late years been recorded.

At daybreak on New Year's Day we foregathered to the number of some forty-five huntsmen, thirty splendid hounds, and about fifteen negroes at the head of the famous Eagle's Nest Drive—a dense thicket of bays and gall-berries, pines and scrub oaks, a half-mile wide and some two miles long. Some of the hunters were mounted; others were taken to their stands in cars. The drive started about sunrise. Nature in that clime is kindly, the air was warm and still, and fragrances from the spicy pines filled the great forest, silent for the moment but not to be silent again for at least two hours.

The quiet of the morning was first broken by the deep bell-tones of one of my hounds, Old Jack. Then a sudden outcry of the Negroes told that a stag was up. Soon all the dogs joined Old Jack and from the general tumult headed our way we knew that there must be other deer afoot. Shots began to ring out. The hunt was fairly on.

Whatever may be said against hunting deer in the manner I am describing, two things are sure: the sport is heightened by the wild clamor of the hounds, which in itself is enough to give the tyro buck fever; and the hunter must nearly always shoot his game on the dead run. And what target is more difficult than that presented by a wild stag in full flight, his easy, undulant motion taking him over the ground at forty miles an hour?

My stand was close to the western edge of Eagle's Nest and my three boys were just below me, the nearest one in sight. For a time we had to content ourselves with listening to the bombardment from the other side of the drive. At least thirty shots must have been fired before we saw a thing. Then, with no dogs pursuing, but in no way slowed up for that reason, a great stag burst from the dense greenery of the thicket and raced past me at thirty-five yards. I got my gun ahead of him and let him have the choke barrel behind the shoulder. He fell as if struck by lightning. Later, upon examination, I found that eleven of the sixteen buckshot in the shell had struck him. When I hear people express doubt as to the killing power of buckshot I suspect that they are either unfamiliar with its use or else are able missers. One of these critics thus complained to me one day after he had missed a ten-pointer at twenty yards: "It was not my fault. I held right on him but just as I pulled the trigger he jumped over the shot." Deer will jump, they say.

I went over to make certain that my buck was dead. He had lost interest completely in things of this world. Even while I was looking at him, though, I had to be wary, for an infernal racket was boiling through the thicket immediately before me: deer crashing wildly through the thickets, hounds going mad on the trail, and Negroes whooping as if they had just been converted and were seeing the Light. I backed to my stand and as I reached it I happened to glance down the line of standers. I saw my eldest son get his gun to his shoulder, but he had it pointed almost straight upward! What a jump that buck must be taking, thought I. But then Black Majesty came in sight—a great gobbler he was—beating his way powerfully to freedom out of that in-ferno behind him. I was close enough to see his long beard streaming, his lengthy legs straight out behind him. At the crack of the gun he folded up and a moment later struck the pine-straw with a mighty thud. I saw him safely retrieved and the proud gunner hanging him on a sapling beside his stand.

On hunts like these there is a friendly rivalry among the

groups of sportsmen from the various plantations. Ours is Hampton, and so far we had done well—a stag and a gobbler.

The drive had almost passed us but experiences of other years had taught me that the fun was not over. These wily stags of Eagle's Nest have a way of running into the cannonade at the head of the drive and then turning back, to slip out of the thickets at any vantage point. In a few minutes, two stands below me, I heard my son Middleton let go with both barrels of his Daly. I said, "That's another, maybe two." I found later that he had killed a fine six-pointer. As yet my youngest son, Irvine, had not shot. But I heard two of my pack, Blue and Music, heading toward him. However, little did I realize the dramatic nature of the situation that he was about to face. A wind had come up, a gentle warm wind, but in the tall pines it made enough music to prevent our hearing with certainty the approach of a deer.

To one who knows and loves dogs, especially hounds, there is a singular delight in recognizing a favorite's voice in the chiming melody of a great pack. I distinctly heard Music's soft tenor, insistent and pleading. Then, unaccountably, there was a complete lull in the proceedings. The wind hushed, the hounds let up. A silence, impressive because of what had been going on, suddenly fell over the whole Eagle's Nest country. It was interrupted, at least for me, by the sound of two Negro voices. They were in the drive in front of me.

"Where he done gone?" one excited African called to his fellow.

"Where who done gone?"

"Big boy, is you libin' and ain't seen him?"

"Who I ain't done see, Sam?"

"Great Kingdom and the angels! Ain't you know we done jump Sebastian hisself? I ain't done see dat buck for two years, but I see him just now. Where he gone? Eben de dogs don't know where he gone."

"Must be he might be a sperit," Sam suggested fearfully. "I comin' right now out of these here thick bushes. I ain't done lost no sperit what I am aimin' to find."

"Look out! Look out!" suddenly yelled the other darky, as a great crashing of brush told that they had almost stepped on a deer.

Sam took the admonition seriously for in a moment I saw

him come out of the branch, apparently sailing over the bushes without even touching his feet to anything. He dashed incontinently past me, and took shelter at my car standing on the road. He firmly believed in not interfering with spirits.

Far off, amid the tall greenery, I saw a prodigious white tail, stiffly erect. It must be a deer's, I thought, though I had never seen such a flag before. It must be Sebastian's, that famous buck that for years the Kinloch Club had hunted so vainly that the old stag had become almost a tradition.

Things began to happen fast. Sebastian had thrown the dogs off by skulking through a pond. While the two Negroes had been talking he had been on tiptoe in a dense copse of sweet bay not twenty yards from them. When he dashed out the driver who had not fled had presence of mind enough to get two of the dogs on the trail. Again I heard Music's sweet tenor, and she was headed toward one of my boys, I could not yet tell which one.

At last I heard Irvine's Greener blare forth; then a second barrel. Though it is a cardinal principle in this kind of deer hunting that the sportsman must never leave his stand, this business was too much for me. I can generally resist anything but temptation. The same impulse had made my older sons join their baby brother—but baby only because he's the youngest. When I reached the critical place I saw a memorable and joyous group. The three young huntsmen were standing almost in awe about the fallen stag—a deer that made my eight-pointer look picayune. For here was the great Sebastian himself—the largest and most beautiful stag I have ever seen, dead or alive. To a high degree he had retained his soft red summer coat; his throat was vividly white. He was huge yet immaculate. Later, when we weighed him, he went a strong 205 pounds. As for his antlers I have seen larger ones and horns with many more points; but for massive grace and symmetry, and for a certain high-pitched sportiness, I had never seen their equal. Even his hoofs were exceptional, for they were large yet not the least broken or marred, and they had a lot of old ivory coloring in them. Surely here was a master trophy!

Returning to our stands we held them for some two hours more, with no further chances save that we saw one big buck slipping out of the drive at about 120 yards—a hopeless distance for a shotgun. Sporadic shooting went on for some time on the farther side of the drive. Most of the hounds ran deer clear out of hearing. At last a horn called us to luncheon on the warm pine-straw, in the genial sun, with some corking yarns of who killed and who missed, and the elaborate reasons why missing was altogether reasonable. . . .

Over this happy crowd of sportsmen our genial host presided. He himself had killed a fine stag, but he seemed far more interested in hearing what we had done. When lunch was nearly over a wagon drove up with the quarry—nine bucks in all for one drive; and the drivers reported that more than nine had escaped. They were laid out in a row according to size. As I was sure he would, the stag that had fallen to the Greener was at the head of the line.

"Why," said Mr. DuPont, "it's Old Sebastian! What a deer!"

He turned and with a true sportsman's genuine earnestness he shook the hand of Sebastian's slayer. And I who watched this proceeding felt the pride that only he can know who has brought up a son to be a good hunter.

FLIGHTS OF WHITETAIL FANCY

Part V

T he literature of deer hunting is rich and surprisingly varied. Rob Wegner, perhaps the leading authority in the field, has identified well over a thousand volumes dealing wholly or in large measure with the sport. Yet virtually all of these works are factual accounts. With a few noteworthy exceptions the deer hunt in fiction is a neglected literary genre. James Fenimore Cooper's *The Deerslayer* comes immediately to mind, as does William Faulkner's masterful short story "Race at Morning." Several authors of popular Westerns, notably Zane Grey and Louis L'Amour, also incorporate deer hunting into their tales.

When it comes to the combination of exciting stories and the ability to cast both the deer and the hunter in realistic roles, however, Rutledge may well be in a class by himself. For some reason his fine fictional plots and knack for characterization have been particularly overlooked by modern readers, perhaps because his writing includes an appreciable degree of sentimentality and anthropomorphism. Such approaches once enjoyed immense popularity, as exemplified by the writings of Ernest Thompson Seton, and to Rutledge it seemed perfectly natural to profess a love for deer as "that noble, elusive, crafty, wonderful denizen of the wilds" with human characteristics. Although such a romantic viewpoint is currently unfashionable, a good argument can be made for the enduring appeal of such work.

Here is the acid test of this argument, a selection of five of Rutledge's fictional tales in which deer play a central role. Although Rutledge's love for the dramatic and a tendency to be overly romantic may strike a jarring note, I suggest that the reader cast cynicism aside and let the author's fictional sorties into the deer's world speak for themselves. The result, I believe, will be recognition of Rutledge as a writer whose powers extended well beyond the masterful factual narrative accounts for which he is primarily remembered.

THE WHITE STAG'S TRYST

For a long time Rodney Lee stood looking from his window in the old plantation home of the Lees. Wide sea marshes spread out before him, flat and dismal as his thoughts. It was a problem, and he just couldn't see the way out. He didn't think there was any way out. To leave Roseland would be hard enough for him. How much harder it would be for his mother! "Too bad," he said to himself, "that so much depends on money."

From the window he turned to survey his spacious room, tarried before his collections of bird eggs and specimens of rare birds which he had mounted, and recalled the praise that had been given them by the Curator of the Charleston Museum; and then his eye fell on a little square of parchment that hung framed on the wall—a letter from Stede Bonnet.

"Money was your trouble, too, you old pirate," he said, aloud, as though he were talking to the notorious buccaneer, "and it got you hanged by the neck until you were dead."

He scanned the strange writing again, though he knew its every word. "The white stag's tryst" was the phrase that had always mystified and fascinated him. He knew the story of the letter itself, but nothing of the meaning of its single sentence. The sheet of parchment had come into the Lee family through old Hubert Lee, an attorney, for whom the unhappy Bonnet, in his last hours, had sent, to inquire if a full confession of his guilt would stay the sentence of the law. The lawyer had been obliged to reply in the negative. Nevertheless, as Lee was leaving him, Bonnet, with an impulsive gesture of generosity, seized a pen, and wrote the mysterious sentence concerning the white stag. Hubert Lee had never made an attempt to fathom the mystery.

From *Heart of the South* (1924).

The parchment sheet had passed from one member of the family to another until it became Rodney's property.

Facing the sea islands and the ocean, Roseland overlooked what had once been the pirate Bonnet's domain; for the view from its eastern side included Bull's Island, where both Stede Bonnet and Captain Kidd had undoubtedly buried treasure. Somewhere there were sea chests crammed with gold and jewels, somewhere in the secret fastnesses afforded by the dense groves of red cedar and the lonely woods of pine. Rodney had always believed it; but never until now had he thought of carrying out a search that his family had neglected for two hundred years. Yet, he reasoned, perhaps no one of them had ever been put in such a position as he now was, when the loss of a home, poverty, and something akin to disgrace threatened his mother and himself. He came to his decision as he looked at Bonnet's letter. He would go to Bull's Island that very day to search for the white stag's tryst.

Hurrying down the stairs, full of excitement over his expedition, he ran into the back yard, shaded by its immense oak trees, and called Samson. In answer to his shout, a powerful Negro of giant proportions came hulking out of a cabin. He was, as usual, smiling amiably. He loved Rodney's enthusiasm.

"Samson," said the boy, "get the big oars and loose the yawl; we are going to Bull's Island."

Samson who delighted in such excursions, vanished into the cellar of the big house, whence he soon emerged bearing the long oars which he bore over his vast shoulders down to the wharf. Rodney followed him, carrying a short shovel. As he came to the front of the house, he leaned this up against the steps and ran up on the porch to tell his mother good-bye. He could see how hard she was trying to be brave and smiling; but her eyes were misty and wistful.

"Samson and I are going down to the island," Rodney announced. "We shall be back by dark, or a little later."

His mother looked at him a little strangely, as if she were surprised and disappointed; surprised that he should leave her on such a day. But she said nothing of her feelings and came down to the landing to see the yawl start, waving good-bye to Rodney, before the boat was hidden by a bend in the creek.

When they were well on their way, Rodney began to tell Samson the purpose of the trip.

"The other day," he said, "Mr. Saunders told Mother that

he had lost money in a lumber deal, and that he would have to foreclose his mortgage on Roseland. I hardly blame him. He loaned us the money when we needed it, and now he wants it back. As we don't have it, Samson, he is going to force us to sell."

"Sell?" the negro said, in an awe-stricken voice. "Not sell Roselan', sah?"

"Yes, sell Roseland. But you know, Samson, if we could—"

Then he unfolded to the wondering Negro his purpose of visiting Bull's Island in the hope of finding the tryst of the white stag and Bonnet's buried gold.

"I suppose, Samson, there must have been, in Bonnet's time, a white stag on Bull's Island, a well-known albino buck. My idea is that this buck must have had a favorite stamping ground or trysting place—a marked spot; and that there the pirate hid his gold. Bonnet's buck has been dead centuries. But if we can find the trysting place of the present leader of the Bull's Island herd, we might come upon the secret."

"If we could just see a white deer, sah," said the Negro, "then we could follow him until we find dat gold." Samson's tone showed that he had small hope in the outcome of his young master's adventure. But Rodney knew well enough that he could count on Samson to stand with him to the last in any such enterprise.

An hour's row down the tortuous salt creek brought them to the back beach of the lonely island. Here they tied their boat to the sunken ribs of an ancient wreck that stood rigid in the sands. Though his surroundings were familiar, it was with a thrill that Rodney felt himself to be at the pirate's rendezvous. He had often been here before to study birds and to gather shells, but on account of the exciting nature of this trip, the place seemed different. It looked like a fit place to search for pirate's gold. Long, narrow, densely wooded with palmettoes, pines, and myrtles, Bull's Island is typical of those chains of isles which fringe the South Atlantic seaboard. On its back beach, lisp the sluggish waters of a tidal creek, while on its front beach, rolls the surf of the Atlantic.

"The first thing for us to do, Samson," said Rodney, as the two walked up the beach together, "is to look for deer and especially for the old buck that leads the herd. Then we ought deliberately to stalk him all day, in the hope that he may go to his tryst and betray to us Bonnet's secret. I have a feeling, Samson, that this is going to be the greatest day of our lives. Roseland's being at stake has already made it so in one way; our being here after this treasure may balance the account on the other side."

As they entered the semi-tropical woods of Bull's Island, they separated, with the understanding that they were to walk parallel courses down the island and keep a sharp outlook for deer. In these rich woods, now in the full glory of their late summer foliage, Rodney Lee's love of nature found fulfillment on every hand. He marked the luxuriance of the leaves, as yet untinted by autumn; the brilliance of the birds, which flashed across shimmering forest vistas or warbled like rivulets of the sky high up among the dreamy-crested pines; the far glimpses of rolling sea breakers, glimmering under dusky arches of cedars, or down the fragrant naves of pine cathedrals. And to all these accustomed beauties was now added the glamour of the search for the mysterious trysting place of the white stag.

Rodney and Samson had not penetrated the palmetto brake more than a few hundred yards when three dun does, accompanied by as many fawns, broke cover and went rocking lightly away, their resilient bounds taking them sailing airily through the brush. A moment later, a great buck with red coat and with glinting horns started up almost at Rodney's feet and went crashing off through the myrtles.

"Samson, look out!" he called. Then he drew in his breath sharply, stopping silent, amazed.

For directly in the path of the first buck there now bounded a second—a startling apparition—a pure white stag of marvelous size and beauty. Rodney had but time to glimpse the noble proportions of the body and the size and height of the regal antlers, when the albino vanished into the thicket.

As he was turning in Samson's direction to call him softly, he saw the big Negro hastily coming, his face wearing an expression of superstitious fear, and his eyes wide with apprehension.

"Cap'n Rodney," he said, "I done see a ghost."

"Why, Samson," the other cried, "it's the albino buck. Stede Bonnet's white stag, or one just like him! He has reappeared here on Bull's Island! Now, if we don't find that pirate's gold, we ought to be hanged, just as the old buccaneer himself was!"

As they stood talking excitedly in the myrtle glade, in the

creek behind the island they heard the steady beat of oars. Rodney asked Samson who it might be.

"Whoever it is," the Negro replied, "he can't row. I 'speck, sah, that it's Mr. Jefferson Saunders."

"Saunders!" cried Rodney. "I wonder if he can be coming down here to see me about that mortgage? It would be like him, Samson." Then he added, with sudden determination, "Let's go down to meet him. And not a word about your ghost, Samson," he cautioned.

When they emerged from the woods, Jefferson Saunders had already tied his boat beside theirs and was coming up the slope of the beach. For many reasons, the man looked out of place on Bull's Island. There was nothing rangy and elemental about him. Rodney Lee, muscular, brown, with deep blue eyes and with wavy hair, seemed to be at home where great ocean surges were breaking, and where giant pines rocked against a vast sky. But Saunders was a small, wiry man, dapper in his dress and quick in his movements. His features were irregular, and years of keen business dealing had sharpened them like a fox's. His eyes were small and colorless; his mustache sandy and frayed. That life had been to him solely a business of getting money could be seen readily, because for the beauteous lonely island, the tossing ocean, and the wide, mysterious marshes he cared nothing. Indeed, he had a scorn for those who loved nature, and some of this scorn was now veiled under the apparent friendly manner with which he greeted Rodney.

"Still after the woodpeckers and the sand chickens, are you, Rodney?" he asked. "I might be after them too," he added, "if I could make it pay."

"You've brought your gun with you," Rodney remarked, ignoring the pleasantry of his visitor. "What are you going to hunt, sir?"

"Meat," came the instant response. "I am a practical man, Rodney, and when I carry a gun it is because I am looking for something to hang in my smokehouse."

"I see," the other assented dryly.

"But I really came here on business," he hastened to explain. "Your mother told me where you were, so I decided to follow you. After we have had our talk, we might take a little hunt for some of these island deer. But business first—always."

On an old stick of yellow pine timber, half buried in the

sands, the two sat down to talk, while Samson, who could not hide his impatience, took occasion to work off his energy by retying the Roseland yawl with such elaborate security that the stout boat would have rotted to pieces at her moorings before she would have broken away.

"Now, Rodney," Saunders began, "you must know what business brings me here. It's about that mortgage, the details of which your mother has already given to you. I had a letter this morning from my lawyer in Charleston who tells me that I shall be obliged to do something this week. So, much as I regret it, to protect my own good name in the city's business circles, I will be forced to bring on a sale of Roseland. I have come to you, Rodney, to put the matter squarely before you and to ask if you know of anything that can be done. I know that you are young to handle such matters, but you are all the help your mother has. I should think," he added, "that you would be trying to do something about it, rather than fooling away your time down here. The way to save Roseland isn't by picnicking on Bull's Island with Samson."

"Mother told me," Rodney replied, "that she had offered you three hundred dollars that we got for the cotton crop. Couldn't you make that do until we can sell some timber or get some money from other sources to pay you?"

Saunders looked impatient.

"I refused the three hundred dollars," he said, "because it would hardly help me. My obligations are large, and I owe it to myself to meet them in full."

For a moment, while Rodney's blue eyes were turned seaward, Jefferson Saunders looked keenly at that fine face, with its rich coloring showing beneath the deep tan and the first lines of manhood's determination marking the firm mouth. The man could not help having a moment of pity for this boy, whom circumstances had made his victim. But he resolutely stifled the feeling as one not calculated to further good business.

"I say, Rodney," he suggested, thinking that nothing would come from their talking further, "call up Samson and let's take a deer drive. I hardly hoped that you would be able to do anything about that other matter; but I had, of course, spoken fully to your mother, and I was determined to let you know just how the affair stood. Where is your gun?"

"I brought none this time," Rodney spoke in a detached

manner, for he was thinking very hard. He did not like to refuse to hunt with Saunders; yet to hunt might expose the white stag to danger. But in a moment he said, "If you will take your stand on Cedar Point, Samson and I will drive something to you from the far end of the island."

"Samson," said Rodney, when the two were well down the beach, "do you remember where the woods down here narrow down to a neck? That is where I am going to stand. You will go about a mile father, and then drive back. I will let any deer but our white buck pass me and go to Mr. Saunders. But if the big albino comes, I will turn him into the surf."

"You mean the breakers, Cap'n," the Negro said.

The deer on the island, as Rodney knew, did things that ordinary deer would not do. When driven from the woods, they took to the surf. The fall of the island was so gradual that a buck could stand up in the surf two hundred yards off shore.

Rodney then parted from Samson, and fifteen minutes later he heard the Negro coming up through the island woods, whistling and shouting.

"I don't believe the old boy relished going down there alone," Rodney said to himself, smiling. "That ghost idea is still with him. What a voice!" he added, as the Negro's melodious tones echoed through the woods. "It's enough to wake Stede Bonnet himself."

And now Rodney heard the thudding bounds of a running deer. Then, with a thrill, he glimpsed the helmeted head of the great white stag. The big buck was bounding high over the scrub palmettoes, with all the grace and rhythm of perfect muscular control. The snowy creature hardly broke his stride at sight of Rodney; but at the height of one of his bounds, he partly turned in the air, his antlers pointed toward the beach. Out of the woods and down the open beach he plunged. The boy, knowing full well how much depended on that extraordinary creature, watched him, fascinated, saw him enter the breaking waves, and forge his lordly way onward, nor pause until he was a hundred and fifty yards off-shore. There no part of him remained visible save the mighty rack of chestnut-colored antlers standing above the surf.

As Rodney turned his gaze back toward the woods, he saw a spike buck coming. He remained motionless, and the lithe creature passed him like a flying shadow.

"That's the Saunders species of deer," he said smiling; "the Bonnet species is in the breakers."

It was only a few moments before the gun of Jefferson Saunders roared out on the island stillness. Then Samson came up, and the two hastened together in the direction whence the shot had come.

"I turned your ghost into the surf, Samson. You did not see him? He looked bigger than ever; and our plan worked perfectly."

When they came up to Saunders, they found him mightily elated over the deer that he had killed.

"Just what I said, Rodney," he remarked; "something for the larder, and a large one for Bull's Island, isn't it?"

"They sometimes get larger," Rodney answered quietly; "but this is good enough."

They carried the little buck down to Saunders' boat, and immediately he got ready to leave the island.

"We'll be coming on a little later," said Rodney casually. "Mr. Saunders," he questioned quietly, "you don't expect to take any definite action against Roseland before Friday, do you? This is Wednesday."

"Do you see a way out?" asked Saunders quickly, looking with sharp and narrowed eyes at the speaker.

"I can tell you tomorrow night."

"Well, my advice to you, Rodney, is not to waste your time down here so far away from your mother, who ought to be able to begin to lean on you now for strength. It won't pay, just now, to have any more jaunts down here."

Saunders spoke in good faith. Rodney did not answer him, but he tried to look contrite. No sooner was the Saunders boat out of sight than the two treasure hunters passed quickly up the beach and re-entered the woods.

"Now, Samson," said Rodney, "this is where we win or lose. My plan is for each of us to climb a palmetto so that we can do our watching from an advantageous height. I have shown you the big albino in the surf. He will come out on the beach at sundown. What will he do then? He may stay on the beach; he may disappear in the woods; and Samson, he may go to his trysting place. Do you understand? This is our chance, and our only one to save Roseland."

Rodney laid his hand on the faithful Negro's arm; and Sam-

son needed nothing more than that touch and the depth of appeal
from the blue eyes looking into his to make him do anything
that might be asked him that night.

The watchers had already settled themselves on the crests
of two stout palmettoes when the September moon rose over the
ocean, transfiguring the wide expanse of waters into ridges and
levels of shimmering movement. And with the rising of the yellow moon, the great white stag began to make his way out of the
surf.

Rodney Lee knew from experience how difficult it is to
watch a deer by moonlight; its movements are silent; its form is
shadowy, seeming to blend with the wavy thickets; and it always
appears more phantom-like than real.

The albino's progress out of the surf was unhesitating, but
on reaching the beach his movements were less positive. He
paced a short distance up the sands; then he turned and lifted
his grand head, scenting the sea. Then slowly up the rim of the
foam-edged beach he passed. At length he mounted a spectral
dune, and there stood, a marvelous statue, marbled in the
streaming moonlight. Presently the lordly creature left his silent
watch on the dune and came noiselessly up toward the woods on
whose borders the two men were waiting. The stag's deliberate
movements showed that for all his long vigil in the surf he was
now without fear.

On the brink of the woods, and not more than fifty yards
from Rodney, the albino began to crop at a patch of lush grass.
He was coming closer to Rodney's palmetto, but his course was
taking him deeper into the woods. Once, when almost beneath
the tree on which the young treasure hunter was perched, the
buck paused indolently to rub his antlers against the rough bark
of a cedar. The velvet of the horns had recently peeled, and the
tines were sharp and clean. For a moment the buck stood in full
view; then, as if a sudden frolicsome mood had come to him, he
bounded lithely over a hedge of bush palmettoes and was lost to
view.

Rodney's heart sank; yet he knew that as the stag passed
out of his own range of vision, he would enter Samson's.

An hour passed, the longest hour of suspense that Rodney
had ever known. A silent hour it was of moonlight and glamour,
an hour when strange bird voices came out of the marshes, and

stranger silences wrapped the lonely forests of the island. Then suddenly, in one of the little paths of the woods, Rodney saw a shape. It was a slim white doe and behind it came a second. Both, beautifully graceful and alert, seemed enhanced in beauty, grace, and alertness by the delicate tinge that the moonlight gave them. Indescribably dainty they were, and full of fairylike woodland charm. A moment later, Rodney saw, with a catch in his breath, the form of the great white stag following the does. When he had come up to them, the three turned sharply to the right. There, surrounded by a group of gnarled and stunted cedars, was a small open space into which Rodney could see. The group of deer, once within this sequestered haunt, paused momentarily; then they quietly separated, their heads low to the ground, as if searching for something. At last, as the watching boy's nerves tingled, the big albino began to paw the ground. Soon he went down on his knees and buried his nose in the hole he had dug.

At that moment Rodney thought of his mother; and he knew that she was thinking of him. It was a great moment for him. With the wide eyes of wonder and dawning hope, he looked on the strange scene before him in the moonlight. He knew that he must have found a tryst of the white stag. Could it be Stede Bonnet's tryst as well? Here was the albino's haunt. Was it the burial place of the treasure?

"It is enough," Rodney said to himself. "If the gold is anywhere on Bull's Island, it is where that old buck is digging."

As he began to clamber down the palmetto, the deer heard him and bounded off. Once on the ground, he gave a shout for Samson. In immediate response, there came the sound of precipitate scuffling down the tawny sides of a palmetto.

Rodney would say nothing when the giant Negro, panting from excitement, from his thoughts of ghosts, and from the speed of his running, had joined him. He silently led the way to the cedar-circled space where the sand was heaped and hollowed.

"Well, Samson," he asked, "what do you make of it?"

Without waiting for a reply, Rodney stepped across the space toward the little pit that the white stag had pawed out. Stooping down, he twisted something off. This he handed to Samson, who stood big-eyed above him.

"Taste it," said he.

Bewildered but obedient, the Negro put the substance to his lips.

"Dat's salt," he said, disappointed, and yet reassured, as if he had feared it to be some terrifying chemical which the touch of his lips would cause to explode into gold.

"Now, Samson," said Rodney, "we know why the deer came here. This place is, and has evidently been for a long time, a regular deer lick. It must have been here in Bonnet's day. Suppose he himself, that crafty old pirate, put the salt here? The deer may not have been coming here regularly all the while; but if they lost the place for a few years, they would be certain to rediscover it. If Bonnet (and he was noted for doing odd, unexpected things), disposing of some captured shipload of salt, for which he cared nothing, had put it here, what was his purpose in doing so, and what did he bury under it? Or, perhaps, he merely discovered here an outcrop of salt, with a deep underbed of it beneath these sands. Go down to the boat, Samson, and bring up that short shovel and we'll soon see if there's anything besides salt in this hole that the albino has been digging."

It took a very few moments for Samson to return. Then, directed by Rodney, he began to dig. Great slabs of salt were pried off, and these the boy lifted and tossed aside into the thicket. All went well until Samson, his back doubled and his right knee arched to drive the spade deeper than ever, paused to say:

"I must be striking a rock, sah, or else some cedar roots. I can't make this spade go in."

Rodney, instead of being dismayed at this, stooped quickly over the hole and thrust his hand to the very bottom, where the point of the shovel rested on some object through which it could not be driven. He felt about for a moment, as if making sure of what his hand was touching. He went down on his knees, and guiding the spade with his hand, he directed Samson's digging. All the while his heart was throbbing with wild expectancy. He believed he had his hand on an iron sea chest; if he did, it could hold but one thing. At last he jumped up with an exclamation.

"We've found it! We've found it, Samson!" he cried. "It's the white stag's tryst, and here is the gold of Stede Bonnet!"

From the partly exposed top of an ancient black chest, deeply bedded in the pit, further great slabs of salt were pried away with the shovel, and soon the chest was loosened from its earth moorings. The treasure hunters hauled it up into the moonlight. Even as it came sliding slowly up the sides of the pit, Rodney saw within through the wide cracks that corrosion had made in the thick metal, dull gleams of gold, and flashings of something far brighter. At Rodney's word, Samson laid his mighty hands on the edge of the box's top and tore it slowly back, the deeply rusted iron falling in slivers and flakes under the stress. Bared to the streaming moonlight lay Bonnet's jewels and gold that for centuries had been hidden under the sands of Bull's Island.

Samson saw that they had found what they had hoped to find, but his mind could not particularize, nor could he know the value of the treasure. But Rodney saw great diamonds glittering, and emeralds greenly glowing, pale opals, and pigeon's-blood rubies.

To another, such a discovery might have meant the beginning of dreams of power that wealth can bring. But Rodney Lee had but one thought. It was of his mother and of that beloved old plantation home.

"Samson," he said, with something like a break in his voice, "we've saved Roseland, we've saved Roseland!"

"Yes, sah, I know, I know; and that ghost deer done it." The giant Negro might have said more, but his voice was husky.

It was nearly two hours later when the Roseland yawl, with her gunwales almost awash, drew slowly up to the plantation wharf. Rodney's mother was there to meet the boat.

"Are you all right, Rodney?" she asked. "What has made you and Samson so late?"

"We'll show you in a minute," Rodney answered; "nothing is wrong, Mother."

THE KINGS OF CURLEW ISLAND

It was Richard who showed me the huge antler—a dropped horn from a whitetail buck. Massive to a degree rarely seen, not less than five inches it measured around the handsome beading. Moreover, there were nine clear points, none mere craggy excrescences; they were genuine tines. Architecturally the beam was perfect. Of course, it was gray from weathering, and it had lost some of its impressive weight; nevertheless, I had never seen a trophy which interested me more. Wild woodland beauty and romance, caught and made permanent, were in such an object for me.

"Well," I asked, "and where did you find it, Richard?"

"Cap'n," said the smiling Negro woodsman, "you done already know."

"On Curlew Island?"

He nodded.

"This year?" I asked.

"I picked up this horn a month ago," he replied—and here his tone took on a seriousness which actually thrilled me—"and this same buck I done see no later than Wednesday, this same week Wednesday."

"And you mean to tell me, Richard, that he was wearing a top hat like this?" I questioned, eyeing the tremendous antler and then the dusky trapper.

"He done ordered a larger size this season," the Negro assured me, a smile creasing his face as a crack in front of a knife creases an overripe watermelon.

When it comes to sporting matters of this kind I am inclined to be abrupt. "When do we start?" I asked shortly.

From *Heart of the South* (1924).

The suddenness of my question did not surprise Richard. He knew me too well. Almost from the cradle we had hunted deer together in the wilds of the Carolina coast country. And he was very well aware that while the years may change the color of a hunter's hair, and perhaps the sprightliness of his step, they cannot touch the fiber of his heart.

"Today would be a good day to go, Cap'n," Richard suggested.

Toward the westward-sloping November sun I glanced appraisingly. Then I looked toward the lonely barrier island, five miles away across the lonely sea marshes beyond many a solitary bay and creek and sound. To reach Curlew Island we would have to row through winding creeks, which from the stormy inlet north of the island spread octopuslike arms far through the vast retiring marsh.

"Your boat—you have it here, Richard?"

The Negro pointed toward the landing before my house. "I didn't even tie her up," he answered, "'caze I knowed you would go."

Yes, he knew me well.

Four hours later Richard and I were actually on Curlew Island. Darkness had fallen, but it was a scented mild and starry darkness. To me it seemed that we had come to a world of sea-winds, sea-stars, and strange lonely beauty. To us came the perfume of dew-drenched myrtle and oleander, the mournful organ-music of the mighty pines, the fluting of a passing flock of yellow-legs. I heard the wings of wild ducks winnowing the warm air. The roar of the surf from the front beach sounded incessantly. We had come to a strange, wild place, Richard and I; and we had come for a romantic purpose. And despite the fact that his name may spoil the romance of it all, I must mention that Scramble, Richard's dog-of-all-work, was with us. You will look in vain among the ancestors of the First Families for Scramble's forebears; nevertheless, he was all dog. When I questioned Richard concerning his favorite's lineage, he told me that Scramble's mother was a fice and his father a woolly dog.

Having hauled our boat into the myrtle thicket, we made our way down the dim trail, glimmering now in the starlight, which led to the old cabin, which the Negro on his occasional trapping trips to the island was accustomed to occupy. On either side of us were black thickets, full of perfumes, rustlings and the hush of listeners. Three times I distinctly heard deer bound away from our approach. You can't mistake the running of a deer; that light, incisive thudding of his precise and trimly handled hoofs. And once I saw a tall flagtail, vividly white for a moment, and then suddenly vanishing down a dark woodland aisle.

"I think, Cap'n, we might walk a little careful," Richard said casually.

"We are liable to fall over ourselves," I agreed, not understanding just what he meant.

"Not that," he corrected me; "but I mean you mustn't make no mistake and tramp on that big rattlesnake what done kill my other dog."

His calm warning nettled me.

"Richard, what are you bringing me into—here in the dark? Why in the world didn't you tell me about this business before we left home? We shouldn't have come down here in the night. . . . I suppose," I added bitterly, "if the stag has eighteen-points on his head, the diamond back probably has as many on his tail."

Like most men on a dark and lonely road, my attitude toward a rattlesnake is wholly conciliatory. I would just as lief let him have the broad highway to himself if he wants it.

"I done kill the mate," Richard told me.

"Large one?"

"My dogs ran into them by an old oak stump, Cap'n. I kill one snake, and the one snake done kill my dog Poacher. The other snake get 'way under the stump. I lost one snake and one dog," he ended.

"How long did Poacher live after he was struck?" I asked.

"He didn't live at all. Nothing don't live after getting what he got. The snake strike at Scramble, too, but Scramble make a sharp dodge."

"That's what I feel like doing now, Richard. Confound you! I suppose the island is full of these little friends of the hunter."

"Just these two," the Negro assured me; and I knew him well enough to trust his word on matters of woodcraft.

"How long was your snake?" I persisted.

"Bad luck to measure a rattlesnake, Cap'n. But, if you had his rattles at a frolic, you wouldn't need no jazz-band. He was a swamp rattler—about eight feet long, I think. But he was the smaller and the tamer of the two."

"Real thoughtful of you, Richard, to save the big one for me, and me for the big one. But yonder's the old cabin in the clearing."

Dimly in the open space in the forest before us there appeared the squat and staggering building that I had dignified by the name of cabin. It stood in an arena-like place of sparse bushes and white sand. About it gathered huge oaks, seeming to meditate in the calm starlight. It was with real relief that I left the darksome, haunted woods and entered this old clearing. An object could at least be discerned on the pale sand—an object like an eight-foot diamondback, let us say.

But whatever resentment I had against Richard was soon dissipated. With a bright fire of dry driftwood he soon had the cabin cheerful. He prepared an excellent supper. Then there were smokes. All seemed well. Life was worthwhile, despite reptiles and such. When I retired it was to dream of stags with tree-like antlers parading before me, begging to be favored with a soft-nosed bullet from my .250-3000.

Next morning, before the dew was thinking of drying, I began in earnest my stalk of the great buck of Curlew Island. And I had not been out an hour before I knew that Richard had told me a true thing when he said that this particular deer made his home on this island. I first struck the master stag's track in the black mud on the marshy edges of a fresh-water pond. Wonderful was that track. The mud's consistency was tough; the track was therefore not exaggerated in size.

"But this must be a calf," I said to Richard; "aren't there still some wild cattle on the island here?"

"Yes," the Negro agreed, "but the track you see here is the track of the Curlew King."

"Sounds romantic," I said, 'the Curlew King.' Well, we're here to do a bit of dethroning."

We followed the track—Richard and I. It led from the pond side into a marshy basin; thence it traversed a wild reedland, wherein wound many animal paths. In this wilderness of reeds were hummocks of cedar, underbedded with soft golden broomsedge—ideal drowsing places for deer. And thrice out of such shelters were jumped deer—two does and a sprightly buck bearing spikes. They rocked away in standard fashion. We were hardly interested in them. The track we were upon belonged to an entirely different kind of creature. But it led into the gross myrtle jungle between the reedy wasteland and the sea. We seemed to lose the trail on the margins of this desperate thicket.

While each of us was wondering just what to do, and while the light and warmth of the morning sun sifted genially down upon us through the piney boughs, both of us detected some object dying down. It was not thirty yards off, and it was nestled in the most deer-like fashion on the brink of a vivid green savanna.

Richard caught my arm and pointed with a steady black finger.

Slowly I lifted my rifle; but then I lowered it.

"Did you think it was the King?" I asked him in a whisper. Then, with more assurance in my tone, I said, "It's nothing but a cow. I can't see its head; but if I'm not mistaken, Richard, it's a dead cow."

Together we approached the prostrate creature. It was a heifer, newly dead. So clean and beautiful was her coat and so prime was her condition that I knew her death must have been a violent one. I thought she might have tripped in a hole and broken her neck. Such an accident sometimes occurs. But Richard discovered the truth concerning her fate.

"She did fall," he said, in answer to my guess as to the cause of her fate, "but she was like Poacher; she was dead when she fell."

"A snake?"

"Not *a* snake, Cap'n, but *the* snake. There's just one snake can do a thing like this."

"I suppose so," I agreed, feeling creepy and beginning to eye the near landscape with that singular alertness that awakens in a man who senses he is in sudden and deadly peril.

"In the neck," Richard was saying, lifting the cow's lank head and pointing to a dread swelling at a place where the great artery comes from the heart.

"Come on, Richard," I said impatiently, "don't start that snake talk of yours. We are after a deer, not a diamondback."

"That's so, Cap'n," the Negro agreed; "but if that cow couldn't smell him, and so done tramped on him, I might do the same thing. . . . I ain't ready to tramp my last tramp yet. The Lord knows I ain't quite ready to sail on the Jasper Sea."

Now, as you know, I had come to the island for pleasure and excitement, yet a sense of dread and distaste was coming over me. But I was determined to shake it off.

"We should have brought Scramble," I remarked, changing the subject.

"He is a good varmint dog," Richard said, "but he ain't so good on snakes—'cept in the dodging line."

"Snakes be hanged!" I exclaimed; "I'm thinking of deer."

Down an old wood road that was densely flanked by a semitropical jungle we trudged. Richard had put me a little out of humor; and no man in a bad humor can do any decent stalking.

"Cap'n," said Richard after awhile, "do you know what I done think?"

"Well?" I queried, hinting by my tone a certain disrespect for any thoughts that the Negro might be having.

"I done think," he said "that Curlew Island ain't got just one King. There's the master buck and there's this same thing that keeps crossing our trail."

"Well," I replied, "perhaps there are more than two kings of this island country: you are the King of all Fools and you've made me the King of Uneasy Walkers. Do you know what I think, Richard?"

The Negro admitted that I had the advantage of him.

"I'll tell you frankly, then. The trouble with us is that we are almost in a funk. Every time I hear a jaybird snap a twig I feel like breaking into a sprint. It takes real men to follow, stalk, and bring down a stag like the one we're after. Do you believe we are men enough to do this? Suppose you let up on this infernal snake talk of yours. I for one have the creeps and the jumps, and I know if I see a lizard I'll do a Brodie over these pine tops."

"All right, Cap'n," the Negro agreed, not in the least out of humor. "But please be careful."

"Hang it, Richard, suppose you go back to the cabin. I'll try to trail this deer alone for a while. You take Scramble out and see what you two can find in the way of varmints. Then you can get a good dinner ready. Look for me about dark."

"All right, Cap'n. . . . If you don't come back," he added with kindly, unconscious gruesomeness, "I will come to look for you."

"Thanks," I said shortly, "but I will be able to get home myself."

Litle did I then realize how much, ere that day was over, I should need the grim good man I was sending away.

With no further words we parted in the lonely road. Richard returned to the cabin, and I struck off at left angles into a dim trail through the fragrant woodland. I was in the wrong mood to traverse such country, for I was too angry to be very quiet, as a stalker should be, or careful, which had been Richard's sound advice. Yet this mood did not remain long upon me. I remembered the cause of my coming to his wild island. The vision of a stately crown of antlers once again rose before me. Yet in such country stalking is not easy. A hunter might pass within twenty feet of the couched king, reposing in the brush, yet never see him.

Semi-tropical, languorous, baffling in its thickety beauty, the virgin dewy wildwood flanked my path. Tawny jungles of palmetto there were; dense greenery of cassina and of myrtle; beds of ferns of majestic height. Overhead there were moss-bannered oaks and old giant yellow pines murmuring musically.

On I walked through scented scenes that made me believe that in these woods the flowers never faded and the dew never dried. Yet they were silent woods. Few birds ever come to the island except shorebirds, which in the migrations descend upon it in countless thousands. Here and there I flushed a woodcock, which went away in his swift, enigmatic, thoughtful way, the thin sweet music of his wings sounding far. Under almost every live-oak I could see where wild turkeys had torn up the trash; and under the big pines they had raked the straw into long windrows. There's no food they prefer to the sweet mast of the long-leaf pine. Twice I started does from the thicket-side. One of these pushed itself gracefully through the myrtles, came to a halt in the dim road, and stood for a moment gazing in startled fashion in my direction. She was just the sort of graceful, mysterious creature to inhabit woods like these. Indeed, she seemed a fairy palpitation out of the heart of the lonely beauteous forest.

But all this was not coming up with the King. It was now past noon, and November afternoons are short. From the forest trail I turned eastward toward the front beach. The deer of Curlew Island have always had the greatest liking for the sand dunes. For all I know, they may, like human beings, love to watch the

plunging surf and to listen to the rolling anthem of the beach.
It is more likely, however, that their fondness for open spaces is
in proportion to the density of the forests which by day they
frequent.

A hundred yards from the beach—and while I was still in
the woods—and for all my following of a mazy trail not so very
far from where Richard and I had parted hours before, I came
upon a long sandy slough. It was the kind of a place where
shorebirds would delight to wade and feed, for it was marsh-
margined, and it was about a half-inch under clear water. In the
packed sand were scores of blurred trails; and one of these, seeming very large, I followed.

Just as it entered the forest to seaward of the savanna I got
one clear impression. There could be no doubt of it; it was the
track of the King. Nor was it an old track. A piece of damp
sand, displaced by the heavy tread of the giant deer, still hung
clingingly on the top edge of the impression. The thing looked
hot; and I knew that if I had been a hound I would have begun
to trail.

I examined the ground further. I came to a wide bayou, the
consistency of chocolate. And what track did I see crossing it?
The buck's was not here, but here was a wide, deep track, almost
straight, for the rattler does not wriggle when he crawls, and
there were tiny cuts and creases in it which I knew had been
made by a reptile's scales. Judging from the width and depth of
the track, my friend had a body not less than a foot in circumference.

Apparently, I was on the trail of both Kings. One I was eager
to see; the other I loathed and dreaded. And why was it that this
second sovereign kept crossing my path with sinister insistence?
But I made up my mind not to be diverted from following the
stag. A curious stalk this was—trying to come up to one creature
and at the same time trying to avoid another. I was, in a sense,
both a follower and a fugitive.

Cautiously I stepped forward, stooping under dense bough
tangles, insinuating myself through ti-ti thickets and trying to
be as noiseless as possible. Quite near me I heard a wild
turkey run. A gray squirrel must have seen the turkey, for he
barked coughingly. He knew that there was some cause for
alarm. I was still on the track of the stag. I had managed to
follow it, even in this jungle, because the earth there is soft

and almost clear of grass. Slow was the work, for sometimes the very darkness of the shadows prevented my picking up the trail readily.

Northward turned the stag; and northward I followed. Two full hours I held the baffling winding trail. Then I found the track making for the beach.

The sun was down when I came to thinning trees and felt the hale breath of the sea wind. Then I saw the mystic sand dunes, topped by their waving tufts of gray beach grass; and beyond them, in foamy tumult, the ocean.

Keeping the lee of a bulky storm-scarred red cedar, I came up quietly under its shelter. From this position I looked carefully up and down the beach. It was the very time of afternoon for deer to visit the sands. But the rolling high dunes shortened the range of my vision. I therefore laid my rifle on the sands and pulled myself up into the first limbs of the cedar. Thence I could see as far as my eyes had vision for seeing. To the southward the beach was bare—unless, nearly a mile away, the shadowy objects which I saw might be a troop of deer. Northward I turned my eyes.

At first I did not see the stag. He was between two huge dunes, and he must have been holding his head down. But now he walked boldly, majestically forward, mounting a bare sand hill. Before my very eyes stood, all unconscious of his peril— the King of Curlew Island. More than a hundred yards away he was—larger than life in clear relief against the sunset line. He was within range, but my rifle lay on the sands under the tree. Though deer hunting has been my pastime since early boyhood, I was greatly excited.

"Richard didn't lie," I kept saying to myself as I eased my weight carefully down the tree. "That's the greatest buck on this island and in this country. His body isn't that of a giant—but his horns! I've seen antlers in my time, but not kingly crowns and chairs of state and all that. No; Richard didn't lie."

For a shot at the great stag I had to do one of two things: either reclimb the tree—which was mightly awkward business with a loaded rifle—or reenter the woods, pass down parallel to the beach for thirty yards or more, so as to get clear of the shielding dunes, and then take a close shot from the forest edge. I decided on the latter course.

Sinking into the darksome cedar grove, I made my way as silently as possible through the borders of the dusky, fragrant wood. The twilight was fading. Momently I expected to be able to make my little maneuver toward the beach, but darkness was coming. And rather than lose precious minutes dodging in and out, I bided my time. At last however, I turned beachward. And simultaneously with my turn I heard the diamond-back! My God, the thing seemed to be under my feet!

Insistent, shrill, querulously warning, the rattles whirred. The sound seemed everywhere. I was afraid to move. Always difficult to locate, this perilous note of menace was hopelessly so on the borders of this thicket. There was no light save a dim jungle glow, eerie and misleading. Moreover, I knew this to be the snake I had been dreading. None other could sound his warning so formidably. I was so close that I thought I smelt the snake. I could not locate him, could not see him; but very well I knew what his appearance was. I knew he was slothfully heaped in his rasping cold coils. Loathsome death was under my feet. Behind those grim jaws, articulated with the strength of steel, behind the faint chill pallor of his contemptuous lips, there lurked a dread secret.

All this I knew. And I knew that my business just now was not to kill a buck but was rather to keep from getting killed. A single movement in the wrong direction might be my last one. I remembered that when my dear friend Bob King had been struck in the femoral artery by a diamondback, he had fallen to the ground unconscious; nor had he ever awakened again in this life. Such a fate seemed now upon me.

Suddenly I heard the patter of running feet. Then there came a dog's sharp yelp. And out of the darkness behind me I heard a human voice call; it seemed to me to be coming out of another world.

"O, Cap'n!" shouted Richard cheerfully. The voice called me back from the realm of terror to the realm of reality. It brought me to myself. I forced myself to try to locate the snake. I heard the dog. He was baying the reptile. They were between me and the beach. I stepped backward into the thicket. A few moments later I had joined Richard in the dim woodland road.

"I thought you might need me," he said almost apologetically.

I thought of Kipling's,

> "Though I've belted you and flayed you,
> By the Living God who made you
> You're a better man than I am, Gunga Din!"

"Is that Scramble back there in the thicket?" I asked.

"Yes, Cap'n. What he been baying near you? I don't hear him no mo'."

"He probably saved my life," I said. Then I told Richard of having seen the stag and of having heard the snake.

"Scramble is good at a sharp dodge," he said, "but I don't know how well he can dodge in the dark."

Here Richard gave a long whistle. To this there was no response.

"I was in danger, Richard," I said; "you came just in time."

"And we is such a long way from home," he responded, "to make 'rangments for a funeral."

"You've such a nice tactful way of putting things," I said.

But the Negro did not get my scorn. He was a dealer in elemental thoughts. To be struck by a big rattlesnake was almost surely to die; to die would undoubtedly necessitate certain arrangements, and in the nature of the case these would devolve upon him. Thus he reasoned simply, naturally; and thus he spoke his thoughts.

And what of the buck? We left him for the night. It was now too dark to shoot, even on the glimmering dunes, and one of my strong aversions in deer hunting has been this business of wounding a fine deer and of letting it get away. But in my mind I could still see that magnificent creature gazing out over the somber twilight sea. Almost a phantom buck he was—a romantic shape of the rolling ghostly dunes, a comrade of the wild sea waves, the mysterious marshes, the lonely forest.

"Is one thing good 'bout this cabin," said Richard as we made up to the staggering structure bulking blackly in the faint starlight.

"So?" I asked disinterestedly, for its virtues had not impressed me.

"No rats," said the emotionless Negro. "A rattlesnake," he explained, "especially a large one, likes to stay 'round an ole place like this and catch all the rats."

"Cheerful little thought," was my comment. "And, Richard,

if you have any more of these happy snake ideas, suppose you give all of them to me in one spoonful. I don't care for the broken doses."

As we entered the cabin, I felt uneasy all over, but Richard's blue-flame driftwood fire and his good dinner relaxed all my tension.

"Tomorrow," I said to the Negro, "is the day. By the way, I hope Scramble gets back safely."

Richard laughed without feeling.

"Scramble, if you could see him now, would look like an accident that is done already happened."

"A daylight start," I said, "and tomorrow will be our last day on the island."

Dawn with its aromatic sea winds, its blazing eastern star, and the dewy spiceries shed by pines and myrtles found us once more abroad in the island woods. Silent and faithful, Richard trudged beside me. He was grieving, I knew, over the loss of his second dog. Within half an hour we were near the scene of our encounter of the evening before. Here the island begins to narrow to its northward point. The end of it, jutting out into a tawny inlet, was not more than a half mile from where we emerged from the woods upon the gray dunes. We mounted a high sand hill.

"It was off yonder, Richard, that I saw him," I said, pointing to a group of dunes down the beach.

It was not yet sunrise. Sea mist hung over ocean and beach and forest, yet beneath its filmy canopy we could see far. The twilight of the morning shed its soft luster over the lonely ocean, the solitary sands, the silent fragrant woods.

"But, Cap'n," said Richard, with more excitement than I had ever known him to show, "ain't that the King down yonder?"

My fascinated eyes followed his pointing finger. Far down the northern end of the beach I saw a shadowy form. There could be no doubt of its identity—we were looking at the stag of Curlew Island. What I had last night left on the sands was, after a long night's wandering, here again. He was taking a last look at the ocean before retiring into the forest for the day.

"Cap'n, I'm thinking that he can't get away from us today." Richard's voice was quiet and assured. "He is at the narrow end of the island, and to get back into the wide woods he will have to pass us."

"We've cornered the King, Richard. But look. He's going up the beach now. He's going into the woods."

The splendid stag faded into the margins of the misty forest.

"Dat's all right," said Richard; "he's going to Eagle Pond to drink before he lies down. Come, Cap'n. I know the way."

No more perfect screen for a stalk could be imagined than was afforded us by the dense undergrowth through which we now, by winding animal paths, made our hurried and silent way. Richard led me ere long to a big palmetto whose broad fronds spread fanlike to the ground. Crouched behind this perfect screen, we looked out over the broad savanna before us. The place was about three acres in extent—a reedy clearing in the forest. Here and there were spaces of damp sand. Near the center of the savanna was Eagle Pond—dark and deep, and just now fairly alive with mallards and teal.

"He will have to cross this place," Richard was telling me.

I am not familiar with the kind of buck that has to do as a hunter thinks he should, but I felt this deer would walk out into the savanna. It practically spanned the woods here. Moreover, it must have been a singularly attractive place for him.

Silence and stealing morning sunshine and the sweet music of wild ducks' wings attended our watch. A lordly eagle beat his way powerfully over the amphitheatre. I heard a wild hen turkey give her plaintive call. The surf fell sleepily on the drowsy shore. I was crouched low, my rifle thrust forward. I had everything in my favor for the shot of a lifetime—everything except the target itself.

Suddenly, silently, out of the mysterious forest he appeared. I felt very much like a friend of mine who, when his first buck walked out to him, exclaimed in a loud amazed voice: "Lord, look at that!" and never thought of shooting. But I tried to be cool and sensible. I measured the antlers with my eyes. Craggy, chestnut-colored they were, massive, symmetrical, and with long tines. I knew he must be an eighteen or twenty-pointer. And the spread of the beams was phenomenal; it could not have been under twenty-six inches. What a head!

A hundred yards away the myrtles had parted, and now he came forth clear.

"Shoot, Cap'n!"

It was the voice of Richard, and over my hesitancy he came as near groaning in spirit as he will ever come.

I lifted my rifle to take the bead. The buck lowered his

great head. Now his head came partly up, and I could see the bulge in his neck. Even at this distance I thought I could detect a defiance, a challenge in his aspect. Suddenly he whirled toward us, and for twenty paces he came head-on. Distinctly I heard him snort—the strange whistling snort of a buck's defiance.

Then he charged down a stretch of open sand toward us.

I was amazed, for I saw no enemy. It could not be that he was charging us. A wild buck doesn't charge a man when he can do anything else. I had my rifle on him. But my finger did not touch the trigger. The buck's behavior compelled me to watch him. I stood up. On the white sand in front of the stag was the object. This was the King's antagonist.

Parting the palmetto fronds with a cautious hand I saw the two fighters distinctly—the huge buck with his hair ruffled angrily forward, and the monstrous diamond-back heaped in his ponderous coil. And Richard and I were witnesses to this combat of the Kings.

The stag backed away, his grand head lowered and lolling with fury. He halted on the wet rim of the sand. I saw the reptile bulge himself, rising in his massive coils. I saw the spade-shaped head drawn back for the mighty drive. Then the buck charged.

When within ten feet of his enemy he leaped into the air, drawing his four feet together into a close-bound sheaf of incisive spears. With deadly precision he dropped on the chimera; and as quickly as had been his descent was the speed with which he cleared himself. With the grace that is born of wild strength he rebounded from his wondrously accurate spring. In another moment he had whirled and had repeated his savage maneuver. We watched, fascinated. We were there to kill the buck, but I could not shoot him. He now desisted from his work. Standing with regal head held high, he was the picture of angry triumph. He had trampled the monstrous serpent to death. I saw dark blood running out on the white sand. The fight was over.

"Richard," I whispered, "you aren't saying 'shoot!' any more."

"He done make that snake pay up for killing Poacher and Scramble," he replied, frank admiration in his tone.

"Well," I said, "a hunter may on occasion be a killer, but he must first be a gentleman. Look what that stag did for us. We've no right to kill him."

"He is sholy the King," said the Negro.

"Yes," I agreed, "and because of what he's done for us, we are going to let him reign."

"And to think, Cap'n," said Richard with a smile as we turned away from the strange close of our memorable stalk, "I don't even have to tell you no mo' to be careful how you walk."

THE WHITEHORN BUCK

He stood with his head above the gallberry bushes, his antlers gleaming softly in the white winter sunlight. Nearby a wild sow, of gaunt frame and thin gray bristles that made a horror of her spine, was searching for her breakfast in the black rooty mud in the pine-barren swamp. In the tangled thicket of myrtle, water-brier and sweet-bay, birds were hopping about and singing. On all sides the great pine-woods stretched away into a silence that held a deep rapture and a perfect peace. The sun, deliciously warm, filtered down through the fragrant pine-crests, shone on the tall brown broomgrass and the dewy swamp, and rested tenderly on the pale blue flowers that starred the sheltered places. The sun shone on the whitehorn buck, and he stood still, drinking in the comfort and beauty of the scene.

He carried the largest and handsomest horns of any deer in the Santee woods; their spread was thirty inches, and there were six tines on each branch. His eyes, like those of all whitetail deer, were singularly full, wild and liquid. His deep chest was covered with a rough growth of shaggy black hair that seemed to increase the appearance of his size and strength. His legs tapered until it became marvelous how they could support his weight. His whole body was shapely, muscular, beautiful; and his bearing was that of a monarch.

Aside from his size, the one feature that would distinguish him from his fellows was the color of his antlers. They were almost pure white. And instead of giving him a freakish appearance, they seemed but in keeping with his carriage, and adorned his noble head.

From *Old Plantation Days* (1921).

The normal color of the horns of the Southern deer is a brownish amber, with a few white knobs here and there near the bases of the forks. Of the two varieties, the swamp- and the hill-deer, the swamp-buck's antlers are of a richer, darker brown, and their spread is more basket-shaped than those of his highland brothers.

Now the whitehorn buck was a swamp-deer, and just how he came to have antlers whiter than any hill-deer's will perhaps never be known. But why they were white makes very little difference. The fact is that they were, and that he carried them. And for many years before this story begins he had become a living tradition on Santee, a breathing evidence of "the biggest old buck," the kind that always gets away.

For he was known to all the hunters on that section of the South Carolina coast. His horns were "yarned" about and coveted. And as with each succeeding year they increased in size and symmetry, the sportsmen, poachers and market hunters all longed with increasing desire to drop their gun-sights on him.

One February a Negro turpentine hand picked up a branch of his antlers on the edge of the swamp and brought it to the Santee Clubhouse, where were gathered many hunters. Men who had killed moose in Maine, elk in Wyoming, and blacktail in the Dakotas, broke off in the midst of memorable yarns to gather in a circle, to handle the glorious antler, to admire it, and to resolve silently but vehemently to take back North as trophies the new and full set of horns when another season should have developed them.

But they had set their hearts on no ordinary game. They were no match for the whitehorn buck. They might surround a branch,—as a small swamp or thicket is called,—and put the best pack of hounds in the country on his trail; but the wary old buck would always slip out. When startled from his haunts among the bay-bushes, he had a habit of throwing his head back on his broad shoulders and racing down the drive, with the pack in full cry after him; but when he had drawn the hunters to that end of the swamp, he would double, and before he could be cut off, would be "stretching forward free and far" through the open woods. Then the only thing left for the chagrined hunters to do would be to stop the dogs and put them in other swamps after inferior deer.

Times past number the whitehorn buck eluded his pursuers.

Nor was it because of his wildness. On the contrary, he was frequently seen. Negroes in the turpentine woods continually brought home stories of him.

One had seen him peacefully feeding on the edge of a bay thicket. One had seen him loping gracefully along under the pines. Again, his wide, deep track would be marked in the white sand of the road just outside the plantation gates. Up to the settlements he would roam in the night, browsing on the tender ferns and grasses and rubbing himself in the scrub oak and spar-kleberry copses. Many times he had been shot at, and if stories were to be believed, he had received mortal wounds on numerous occasions. But no hunter ever had a hair or a drop of blood from the monarch that bore the gleaming antlers to substantiate his story or prove the fatality of his aim.

There were not a few sportsmen who would have gladly taken the trip from the North to Santee just to get a shot at the buck, but most of them realized that their desire was a vain thing. There were grizzled old hunters, natives of the deep swamp, who knew the lure and magic of the woods, who thought nothing of bringing home six wild turkeys and a black bear in a single day, desperate men, too, they were, who knew more than one use for the hunting-knife. But even they failed to get more than a sight or perhaps a hopeless shot at the whitehorn buck.

There were pale business men from the city, come up to spend a week under the pines, on the ample, sweet bosom of nature, and they secretly determined to give the old hunters a surprise. They had often heard of the buck, and wished in a vaguely spectacular way to kill him, although they would probably have fainted away had he so much as given them a sight of himself.

Then there were the wealthy, wholesome sportsmen of the Northern Club, robust, good-natured, and fair shots, who longed for a chance at the whitehorn buck. But one and all were foredoomed to disappointment. If hunted too frequently, he would disappear entirely for a month, and all the whooping of drivers and trailing of dogs through his favorite haunts and cover would fail to rouse him. He had gone no one knew where.

So, year after year, the whitehorn buck was hunted, mortally wounded, storied about, and despaired over until, through the whole length and breadth of the Santee country he became a myth, a proverb, a spirit of elusion. And as he stood that winter morning in the gallberry bushes on the edge of the swamp known as the Rattlesnake Drive, he was indeed a fit subject for imaginative stories.

His bearing was superb. The wide, thin-edged nostrils, breathing in the damp and fragrant morning air, the proud defiance of the regal head, the soft, liquid eyes, expressive of so much grace and pride, and the glistening sheen of his dun coat—all made him past description, as his cunning and speed made him beyond the power of men to capture or to kill.

Yet in that coast country there was one hunter whom the lordly whitehorn buck would have to reckon with. He was the Negro poacher, Scipio Lightning.

Scipio was built for the woods. His physical senses were developed like those of a wild animal. His eyesight was that of a harrier hawk; his sense of smell that of the ravens that sun themselves on the lone cypresses along the river; his hearing was as keen as that of a wary old gobbler.

As the years passed, he had seen the woods and the fields over which he had once roamed and hunted at will taken up and posted by rich clubmen. Not that the posting made any particular difference to Scipio; he still hunted about where he pleased, for because of his good nature he was on terms of smiling tolerance with all the watchmen of the game-preserves. And there was not a man on Santee who did not love him for his woodcraft, his strength and endurance, and the stories that he could tell of hunting. From sand-chickens to swamp-bear, there was nothing about the Santee woods or river with which he was not thoroughly conversant.

Yet for all his prowess as a hunter, and for all his matchless skill as a woodsman, Scipio was weak enough to be superstitious. He said once that he knew where a wahwoo-cat lived. Now a wahwoo-cat is a creature that is supposed to be invisible, and which whimpers and snarls at you out of the darkness. Scipio looked askance at rabbits, and no one ever found him eager to kill a mink. He had his superstitions about them all. And this weakness had a great deal to do with his relations with the whitehorn buck.

He knew almost all that there was to be known about the whitehorn buck. He could show you the warm, sunshiny bed between the green tussocks of broomgrass where he had been dropped as a fawn. He knew in what clump of myrtle-bushes his mother used to leave him when she went far away through the lonely forest to feed. And as for his habits and his haunts, Scipio had them by heart.

He knew that the Rattlesnake Drive was his home; but that when he was hunted hard he went back four or five miles in the woods, and there took refuge in a great swamp known as the Ocean, a vast, impenetrable morass, silent, dreary, haunted.

Yet Scipio took little stock in all the glory and glamour that were gathered about the name and fame of the whitehorn buck. To the unromantic Negro hunter he was only a wary old deer that no white man would be likely to kill. He knew that he himself could shoot him, for Scipio knew how. He would take no dog with him, no horn, no turmoil of galloping horses and loud-mouthed men. He would take only his old musket, loaded with thirty buckshot. Such a charge would stop a dozen deer; but Scipio never made the mistake of undercharging his gun.

So it came about that after the whitehorn buck had been made famous by the sportsmen who had missed him, and after rumors of the great price which would be paid for the horns had been in circulation for some time, Scipio decided to go after the monarch of the pines.

Therefore it happened that on the very same day on which we saw the buck standing so proudly on the edge of the branch, Scipio began his preparations. He gave his musket a thorough overhauling. In the mellow sunlight behind his cabin he cleaned it, washed it inside and out with warm water and soap, dried it, oiled it and loaded it. He primed the nipple carefully, and chose from the shiny box the brightest-looking percussion-cap that he could find. Then he lay down on a bench in the sun and slept till the late afternoon.

The sun was setting in a fire of glory behind the tall, somber pines when Scipio left his cabin. The Rattlesnake Drive was only a mile away, and an easy walk. The Negro's long strides would take him there in fifteen minutes, for what he would see on the way—and there woud be much to see—would not deter him, now that he had a fixed purpose in mind. All the beauty of the sunset, of the twilight, of the soft coming of the dewy stars, of the mysterious rising of the ghostly mist—these meant nothing to the Negro. A single purpose reigned in his heart: he was going to kill the whitehorn buck.

As he walked swiftly down the narrow path that led through

the high broomgrass under the pines, he saw the wild life of the
night begin to come forth. Once a gray fox came trotting up the
path towards him, and seeing him suddenly, almost turned a
somersault, and dashed wildly away with his fluffy tail bobbing
over the fallen timber. Once a great horned owl on velvet wings
floated softly over him:

> Not with a loudly whirring wing,
> But like a lady's sigh.

Once, too, an old raccoon paced sedately down the length of a
hurricane-thrown log without seeing the Negro.

Scipio soon came to the Rattlesnake Drive, and entered the
thicket. The gallberry bushes, cold with the dew, wet him up to
his knees. He made his way carefully and knowingly to a little
strip of high ground in the middle of the branch, a little white,
sandy hillock that on the coast would be called a hummock,
where stood a few giant pines and a little gathering of scrub
oaks. It was near the plantation end of the drive, and here, he
knew, some time during the night, the whitehorn buck would
surely come. It was a habit of his, and all his habits were known
to Scipio.

So Scipio waded through the swampy thicket, where the
sweet-bay bushes brushed him fragrantly, where the huge green
water-briers, with their poisonous thorns, caught at him out of
the shadows, until he came up on the warm, dry hillock. Here
he found two pines fallen across each other. Gathering some of
the soft pine needles, he heaped them in one of the corners
against the logs, and sat down to wait.

He knew that the buck, after feeding on the deep edges of
the branch, would come up on the hill to walk about, to rub
himself, and to dry his legs. Scipio knew that he would be able
to hear him far down the swamp, and could see him, too, after
moonrise, which was not now more than an hour away.

The Negro settled back for his long wait. Across his knees,
and grasped by his gaunt and powerful hands, was his musket,
the lock covered with the edge of his coat to keep the cap and
the powder perfectly dry. About him the great pine woods
stretched away in unbroken beauty and stateliness. Mile after
mile, like the solemn aisles of some fabulous cathedral, the dark
shafts and luminous corridors withdrew into the night. And the
music there was the rolling anthem of the pines that softly rose

and triumphed and fell, like the waves of some mighty, dreaming ocean, to break at last in far, melodious foam.

After a while the moon rose, and the woods for half a mile in each direction were as clear as day. Once a doe came feeding up to where Scipio sat; he could have touched her with his musket-barrel, but he did not stir. Once a gaunt old red fox trotted swiftly over the hill, urgently bent on business of his own, and Scipio let him pass unmolested.

The radiant moon climbed higher, and the stars wheeled up and by. The infinity of the night grew vaster. Midnight, with its mystery, came and went. Scipio was growing chill. So far there had been no signs of the great personage whom he awaited.

It would soon be too late for him to feed. Scipio grew anxious. But he need not have been, for when the Negro entered one end of the drive, the buck had come in the other, and had been browsing up toward the sand-hill.

When he was still two hundred yards away, Scipio heard a bay-bush crack. Ten minutes later he heard the petulant rap of horns against a young tupelo-tree. Five minutes more, and Scipio saw clearly, not more than fifty yards away, the gleam of snowy antlers.

He ran no risk with a long shot, for after forty yards buckshot are very uncertain. He waited. The whitehorn buck came up to the edge of the sand-hill, quartering to the Negro. Scipio, who at the first sound had rested his musket on the log before him, now tilted it gently until he saw the brass sight shine against the white patch behind the buck's fore leg. The gun tightened against his shoulder; he steadied it with all the strength of his powerful arms; he pressed the trigger!

"Ti-a-a-rr!" echoed the cap, derisively, and the buck, seeming to jump seven ways at once, and fifteen feet in each direction, straightened out at a tremendous speed down the branch. The powder had slipped down in the nipple, the cap had popped, and the whitehorn buck was getting away!

Yet Scipio held his sight on him, hoping that the charge might still ignite. But all in vain. The great buck thundered on down the edge of the drive, and was soon lost to sight among the glimmering pines. Scipio lowered his musket in disgust. Yet there was more than disappointment and chagrin on his face; there was superstition and downright fear. He looked furtively about him, and then struck off in a fox-trot toward home. Nor did he slacken his pace until he was in sight of his lonely little cabin that slept in the peaceful moonlight.

If one might read Scipio's heart, one would find that the Negro believes that he was trying to shoot at a spirit, or that some strange power was working against him. Never before and never since that night can he remember his musket's failing him. So he goes no more to stalk the whitehorn buck. And that old monarch who bears the glorious antlers should be thankful in the thought that the best hunter in that country is superstitious.

THE FAWN

A state of affairs had come to pass on the old plantation that, if tolerated, would completely crush Colonel Jocelyn's hopes of abundant crops. It was in May, the vital month for growth in the South—the time when crops are made or lost. The colonel had a fine stand of corn; he had been spared both late frosts and high waters; and but for this new and unheard-of situation, he could now be counting on a good harvest.

Every night for almost a fortnight deer had been coming into the fields and committing what Colonel Jocelyn hotly declared to be "marauding practices." A big buck would lope over the rotting rail fence, strike the end of a long corn row, dew-drenched and succulent, and eat calmly down to the other end, only to start back on the next row. Two or three sleek does followed each buck. The colonel, who came up daily to the plantation from his summer home on the seacoast ten miles away, estimated from the amount of depredation committed that there must be ten or fifteen culprits. Night after night the crops of cowpeas, corn, and peanuts rapidly diminished.

Once or twice Colonel Jocelyn hunted out the thickets on the edges of his field, and jumped many deer; but he was an old man, and the sun was very hot, and disheartening to strenuous effort, and the one deerhound that the colonel had was decrepit. He was so infirm that often when he struck an excitingly fresh scent he would merely stand in one place and vent his feelings in a futile, emotional bay. Once the colonel actually walked up to two does that had been lying on the margin of the field, dozing in the high, warm broomgrass.

From *Old Plantation Days* (1921).

One night he tied the old hound to a stake in the field near the border of the pine thicket, hoping that his presence might frighten the marauders away; but Prince Alston, one of the Negro hands on the plantation, told the colonel the next morning that the dog had yelped all night, and that he must have had a bad scare. Sure enough, when his master went to untie him, he found him shivering and sick. Near by, he saw where a great buck had circled the hound, and pawed and stamped the black loam with his sharp hoofs.

Colonel Jocelyn decided to take the law into his own hands. He had heard that one night hunt, if successful, would so intimidate the deer that they would ever afterward keep a safe distance away from the field where one of their number had fallen. Not another night should pass, resolved the colonel, before he would put a stop to his losses and his anxieties. He would stay on the old place that night.

The full moon was fringing the broken forest line with light when Colonel Jocelyn, with his shotgun in his hand, left the house and walked down toward the cornfield that had suffered most. He did not feel exactly at his ease; for night shooting is always exciting, and especially so to one who is going beyond the law to kill deer.

Passing beneath huge, shadowy oaks and across velvet strips of moonlit lawn, the colonel came at last into the corn, green-bladed, burdened with misty dew, lustrous in the mellow light. Far down on the edge of the black thicket he found a fallen pine, with dry pine trash underfoot and a screen of broomgrass in front. Here he sat down and waited for the deer.

Meanwhile, from distant ferny solitudes, through the deep-gladed pine wood, into the dark depths of the thicket, a shadowy troop of deer came toward the cornfield. A splendid old giant buck with towering antlers led them. Two slim does followed, and farther back came two peghorns and four does. On they came with wonderfully little noise for their size. The old buck led his band to the edge of the field, perhaps a hundred yards from where the colonel sat. There the leader stood; his tall horns gleamed gray above the fringing bushes, but his body was lost in the shadows behind. The shot was an easy one for a rifle, but hardly for an old shotgun; besides, the colonel's object was to shoot a deer actually at work in the field, so that there should be no doubt as to the purpose of the deed.

But no creature in the woods of the South is so wary as a

buck that carries great antlers. The proud head was lifted high in the breeze; the antlers shook impatiently, and then steadied suddenly. For a second, as the keen nose detected the presence of the crouching colonel, the wise old "bayleaf" paused; then with a mighty plunge, he disappeared into the thicket.

One of the does, startled and misunderstanding, darted into the field, where she crouched with ears thrust forward, eyes dilated, and slim legs set and tingling; but before she could make a jump, the colonel, knowing that he would get no more chances that night, threw his gun to his shoulder and fired.

He walked over to where the doe lay between two corn rows, with her white sides gleaming in the moonlight, and her lithe limbs, so fleet only a moment ago, now helpless and growing chill. He did not face the rebuke of the doe's great eyes; he went only near enough to see that she was dead. Then with a strangely heavy heart he walked through the dripping corn back to the house.

But real and deep as was his regret over the occurrence, Colonel Jocelyn forgot it almost completely during the next few days. A far more exciting and pleasurable interest had come into his life—an event for which he had waited twenty years. At last the fine tract of yellow pine, a part of the old Malbone estate that joined his land, was to be sold at auction.

Although Jonathan Malbone, the eccentric owner, had never lived on the place, he had always flatly refused to sell it to the colonel, who knew and loved nearly every stick of timber on it. However, after wretched health and more wretched temper, old Malbone died; and the heirs had put the property up for sale. It was to be sold at auction in Cummings village that Friday night; and when, on Friday morning, Colonel Jocelyn rode through the village on his way toward his plantation, he heard some talk of the bidding.

Herman Peckham, the German storekeeper, came down from his white porch into the road to greet and congratulate the colonel.

"Your chance is coming to-night," said he, pointing with a fat thumb toward the schoolhouse, where the auction was to be held.

"Yes," replied the colonel, reining in his bay mare, "and I wouldn't miss it for a trip to the moon. Who's against me, Herman?"

"Fred Baker's talking about it, and Ben Whitmore; but the

man you must watch is young Lou Sands. I have Lou's acquaintance. He comes from Georgetown to bid for the Coast Lumber Company."

"Well, come down and see the fun, Herman," said the colonel.

The journey that morning was short and happy. The pines were fragrant; the green, level woodland was starred with flowers; far off on the edges of the shadowy cypress swamps, where lush savannas lay in tropic luxuriance, flamed strange, sultry flowers; the pleasant sunlight filtered through the pine needles; and the birds sang joyously.

At last, turning a bend in the road, he came within sight of the gate of the plantation and saw the great white house in the clearing beyond. He shook the reins, and the mare broke into a light canter that soon brought him, flushed and smiling boyishly, to the line fence and the gate, which Prince was even then opening for him.

Prince looked conscious and abashed.

"Have they been in again, Prince?" the colonel asked sharply.

"No, sah," answered Prince slowly, coming forward and laying his huge hand on the mare's mane. "But I find dat fawn," he added, without looking up.

"Fawn!" ejaculated his master. "Did the doe I shot have a fawn?"

"Must be," murmured the negro.

"Oh, what a pity, what a pity!" The colonel shook his gray head sadly. "Is it dead, Prince?"

"No, sah, but it's sho' gwine die."

"Where did you find it? Where is it now?"

Prince told him that as he was following a raccoon track into the thicket behind the cornfield early that morning he had come to a little open, sunny space beneath the pines, where he had found the fawn lying, too faint to struggle. And there certainly it must have been since Colonel Jocelyn killed its mother; for it is well known that when a doe leaves her fawn and goes away—sometimes for miles—to feed, her little one will not stir until her return. Prince also told his master that he had put the fawn on a rug in the dining-room, and asked in the same breath whether he could be spared that day to go across the river to a great "jubilee picnic."

The colonel nodded his assent, put sudden spurs to his mare, and galloped across the field to the great house. Under the big live-oak before the wide piazza he dismounted, slipped off the saddle and bridle, and leaving the mare to graze, ran up the broad steps.

The fawn lay where Prince had left it, stretched on a worn rug on the floor, with its great brown, pitiful eyes mutely appealing. It was young, with starry white spots on its glossy golden coat. Its shapely legs seemed no larger than the colonel's fingers; its delicate hoofs were soft and pearly. It tried to move and lick its lips, and its sunken sides heaved with fright and the eagerness for food.

The colonel knelt down by it and stroked its back. He sat on the floor and took its head into his lap. He looked into its wonderful eyes, and saw in them fear and yearning affection. Yet it was only after the tiny creature had licked his hand with its rough tongue that he realized its crying need.

He brought some milk, and again taking the fawn's head in his lap, fed it with a spoon. In spite of the strangeness of a silver spoon in its mouth, it drank eagerly; but it seemed too weak to respond to the nourishment. It gasped and struggled with each mouthful. It shuddered and nuzzled up to the colonel.

Meanwhile the afternoon sun was stretching the pine shadows across the wide fields, and a yellow shaft of light stole into the hushed room and lay at the colonel's feet. It roused him to a realization of where he was and what he was doing. It was Friday, and four o'clock in the afternoon. Yes, and on Friday at six o'clock the coveted Malbone tract was to be sold to the highest bidder. The fawn had so distracted Colonel Jocelyn's mind that it seemed years since he had heard of the sale; but gradually he came to himself, and his intense desire to purchase the timber returned.

And here indeed was a plight! With every Negro on the place gone to the "jubilee picnic," with no way of taking the poor little fawn home with him, and with the sale for which he had prayed for twenty years taking place within two hours, what was he to do?

He could not count on Prince's return; for among the uncertainties of Southern life is a Negro's return from festivities of any nature. The fawn apparently could not live unless nourished every few minutes. The village was almost an hour's ride from

264 Flights of Whitetail Fancy

the plantation; if he were to reach the sale on time, he must be starting. But there lay the helpless fawn!

The colonel grew angry, and then flushing with shame at his anger, laid a gentle hand on the tremulous little creature. Easing its head softly to the rug, he rose and tiptoed to the doorway. Under the big oak he saw the mare feeding. He would just have time to ride home comfortably, put the mare away, and go to the sale.

He should be there at six o'clock sharp; for with the strange inconsistency of a sleepy village, official events in Cummings were usually held on schedule time. So seldom did anything of importance happen there that those concerned were likely to be in a hectic hurry. Lou Sands was probably there now. Fred Baker would be on the spot when the time came. And if Colonel Joce-lyn were not on hand, the sale would proceed and the land be lost to him.

Turning back into the room, he saw the fawn's great, appealing eyes looking at him. He could not leave the poor little creature to die. The Malbone tract would have to go; but he could not be such a brute as to kill the mother and leave her baby to perish.

So he went back to the fawn; and it was glad to have him come. Once more his hand rested tenderly on its silken flank, and he could feel its heart beat more quietly and its quivering muscles relax. It nestled close to him, and nuzzled against his sleeve.

An hour passed, and the shadows on the plantation fields were very long. It was nearly six o'clock, and the sale would soon begin. It was hard to wait twenty years for a chance and then lose it! If Prince would only come, he might still get to the sale; but Prince was far away. Six o'clock came and went; then, after what seemed an age, seven. The colonel had lost; but the fawn was safe asleep in his arms.

Shortly after eight o'clock, Prince's long, melodious whoop sounded through the hollow pine wood. Laying the fawn in a big armchair, the colonel took a hunting horn down from a craggy pair of antlers, stepped to the door, and blew a mellow note. Prince came running toward the house.

"Saddle the mare, Prince," his master said. "Saddle her quickly!"

The Negro, half-frightened by the colonel's manner, caught the mare and brought her up to the steps, ready.

"Prince," exclaimed the colonel, "I have kept that fawn alive, and it's in there now in the big armchair by the fireplace! Wrap it up and take it over to your house. Keep it warm and feed it milk every hour in the night. And if you let it die after all I've done—"

Prince could not hear the threat that came over the colonel's shoulder as he galloped down the darkened avenue. The mare was fresh, and she was homesick for the tang of the salt air. As she cantered briskly along the level road, the straight-stemmed trees flitted by in the dusk. Now she tore over a hollow-sounding bridge, now she swept into the cool darkness of a bay-branch crossing, and now she clattered through a long, shining water slash. The colonel knew that there was the barest chance that he might yet be in time.

When, still urging the lathered mare, he emerged from the woods and came up on the high, hard-shell road, the lights were twinkling in the village. Light after light darted past; house after house loomed into view and disappeared. At last the tall white schoolhouse came in sight; a clump of trees partly shielded the building from his view; Colonel Jocelyn leaned forward on the neck of his faithful little mare; then as he passed the clump of trees, he drew rein suddenly, and sighed. His free hand rested nerveless on the pommel of his saddle. The schoolhouse was dark and the yard was silent. The sale was over; his chance was gone.

Suddenly from the roadside a voice called out of the darkness:

"I thought you might be a Valkyrie, riding like that! Where have you been, colonel?"

"Oh, I was kept on the place till too late," Colonel Jocelyn said wearily.

"Yes," returned the other, coming near and reaching up until his hand rested over the colonel's. "But they rise early who beat Herman. I overbid Baker and Lou Sands, and all the rest. I buy the place for you!"

CAESAR

The situation into which Cæsar had been put was difficult
at best; this last turn of affairs had proved it to be perilous.
Arthur Moreland, the owner of the old plantation "Woodside,"
had been called away by a handsome position offered him in far-
off Tennessee. He had decided to close the plantation house for
a time—possibly a few years—until better circumstances would
enable him to reopen it. The planting on the place would be
done by the Negroes, who would be glad enough to have the
use of the land. Cæsar would be left in charge of the whole
thing,—Cæsar, the Negro with whom Moreland had played as a
boy, with whom he had a thousand adventures by wood and
water,—Cæsar, whom he trusted with a great and an affectionate
faith.

The plan appeared a good one; and for the first six months
there was no trouble. But then the deer season opened. Now, if
there was anything about which Moreland was particular, it was
the hunting on "Woodside." On his twelve hundred acres there
he had always had forty or fifty deer; some of these ranged up
to the house; one old doe was a pet of long standing. For five
succeeding years she had reared a fawn in the sparkleberry thickets between the house and the river. Occasionally Moreland
would kill an old stag; but he took great pride in not really
diminishing his stock of these superb wild creatures.

To protect them in his absence, Moreland had carefully
posted the plantation; moreover, to make an understanding of
the business clear, he had written in his own hand on the bottom
of each sign that Cæsar Moultrie was in charge of the place.
Then he had gone away; and for a time all prospered.

From *Heart of the South* (1924).

But there came that morning when Cæsar, out along the pasture-fence to patch it, heard an automobile coming from the ferry. The road from the river passed through "Woodside." Occasionally a car would come through; but as the pineland through which the road ran was wild, it was not often that a car would stop,—as this one now did.

From his work Cæsar paused. The throbbing of the motor had ceased. In the towering pines soaring above him he heard a soft wind murmur. Bluebirds warbled overhead in the clear sunshine. From the road, some two hundred yards distant, he thought he heard someone whistle, then call.

"I must see 'bout this," said the Negro, suddenly feeling very alone and very responsible, but remembering with a stout heart his master, now far away, and counting on him to take care of the old place.

Nor would it be overlooked or denied that in many parts of the South a Negro takes his life in his hands if he takes it upon himself to question the behavior of white men. Moreland had come to know and to care for Cæsar beccause he had always considered him first as a man, and then—well, he seldom gave a thought to his color. This is probably a good and wise thing to do: this business of considering a man as a man,—and then later, perhaps, if necessary, make distinction because of color or race or other differences.

Through the dewy underbrush Cæsar made his way toward the road. Soon the car was in sight; it had been run into a little blind and there parked. Beside the car Cæsar saw a man roughly dressed; with lolling tongues and wagging tails, beside him were two hounds, glad to be released from their cramping in the car, and happy over the prospects of a hunt.

With something like a thrill Cæsar recognized the man as Abel Bramson, from Tawneytown, across the river. A year before, when Arthur Moreland had had some timber cut, this fellow Bramson had been in charge of the work; and at that time he had been suspected of poaching and doing other plunderings. Now he was back; and Cæsar well knew that it was for nothing good.

"Good mornin', sah, Mr. Bramson," said Cæsar as he left the wet bushes and stepped into the road.

"Hello, Cæsar. You here? I thought everyone had gone away. We heard over the river that Mr. Moreland had given up the place."

"He gone away," Cæsar admitted, "but he gwine come back. While he is gone," the Negro added by way of quiet announcement, "I is here to guard it for him."

"Guard it, hey! Well, you don't mind my being here, do you? I've just come over to check up on some timber," Bramson lied glibly. "I'll just cruise over the woods as usual."

To let this explanation of his presence take effect, the white man turned his back, lifted the hood of his Ford, and began to pretend to tinker with the engine. When he finally emerged from this specious ambush, Cæsar had not stirred.

"How do you happen to be out here this morning, Cæsar?" he asked. "You're rather far from home, aren't you?" he added with just a hint of something sinister in his tone. Bramson was a man of burly proportions, hard-muscled, bronzed, with a heavy mustache, and with an expression always somewhat fierce. His motions were truculent, abrupt; he always wore a chip; and he had a habit of staring an intruder out of countenance. He now looked very hard at Cæsar.

"You are a little far from home, aren't you?" he repeated, with a tinge now of unmistakable menace in his tone. Cæsar knew that he was in danger. He decided to bring the whole business into the open.

"Mr. Bramson, sah, you ain't done come for hunt, is you? Mr. Moreland done give me particular orders to ask eberybody what done come to do no huntin'. . . . He done put up sign all over 'Woodside,'" Cæsar concluded, feeling that the duly posted signs put him on the side of the law.

"My dogs are mangy," Bramson said coolly, "and it does them good to ramble through the myrtles. I brought my gun along to shoot a squirrel maybe, or to keep off the rattlers while I'm cruising the woods. We killed some big ones last year. If this isn't all right and regular, I'll make it so with Mr. Moreland when he comes back."

Abel Bramson concluded this last statement with a rather fierce look at Cæsar.

"Dem dogs can ramble the mange off, and I know Mr. Moreland wouldn't mind you shootin' a squirrel, and all the rattlesnakes; but you mustn't kill no deer, Mr. Bramson. You know, Mas' Arthur and me, we don't neber 'low dat."

"Cæsar, you had better, I think, mind your own business. I'm going down here through the Fawn Pond country to look over that loblolly."

"But don't shoot no deer," the Negro said, looking the deliberate invader of "Woodside" clearly in the eye.

"Come, Hammer; come, Trigger," Bramson's voice was full of a quiet determination, and the glance he shot at Cæsar was scornful and menacing. Turning on his heel, he slouched down the road, leaving the negro watchman standing beside the car.

"Now, what must I ought to do?" said Cæsar aloud. His loyalty to Moreland was pathetic. "What would Mas' Arthur do with a man like that? But he could talk to him in a way I can't talk to him. But I must guard the place," he concluded.

The Negro went back to his work. But he could not do it with any heart. Always he kept listening for hounds, for a gun. Nor did he listen in vain.

Within an hour Bramson's two hounds had jumped a deer. It eluded the hunter and headed straight for the pasture. Cæsar, knowing the deer-runs well, got ahead of the dogs. Within a few minutes, the dogs, full-cry, had come up.

Cæsar had gathered to himself a formidable pine pole, and this he brandished before the dogs, shouting at them meanwhile to turn. They paused in their running, bright-eyed and uncertain. But Cæsar seemed so determined that they gave up the chase and slunk away. When they were gone, the Negro went slowly back to the car expecting to meet Mr. Bramson there. But the poacher, sounding a horn far back near Fawn Pond, recalled the dogs to him there.

It was perhaps two hours later, when Cæsar had almost finished work on the fence, that a shot rang out across the road, not a quarter of a mile from the car. The hounds opened wildly, then they suddenly hushed. That behavior meant just one thing: a deer had been started, and the hunter had killed it in front of the hounds. Cæsar knew this as well as if he had seen it. Too long had he been a woodsman with Moreland not to understand such matters. And what he did was as sudden and determined as his knowledge was accurate: stepping to a hollow tree, he slipped his hatchet into it; then he struck through the woods for the ferry, a mile away.

"I'se gwine to Tawneytown," he announced to himself. "Mas' Arthur done tell me that when I run into a business I can't handle, I must go to he cousin in Tawneytown, and he will onrabble the ponderation. He name is Mas' John Sumter. He will know how for talk with this man. He ain't folks like we," he added disparagingly of Bramson; "he is swamptrash; he done float down the ribber in a freshet one time," he ended with a grim laugh.

The ferry across the Santee was a most primeval affair. It consisted of a huge unwieldy flat, poled across the wide river by a negro whose talents in life were certainly not those of a boatman. Departures and arrivals of the "boat" were determined by such uncertainties as wind, tide, cold weather, the wakefulness of the ferryman, and often by the somewhat elemental one of his being at his post. Many a party of long-distance travelers has camped on the Santee wharf awaiting the return of the ferryman from some frolic miles away in the pineland.

When Cæsar came to the river, the flat was on the farther side. He whooped in a voice far-reaching and melodious, and soon the heavy boat was seen to be in motion. Cæsar would cross the river, walk ten miles to Tawneytown, make his report to John Sumter, and then, perhaps, return home that night. But so slight a detail as his getting home afforded him no concern.

While the Negro was standing on the rude wharf, and while the laboring flat was still at some distance away, he heard a car coming. In a few minutes it had been run out on the wharf in a position favorable for its advance into the flat. It was, of course, Bramson's. The owner was at the wheel; two hounds peered over the door in front. From above one of the rear doors there stiffly projected the feet of a deer. The whole thing was as Cæsar had expected—except the matter of his crossing the river with the poacher.

Bramson, seeing that he could not hide the deer, and utterly surprised at the presence of Cæsar, assumed a somewhat jovial attitude.

"I shot that squirrel," he said with a forced laugh; "he was climbing a pine tree."

Cæsar the watchman looked at him gravely and said nothing.

"Where are you going, Cæsar?" asked Bramson, changing his tone.

"Across the ribber, sah," the Negro said with dignity to himself and apparent respect for the white man.

"I might give you a lift," suggested Bramson, a wily light dawning in his pale yellowish eyes.

Again Cæsar decided to bring things into the open.

"Mas' Arthur done tell me that when I get into trouble I must go to Mas' John Sumter to Tawneytown,—him what used to be a judge. Mas' Arthur done say that Mas' John will help me out of any kind of trouble."

"But what's the matter? What trouble do you mean?"

Cæsar pointed at the deer.

"That's all the trouble," he said.

Quick as a blinding flash Bramson slipped under the steering wheel and leapt from the car; three swift strides brought him to Cæsar. The men were hardly a foot apart. Bramson, quivering with rage, towered over the negro, who stood his ground quietly.

"If you ever tell Judge Sumter about this," he said, "it will be the last thing you'll tell. . . . And if I ever see you in Tawney-town, or on the road there, you'll never see home again. Do you get me, Cæsar?"

This question was literally snarled from under the poacher's dense mustache.

The ferry-flat was now almost at the wharf. Ben Jones, the ferryman, called to Cæsar to catch a line. This distraction saved the "Woodside" watchman from answering Bramson. But both he and the white man knew very well how matters stood between them. Just before he stepped into his car to drive into the flat, Bramson called to Cæsar:

"And nothing to Moreland, either, about this. Do you hear? If you do, I'll find a way to reach you. . . . My arm's long enough to get you, you spy!"

It was with a certain alien pity that Ben listened to this speech. But of it he dared say nothing.

"You gwine 'cross?" he asked Cæsar.

The Negro nodded.

"No, he isn't, either!" shouted Bramson. And just then he stepped on the starter and his car moved downward to the level of the flat. It was ticklish business at best, for there was no guardrail at the farther end of the boat, and beyond was a sheer drop into forty feet of water, wild now with a turbulent current. One of Bramson's hounds, afraid of the sight of the big river, whined, then tried to jump out of the car. Bramson caught it by the collar, taking his eyes from the track in front of him. In his effort to seize the hound he struck down the gasoline lever.

At sudden terrific speed the car shot forward, leaped violently from the flat, and plunged heavily into the dread depths of the river.

"He gone! He gone!" cried Ben Jones. "I'se gwine for a

paddle for my little boat," he shouted at Cæsar as he began to run up the road toward his cabin. But Cæsar knew that it might be ten minutes ere Ben had launched his small craft. Swiftly he looked here and there for help. In the bottom of the old flat lay some loose cypress planks. Tearing off his shoes, Cæsar lifted one of these, slid it into the water, and quickly let himself over upon it, swimming out toward the place where the car had disappeared.

Twenty feet from the wharf, in a smother of muddy swirls, there arose the keen black head of a hound. In a soft tone that the dog knew was friendly but imperative, Cæsar called the half-drowned creature. It swam toward him and began to crawl up on the plank. In a minute another had joined him.

"But where is the man?" muttered Cæsar.

As he said this, he was horrified to see blood rising in the water. But in the wake of the red stains came a dim shape, feebly struggling for the surface. Above the water two arms were lifted imploringly, despairingly. Bramson's heavy hunting equipment was drowning him; and the blood showed that he had been injured.

Cæsar, swimming powerfully for the helpless man, shouted to him words of hope. But he was sinking when the negro's strong arm encircled him, drawing him toward the heavy float.

"Don't worry, Mr. Bramson," he said; "you is safe, sah."

Cæsar was almost to the shore ere Ben Jones returned with the paddle. The two negroes carried the white man, cruelly cut by glass, to Ben's cabin, where they revived him and cleansed and dressed his wounds.

"The dogs are safe," said Bramson at last, "but the car is gone, and my gun, and—and the deer."

"I could drive you home, sah," Cæsar respectfully suggested.

"All right," the injured man acquiesced—"but—but you'll see Judge Sumter about me."

"No, sah, not if you say I need not," Cæsar suggested.

"Never again," Bramson agreed. "I was in the wrong, Cæsar, and I knew it. You'll never see me bring dogs and gun to 'Woodside' again to cruise timber."

That afternoon Cæsar, having brought his old horse and buggy to the ferry, drove Bramson home. The hounds trailed disconsolately behind the creaking vehicle. It was after dark when they reached Tawneytown.

As he was saying good-bye to the Negro, Bramson dragged a soaked five-dollar bill from his pocket and pressed it into Cæsar's hand.

"You saved my life," the white man said simply.

BIBLIOGRAPHY

Although deer hunting was Rutledge's first love as a sportsman, little has been written dealing specifically with his involve-
ment in the sport. The most significant treatment of this aspect
of his career, and to my knowledge the only one focusing entirely
on the subject, is Rob Wegner's insightful article "Flintlock: A
Dixie Deerslayer," initially published in *Deer & Deer Hunting*
magazine (June 1990). The piece also is the first chapter in Wegner's *Deer & Deer Hunting: Book 3* (Harrisburg, PA: Stackpole
Books, 1990). Judge Irvine Rutledge, in *We Called Him Flintlock*
(Columbia, SC: R. L. Bryan, 1974), includes a substantial chapter entitled "The Hampton Hunt." In it one gets a feel for just
how significant whitetails were in Rutledge's life. Also of some
note is a little-known volume by Rutledge's brother, Frederick.
Entitled *Fair Fields of Memory* (Asheville, NC: Privately printed,
1958), it focuses primarily on sport and includes reminiscences
of hunts at Hampton and on nearby plantations.

There are a number of other works which, while of lesser
importance for an examination of Rutledge as a deer hunter,
touch on the subject or provide useful biographical details. Idella
Bodie's *The Story of Archibald Rutledge: A Hunt for Life's Extras*
(Orangeburg, SC: Sandlapper, 1980) is written for a youthful
audience. While it lacks depth, the author does give appropriate
coverage to hunting as a central feature of her subject's life.
*Hidden Glory: The Life and Times of Hampton Plantation, Legend of
the South Santee* (Nashville, TN: Rutledge Hill Press, 1983), by
Mary Bray Wheeler and Genon Hickerson Neblett, includes an
interesting chapter, "The Poet," on Archibald Rutledge. This
work also contains three bibliographical appendices which cover,
respectively, Rutledge's books, manuscripts and tearsheets of his
articles housed in the South Caroliniana Library, and magazine
articles in the same collection. Unfortunately, the last two appen-

dices are marred by numerous errors. Much more useful, especially for a general overview of Rutledge and Hampton Plantation, is the main bibliography of *Hidden Glory*. George Bird Evans, a noted writer on upland game, includes typically well-written vignettes of Rutledge in two of his books, *Men Who Shot* (Bruceton Mills, WV: Old Hemlock, 1983), and *George Bird Evans Introduces* (Bruceton Mills, WV: Old Hemlock, 1990).

Several articles on Rutledge are significant. Bob Campbell's "The Nature of Will Alston" (*South Carolina Wildlife*, May/June 1974, pp. 15–17) is a moving profile of the son of Rutledge's close friend and long-time hunting companion, Prince Alston. "South Carolina's Poet Laureate" (*Sandlapper*, October 1968, pp. 47–51), by Virginia Ravenel, scarcely touches on sport, but the piece does provide an overview of Rutledge's literary career. Benton Young's "The Squire of Hampton (*South Carolina Wildlife*, October 1983, pp. 16–21) is well written and draws on the author's personal friendship with Rutledge during the latter's final years. An anonymous piece, "Memories of Archibald Rutledge" (*Sandlapper*, November 1973, pp. 57–58), paints a brief but poignant picture of the man.

All of these sources are helpful, but for deer hunting, as for Rutledge's career in general, his own writings are the fullest and most reliable source. His published tales of whitetail hunting stretch across a period of almost seven decades, and collectively they recount his vast and varied experiences with deer. Every memorable hunt, each remarkable event, was recorded for posterity, for Flintlock published accounts of his deer-hunting experiences with almost as much regularity as some sportsmen maintain entries in field diaries.

The bibliography which follows, while unquestionably incomplete, is reasonably comprehensive. It is based on consultation of all of the author's books, together with research in most of the major outdoor periodicals of the twentieth century. However, many of these periodicals are now rare, and in some cases I was unable to peruse complete runs. Likewise, it should be noted that Rutledge wrote widely in boys' magazines, and while I have done little work in these, it is likely that they include some articles on deer.

Certainly, the entries below suffice to give an indication of the breadth of Rutledge's work on deer. Only those articles which deal wholly or in large measure with deer are included.

Most of his deer stories were first published as articles and then subsequently collected in his books. Where such multiple publications are known, they are identified. It should be noted that Rutledge frequently made minor revisions in his stories when they were included in books. In closing, the editor would like to indicate that additions to the list that follows are most welcome.

"All of a Christmas Morning," *An American Hunter* (1937), pp. 251–60. Also in *Fireworks in the Peafield Corner* (1986), pp. 229–36.

"Am I Surprised!," *Outdoor Life*, August 1942, pp. 26ff.

"A Baby Fawn," *Wild Life of the South* (1935), pp. 72–73.

"Bagging Game with Buckshot," *Days Off in Dixie* (1925), pp. 194–202.

"A Black Buck," *Tom and I on the Old Plantation* (1918), pp. 31–42.

"The Black-Horn Buck," *Wild Life of the South* (1935), pp. 79–82. Also in *Santee Paradise* (1956), pp. 42–63, and *Fireworks in the Peafield Corner* (1986), pp. 349–57.

"Blue's Buck." *Hunter's Choice* (1946), pp. 129–35. Also in *Fireworks in the Peafield Corner* (1986), pp. 267–74. First published in *Field & Stream*, January 1939, pp. 22ff.

"The Boy and the Buck," *An American Hunter* (1937), pp. 325–34. First published in *Forest & Stream*, September 1927, pp. 530ff.

"The Buck at the Secret Crossing," *Outdoor Life*, March 1965, pp. 46ff.

"A Buck in the Rain," *An American Hunter* (1937), pp. 10–19. Also in *Fireworks in the Peafield Corner* (1986), pp. 335–42.

"The Buck with the Palmated Horns," *Hunter's Choice* (1946), pp. 68–74. First published in *Field & Stream*, December 1941, pp. 24ff.

"The Buck with the Wide-branching Horns," *Those Were the Days* (1955), pp. 195–202.

"Bucks Are Like That," *Those Were the Days* (1955), pp. 389–97. First published in *Field & Stream*, July 1938, pp. 22ff.; also in *South Carolina Magazine*, October 1961, pp. 4ff.

"Bucks Don't Want to Be Trophies," *Outdoor Life*, August 1938, pp. 22ff.

"A Buck's Hiding Place," *Wild Life of the South* (1935), pp. 69–71.

"A Buck's Strategy," *Wild Life of the South* (1935), pp. 183–85.

"Caesar," *Heart of the South* (1924), pp. 219–30.

"The Case of the Elmwood Buck," *An American Hunter* (1937), pp. 8–9, 59–60. First published in *Outdoor Life,* January 1929, pp. 61–69.

"Catching Them on the Dew," *Plantation Game Trails* (1921), pp. 88–101. First published in *Field & Stream,* October 1918, pp. 472ff.

"Certain Great Stags," *Field & Stream,* October 1927, pp. 26ff.

"The Christmas Eve Buck," *Field & Stream,* December 1929, pp. 40ff.

"A Christmas Hunt," *Those Were the Days* (1955), pp. 349–56. Also in *The Woods and Wild Things I Remember* (1970), pp. 130–38.

"Critical Moments," *Field & Stream,* October 1945 pp. 34–35, 90.

"A Curious Chase," *Wild Life of the South* (1935), pp. 246–47.

"A Day in the Pineland Wilds," *Days Off in Dixie* (1925), pp. 179–93. First published in *Field & Stream* as "A Day in the Pinelands," April 1921, pp. 1084ff.

"Daybreak in the Ocean," *Field & Stream,* February 1936, pp. 30ff.

"The Deer and the Hound," *Bolio and Other Dogs* (1930), pp. 199–226. Also in *Plantation Game Trails* (1921), pp. 127–59.*

"The Deer and the Hound," *Those Were the Days* (1955), pp. 7–13. First published in *Field & Stream,* February 1919, pp. 752ff.; also in *Sports Afield,* August 1947, pp. 48ff.

"The Deer as a Jumper," *St. Nicholas,* October 1925, pp. 1258ff.

"Deer Hunting in the Southern Woods," *Field & Stream,* February 1915, pp. 104ff.

"A Deer Kills an Enemy," *Wild Life of the South* (1935), pp. 46–47.

"Deer in a Storm," *Wild Life of the South* (1935), pp. 148–49.

"The Deer of Charleston County," *News & Courier* (Charleston), November 14, 21, and 28, 1915.

"The Deer of the Coastal Islands," *Days Off in Dixie* (1925), pp. 87–94. First published in *Country Life,* February 1920, pp. 70ff.

"The Deer of the Southern Woods," *Field & Stream,* January 1915, pp. 948ff.

*Although this story and the one listed immediately below carry the same title, they are two different pieces.

"Deer Propagation on Waste Land," *The Game Breeder*, January 1931, pp. 3ff.

"A Deer's Recovery," *Wild Life of the South* (1935), pp. 117–21.

"Deer Tales: What, No Bladder?," *The Rotarian*, June 1954, pp. 59ff.

"The Demon of the Ocean," *From the Hills to the Sea* (1958), pp. 167–75.

"Does a Staggered Season Work?," *Field & Stream*, December 1934, pp. 17ff.

"The Fawn," *Old Plantation Days* (1921), pp. 246–58.

"Fearless Children," *Wild Life of the South* (1935), pp. 142–44.

"Festival in Nature," *Coronet*, May 1951, pp. 62ff.

"55 Years a Deer Hunter," *Sports Afield*, September 1950, pp. 38ff.

"Flora's Buck," *The Woods and Wild Things I Remember* (1970), pp. 194–200. Also in *Fireworks in the Peafield Corner* (1986), pp. 187–92.

"The Funny Side of Deer Hunting," *Forest & Stream*, November 1925, pp. 646ff.

"The Ghost Point Buck" *Those Were the Days* (1955), pp. 342–48.

"The Golden Robber," *Old Plantation Days* (1921), pp. 84–92.

"The Grey Stag of Bowman's Bank," *Plantation Game Trails* (1921), pp. 264–74. First published in *Field & Stream*, December 1920, pp. 751ff.

"The Horn Architecture of the White Tail," *Field & Stream*, December 1927, pp. 20ff.

"Horns on the Delta," *Sports Afield*, September 1938, pp. 14ff.

"How Guns Shoot Buckshot," *Outing*, December 1919.

"A Hunt at the Kinloch Club," *An American Hunter* (1937), pp. 378–85. First published in *Outdoor Life*, March 1934, pp. 14ff.

"A Hunt with the Oakland Pack," *Days Off in Dixie* (1925), pp. 203–13. Also in *Bolio and Other Dogs* (1930), pp. 187–98 and *An American Hunter* (1937), pp. 30–39. First published in *Field & Stream*, November 1921, pp. 663ff.

"Hunter Come Home," *Those Were the Days* (1955), pp. 309–14.

"Hunting Deer in Dixieland," *Forest & Stream*, February 1921, pp. 53ff.

"Hunting Helmetted Stags," *Forest & Stream*, March 1917, pp. 400ff.

"Hunting with Half a Gun," *An American Hunter* (1937), pp. 434–41.

"Joel and the Marsh-Buck," *Days Off in Dixie* (1925), pp. 148–58. First published in *Field & Stream*, February 1921, pp. 912ff.

"The Kings of Curlew Island," *Heart of the South* (1924), pp. 369–91. Also in *Those Were the Days* (1955), pp. 242–57 and *The World Around Hampton* (1960), pp. 131–56. First published in *Outer's Book-Recreation*, January 1923.

"The Lady in Green," *Hunter's Choice* (1946), pp. 3–12. Also in *Fireworks in the Peafield Corner* (1986), pp. 133–41. First published in *Field & Stream*, October 1941, pp. 26–27, 68–70.

"Let's Stop Night Hunting," *Outdoor Life*, December 1941, pp. 32, 91.

"Master Minds," *An American Hunter* (1937), pp. 90–100. First published in *Field & Stream*, April 1927, pp. 38–39, 98–99.

"The Master Wildwood Sport," *Days Off in Dixie* (1925), pp. 59–72. First published in *Forest & Stream*, November 1922, pp. 483ff.

"Mists Over Montgomery," *Those Were the Days* (1955), pp. 321–28. First published in *Sports Afield*, Nov., 1939, pp. 9ff.

"My Colonel's Last Hunt," *Hunter's Choice* (1946), pp. 25–31. First published in *Outdoor Life*, January 1942, pp. 22ff.

"My First Buck," *Wild Life of the South* (1935), pp. 8–11.

"My Friend the Deer," *Plantation Game Trails* (1921), pp. 1–21. First published in *Country Life*, May, 1918, pp. 45ff.

"My Greatest Thrill," *An American Hunter* (1937), pp. 344–51. Also in *Fireworks in the Peafield Corner* (1986), pp. 143–48. First published in *Field & Stream*, August 1930, pp. 19ff.

"My Hunterman," *Outer's Book-Recreation*, September 1919, pp. 170ff.

"My Life as a Hunter," *Sports Afield*, December 1951, pp. 25ff.; Part 2, January 1952, pp. 30ff.; Part 3, February 1952, pp. 44ff.; Part 4, March 1952, pp. 38ff.

"My Most Memorable Deer Hunt," *Outdoor Life*, July 1971, pp. 44ff.

"My Twilight Stag," *An American Hunter* (1937), pp. 122–31. First published in *Field & Stream* as "My Twilight Buck," 1924, pp. 14ff.

"My 250th Buck," *Those Were the Days* (1955), pp. 374–81.

"The Odyssey of Old Clubfoot," *Field & Stream*, September 1928, pp. 34ff.; Oct., 1928, pp. 36ff.

"Old Five-Master," *An American Hunter* (1937), pp. 301–11.

"A Pine Cone Fell," *Those Were the Days* (1955), pp. 287–91.

"Remarkable Shots," *Forest & Stream*, December 1926, pp. 723ff.

"Riding Them Up," *An American Hunter* (1937), pp. 281–90. First published in *Field & Stream*, August 1931, pp. 20ff.

"Rifle or Shotgun for Deer?," *Outdoor Life*, September 1940, pp. 26ff.

"The Romance of Deer Stands," *The Woods and Wild Things I Remember* (1970), pp. 187–93. First published in *Field & Stream*, May 1945, pp. 16ff.

"Sancho's Buck," *Hunter's Choice* (1946), pp. 100–05. Also in *Fireworks in the Peafield Corner* (1986), pp. 159–64. First published in *Field & Stream*, July 1942, pp. 12ff.

"The Seamarsh Buck," *Heart of the South* (1924), pp. 63–73. First published in *Outdoor America*, December 1923, pp. 201ff.

"Shooting Bucks Over a Bird-Dog," *An American Hunter* (1937), pp. 162–72.

"Shots I Really Remember," *Those Were the Days* (1955), pp. 270–78. The first portion of this article deals with deer hunting.

"So You Missed Him!," *Sports Afield*, November 1942, pp. 24ff.

"Some Kingly Crowns," *Field & Stream*, November 1919, pp. 660ff.

"A Stalk on the Dunes," *Field & Stream*, September 1934, pp. 28ff.

"Stalking Your Buck," *Outdoor Life*, December 1934, pp. 36ff.

"Steve and the Plateye Buck," *Field & Stream*, July 1937, pp. 20ff.

"Steve Knows How," *Sports Afield*, October 1938, pp. 9ff.

"Steve's Masterpiece," *An American Hunter* (1937), pp. 451–61. Also in *Fireworks in the Peafield Corner* (1986), pp. 167–75. First published in *Field & Stream*, March 1935, pp. 34ff.

"Strange Stalks," *Field & Stream*, August 1938, pp. 30ff.

"A Strange Watchdog," *Wild Life of the South* (1935), pp. 239–40.

"The Surprise of My Life," *Those Were the Days* (1955), pp. 363–68. First published in *Field & Stream*, April 1942, pp. 20ff.

"Tales of Deer," *Good Housekeeping*, November 1929, pp. 32ff.

"Tall Man of the Twilight," *Field & Stream*, March 1939, pp. 34ff.

"Tampering with Kingly Crowns," *Days Off in Dixie* (1925), pp. 277–80.

"That Christmas Buck," *Plantation Game Trails* (1921), pp. 216–31. First published in *Field & Stream*, January 1920, pp. 833ff.

"That Christmas Eve Stag," *An American Hunter* (1937), pp. 398–406.

"That Day at Dan's," *An American Hunter* (1937), pp. 219–28. First published in *Field & Stream*, November 1925, pp. 11ff.

"That Hunt at Jasper Hill," *Those Were the Days* (1955), pp. 104–11. First published in *Forest & Stream*, December 1929, pp. 896ff.

"Trophy Hunting," *Outer's Book-Recreation*, November 1919, pp.

"Trophy of a Lifetime," *Those Were the Days* (1955), pp. 28–33. First published in *Outdoor Life*, June 1943, pp. 31ff.

"The Unbelievable," *Days Off in Dixie* (1925), pp. 95–111.

"A Wary Stag," *Wild Life Of the South* (1935), pp. 165–67.

"What Every Deer Hunter Should Know," *Those Were the Days* (1955), pp. 203–09. First published in *Outdoor Life*, August 1946, pp. 48ff.

"What Makes a Deer-Stand?," *Outdoor Life*, January 1940, pp. 36ff.

"What Your Buck May Do," *Saturday Evening Post*, October 12, 1929, pp. 68ff.

"The Whitehorn Buck," *Old Plantation Days* (1921), pp. 46–59.

"The White Stag's Tryst," *Heart of the South* (1924), pp. 329–47.

"A Woodland Courtship," *Children of Swamp and Wood* (1927), pp. 16–25.